Better Homes and Gardens® Books
Des Moines, Iowa

Better Homes and Gardens® Books
An imprint of Meredith® Books

AMERICA'S HOMETOWN FAVORITES

Editor: Kristi Fuller
Contributing Editor: Lisa Kingsley
Associate Art Director: Mick Schnepf
Copy Chief: Terri Fredrickson
Editorial Operations Manager: Karen Schirm
Managers, Book Production: Pam Kvitne, Marjorie J. Schenkelberg
Contributing Copy Editors: Daniel Cubias, Maria Duryée
Contributing Proofreaders: Pegi Bevins, Gretchen Kauffman, Sherri Schultz
Indexer: Sharon Duffy
Electronic Production Coordinator: Paula Forest
Editorial and Design Assistants: Judy Bailey, Mary Lee Gavin
Test Kitchen Director: Lynn Blanchard

Meredith® Books
Editor in Chief: James D. Blume
Design Director: Matt Strelecki
Managing Editor: Gregory H. Kayko
Executive Food Editor: Jennifer Dorland Darling

Director, Sales, Special Markets: Rita McMullen
Director, Sales, Premiums: Michael A. Peterson
Director, Sales, Retail: Tom Wierzbicki
Director, Book Marketing: Brad Elmitt
Director, Operations: George A. Susral
Director, Production: Douglas M. Johnston

Vice President and General Manager: Douglas J. Guendel

Hometown Cooking® **Magazine**

Editor: Joy Taylor
Art Director: Nick Crow

Better Homes and Gardens® **Magazine**
Editor in Chief: Karol DeWulf Nickell

Meredith Publishing Group
President, Publishing Group: Stephen M. Lacy
Vice President-Publishing Director: Bob Mate

Meredith Corporation
Chairman and Chief Executive Officer: William T. Kerr

Chairman of the Executive Committee: E. T. Meredith III

Copyright © 2002 by Meredith Corporation, Des Moines, Iowa. First Edition.
All rights reserved. Printed in China
Library of Congress Control Number: 2001135120
ISBN: 0-696-21459-8

All of us at Better Homes and Gardens® Books are dedicated to providing you with the information and ideas you need to create delicious foods. We welcome your comments and suggestions. Write to us at: Better Homes and Gardens Books, Cookbook Editorial Department, 1716 Locust St., Des Moines, IA 50309-3023.

If you would like to purchase any of our cooking, crafts, gardening, home improvement, or home decorating and design books, check wherever quality books are sold.
Or visit us at: bhgbooks.com

Pictured on front cover: Sour Cream Buns (see recipe, page 48)

Dear Friends,

It's no secret that the tastiest recipes in America can be found in tried-and-true, real hometown cookbooks. You can find the best of these recipes in *Hometown Cooking*® magazine—and now in this cookbook, *America's Hometown Favorites*. Our staff travels the highways and the back roads to discover the most satisfying home cooking  in America and to meet great cooks from California to Maine. Our new acquaintances aren't professional chefs; they're moms, dads, and grandparents who love to prepare satisfying meals for their families. And they proudly share recipes with friends and neighbors in a community cookbook. Now you can sample these honest-to-goodness recipes in your own kitchen.

Hometown Favorites features more than 200 recipes, from quick party appetizers to festive holiday desserts. I hope you and your family enjoy this wonderful collection of America's best home cooking, all endorsed by the Better Homes and Gardens® Test Kitchen.

Joy

Joy Taylor, Editor

***Hometown Cooking*® magazine**

Learn more about *Hometown Cooking*® magazine at www.hometowncook.com

Table of Contents

1.

Appetizers, Beverages, and Snacks

Cheese-Pecan Crackers

From the St. James at Sag Bridge Church cookbook,
Lemont, Illinois

4 oz. sharp cheddar cheese, shredded (1 cup)	1/2 cup finely chopped pecans Nonstick cooking spray
1/4 cup butter	
1/4 tsp. dried thyme, crushed	**Prep:** 20 min. **Chill:** 4 hr.
1/8 tsp. ground red pepper	**Bake:** 10 min. per batch
3/4 cup all-purpose flour	

Hilltop Beauty

The St. James at Sag Bridge Church cookbook was published in 1998 to celebrate the 165th anniversary of the parish and to raise funds to restore and maintain the church. One of the oldest church structures in Illinois, St. James sits at the top of a hill surrounded by the St. James Cemetery, which is listed on the National Register of Historic Places.

1. In a medium mixing bowl, bring the sharp cheddar cheese and butter to room temperature (about 30 minutes).

2. Beat cheese mixture with electric mixer until well combined. Add thyme and red pepper. Beat until combined.

3. With a wooden spoon, stir in the flour and finely chopped pecans until combined. Form into a ball.

4. Shape into an 8-inch log. Wrap with plastic wrap and chill for at least 4 hours or until the mixture is firm.

5. With a sharp knife, cut dough into 1/8-inch-thick slices. Place on cookie sheets that have been lightly coated with cooking spray. Bake in a 350°F oven about 10 minutes or until lightly browned.

Makes about 60 crackers.
Per cracker: 26 cal., 2 g total fat (1 g sat. fat), 4 mg chol., 20 mg sodium, 1 g carbo., 0 g fiber, 1 g pro. Dietary exchanges: 1/2 fat.

Jack's Party Pecans

From the Jack Daniel Distillery.
Lynchburg, Tennessee

1/4	cup butter
1/4	cup whiskey
3	Tbsp. sugar
1	to 2 Tbsp. bottled hot pepper sauce, or to taste

1/2	tsp. salt
1/2	tsp. garlic powder
4	cups pecan halves (about 1 lb.)

Prep: 10 min. **Bake:** 25 min.

1. In a large saucepan, combine all ingredients except pecans. Bring to boiling over medium heat; reduce heat. Boil gently, uncovered, for 3 minutes, stirring occasionally. Remove from heat. Stir in pecans; toss well to coat. Spread nuts in a single layer in a shallow baking pan.

2. Bake pecans in a 300°F oven for 25 to 30 minutes or until nuts are crisp, stirring occasionally. Spread on foil; cool. Store in an airtight container.

Makes 4 cups nuts.
Per 2 tablespoons: 113 cal., 11 g total fat (2 g sat. fat), 4 mg chol., 55 mg sodium, 4 g carbo., 1 g fiber, 1 g pro. Dietary exchanges: 2 fat.

Who Was Jack Daniel?

Born in 1850, Jack Daniel apprenticed to a whiskey maker when he was only 7. He took over the business when he was 13 and started the first registered distillery in the United States. "Mr. Jack" was something of a dandy, dressing in a formal, knee-length frock coat and wide-brimmed hat. He also had a temper, which cost him his life when the big toe on the foot he kicked his safe with became gangrenous. He died in 1911.

Texas Caviar

From Party Snacks from Encino Park,
San Antonio, Texas

2	15-oz. cans black-eyed peas with jalapeño peppers, rinsed and drained
1	cup chopped red sweet pepper (1 large)
1/2	cup chopped onion (1 medium)

1/2	cup snipped fresh parsley
1	or 2 cloves garlic, minced
1/4	cup olive oil
1/4	cup rice vinegar or white vinegar
1/2	tsp. salt
1/8	tsp. black pepper
	Large corn chips

Prep: 15 min. **Chill:** 1 hr.

1. In a large bowl, combine black-eyed peas, sweet pepper, onion, parsley, and garlic. Pour oil and vinegar over black-eyed pea mixture. Sprinkle with salt and black pepper. Toss gently to coat. Cover and chill in refrigerator for at least 1 hour or up to 24 hours before serving. Serve with large corn chips.

Makes eighteen 1/4-cup servings.
Per serving: 73 cal., 3 g total fat (0 g sat. fat), 0 mg chol., 308 mg sodium, 8 g carbo., 2 g fiber, 2 g pro. Dietary exchanges: 1/2 starch.

White Chili Dip

From The Creekside: A Celebration of Cedarburg Cooking,
cookbook of the Junior Women's Club, Cedarburg, Wisconsin

1	15-oz. can Great Northern beans, rinsed and drained		2	tsp. ground cumin
3/4	cup salsa		2	cups cubed, cooked chicken breast
2	cups shredded Monterey Jack cheese with jalapeño peppers (8 oz.)			Tortilla chips

Start to finish: 15 min.

1. In a large saucepan, combine beans, salsa, cheese, and cumin. Cook over medium-low heat, stirring constantly, until cheese is melted. Add cooked chicken; heat mixture through, stirring occasionally. Serve immediately with tortilla chips.

Makes about 3½ cups.

Per serving: 31 cal., 2 g total fat (1 g sat. fat), 9 mg chol., 57 mg sodium, 1 g carbo., 0 g fiber, 3 g pro. Dietary exchanges: ½ medium-fat meat.

The Big Cheese

Since 1910 Wisconsin (aka America's Dairyland) has produced more cheese than any other state—more than one-fourth of the total cheese produced in the United States. Most of the cheese is brick, American, cheddar, Muenster, and mozzarella. However, the state is also known for Colby cheese, which was invented in Colby, Wisconsin, and the aromatic Limburger, which is produced only in Wisconsin. You can also find such specialty Wisconsin cheeses as Gorgonzola, Gruyère, Asiago, provolone, Gouda, blue cheese, and feta that are traditionally produced overseas.

Oriental Cabbage Dip

From Picnics, Potlucks & Prizewinners:
Celebrating Indiana Hospitality with 4-H Families and Friends

PICNIC POINTERS
Some foods, including salads, meats, cheeses, and dairy products, need to be kept chilled. Pack these cold foods with an ice pack in an insulated bag or cooler. You can also freeze cold juices to act as ice. By picnic time, the drinks will still be cold but thawed enough for drinking. Consume perishable foods within 2 hours of preparation; 1 hour if outside in temperatures above 90°F.

1	cup coleslaw dressing
2	8-oz. cartons dairy sour cream or light dairy sour cream
1	tsp. instant beef bouillon granules or low-sodium instant beef bouillon granules
1	tsp. Worcestershire sauce
1	tsp. garlic powder
3	cups finely chopped packaged shredded cabbage with carrot

	(coleslaw mix) or finely chopped green and/or red cabbage
1	8-oz. can sliced water chestnuts, drained and finely chopped
3/4	cup sliced green onions
1	Tbsp. toasted sesame seed

Prep: 30 min. **Chill:** Up to 2 hr.

1. In a medium bowl, stir together the coleslaw dressing, sour cream, beef bouillon granules, Worcestershire sauce, and garlic powder. Add coleslaw mix, water chestnuts, green onions, and sesame seeds. Stir to combine.

2. Cover and chill the mixture in the refrigerator for up to 2 hours. Spoon dip into a serving bowl. Garnish with additional green onion and shredded carrot, if desired. Serve with vegetable or pita chip dippers.

Makes 4 cups.
Per tablespoon: 36 cal., 3 g total fat (1 g sat. fat), 3 mg chol., 37 mg sodium, 2 g carbo., 0 g fiber, 0 g pro.
Dietary exchanges: ½ vegetable, ½ fat.

Hot Reuben Dip

From *What Can I Bring?* cookbook of the
Junior League of Northern Virginia

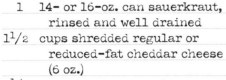

1 14- or 16-oz. can sauerkraut, rinsed and well drained	6 oz. corned beef, chopped (about 1 cup)
1½ cups shredded regular or reduced-fat cheddar cheese (6 oz.)	1 cup mayonnaise or nonfat mayonnaise dressing
1½ cups shredded regular or reduced-fat Swiss cheese (6 oz.)	Party rye bread or baguette slices, toasted

Prep: 10 min. **Bake:** 25 min.

1. Pat rinsed and drained sauerkraut dry with paper towels. In a large bowl, combine all ingredients except bread. Spread into a 9-inch quiche dish or 1½-quart casserole. Bake, uncovered, in a 350°F oven for 25 minutes or until hot and bubbly. Serve with sliced rye bread or baguette.

To microwave: Spoon dip ingredients into a 1½-quart microwave-safe casserole. Microwave on high (100 percent power) for 5 to 6 minutes, or until heated through, stirring twice. Serve as directed at left.

Makes 15 to 20 servings.
Per serving: 223 cal., 21 g total fat (7 g sat. fat), 39 mg chol., 943 mg sodium, 1 g carbo., 2 g fiber, 8 g pro. Dietary exchanges: 1 high-fat meat, 2 fat.

Arline's Crab Spread

From Speedy Specials for Special People,
cookbook of the MATRIX center, Novato, California

WHAT'S SURIMI?
Delicate, slightly sweet imitation crabmeat is actually a chopped and re-formed version of pollack that's flavored with the essence of shellfish and colored to resemble real crabmeat. It can be used interchangeably with real crabmeat in most recipes—but is best in salads, casseroles, and soups. Surimi can be kept unopened in the refrigerator for up to 2 months. Once opened, use it within 3 days.

	Nonstick cooking spray
1	$10^3/4$-oz. can condensed cream of mushroom soup
1	envelope unflavored gelatin
1	8-oz. pkg. cream cheese, softened
1	cup mayonnaise or salad dressing
$1/2$	tsp. lemon juice
	Several dashes bottled hot pepper sauce

1	6- or 8-oz. pkg. flake or chunk-style imitation crabmeat, finely chopped, or one 6-oz. can crabmeat, drained and flaked
1	cup finely chopped celery
$1/2$	cup finely chopped green onions
	Assorted crackers

Prep: 20 min. **Chill:** 4 hr.

1. Lightly coat a $4^1/2$- to 5-cup mold with cooking spray; set aside.

2. In a medium saucepan, stir together soup and gelatin; let stand 5 minutes. Cook over medium heat, stirring constantly, just until bubbly. Add cream cheese; stir just until melted. Remove from heat. Stir in mayonnaise, lemon juice, and hot pepper sauce. Fold in crabmeat, celery, and green onions.

3. Spoon gelatin mixture into prepared mold. Cover and chill in the refrigerator for at least 4 hours or up to 24 hours or until firm. Unmold. Serve with assorted crackers.

Speedy Crab Dip: Assemble ingredients for Arline's Crab Spread, except omit cooking spray and gelatin. In a medium bowl, combine soup and cream cheese. Beat with electric mixer on low speed until combined. Stir in mayonnaise, lemon juice, and hot pepper sauce. Fold in crabmeat, celery, and green onions. Cover; chill in refrigerator for at least 1 hour or up to 24 hours. Serve with assorted crackers and/or vegetable dippers.

Makes about 5 cups spread.
Per tablespoon: 37 cal., 4 g total fat (1 g sat. fat), 5 mg chol., 69 mg sodium, 1 g carbo., 0 g fiber, 1 g pro. Dietary exchanges: 1 fat.

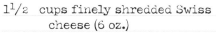

Spanish Olive Spread

From Biggest Hits, cookbook of the Elk Grove Renegade softball team, Elk Grove, California

1¹/₂ cups finely shredded Swiss
   cheese (6 oz.)
1   3-oz. jar pimiento-stuffed
   green olives, drained and
   chopped

¹/₂ cup mayonnaise or salad
   dressing
   Assorted crackers

Prep: 15 min. **Chill:** 4 hr.

1. In a medium bowl, stir together the shredded Swiss cheese and the chopped olives. Stir in mayonnaise or salad dressing. Cover and refrigerate spread for at least 4 hours or up to 24 hours.
2. Before serving, gently stir mixture. Serve with crackers.

Makes about 20 servings.

Per tablespoon: 76 cal., 7 g total fat (2 g sat. fat), 10 mg chol., 140 mg sodium, 0 g carbo., 0 g fiber, 2 g pro. Dietary exchanges: ½ high-fat meat, ½ fat.

Softball and Recipe Sharing

While Shirley Phillips was sitting on the sidelines at her husband Emery's senior league softball games, she decided to write a cookbook. After all, Shirley and the wives of Emery's teammates had been swapping their favorite recipes for years. Shirley and her friends wanted to raise money for the team. Emery's team, the Elk Grove Renegades, is just one of several Northern California over-50 men's softball teams. The result of their efforts was the Biggest Hits cookbook.

Salmon-Cream Cheese Pie

From the St. James at Sag Bridge Church cookbook.

Lemont, Illinois

2/3	cup seasoned fine dry bread crumbs
3	8-oz. pkgs. cream cheese, softened
1/2	cup milk
1/4	cup butter
2	tsp. dry mustard
1/2	tsp. dillweed
1/4	tsp. salt
1/4	tsp. ground red pepper
4	eggs
2	7$\frac{1}{2}$-oz. cans salmon, drained, flaked, and skin and bones removed
2	cups shredded mozzarella cheese (8 oz.)
1/4	cup chopped green onion

Prep: 25 min. **Bake:** 45 min. **Chill:** 2 hr.

1. Lightly grease two 9-inch round baking pans. Coat the bottoms and sides of each pan with 1/3 cup of the dry bread crumbs. In a medium bowl, beat cream cheese, milk, butter, mustard, dillweed, salt, and red pepper with electric mixer on medium speed until combined. Add eggs one at a time, beating just until combined. Stir in salmon, mozzarella cheese, and green onion. Divide mixture between pans. Spread evenly. Bake in a 325°F oven for 45 minutes or until set. Cool completely. Remove from pans. Cover; chill in the refrigerator for 2 to 8 hours.

Makes 32 servings.
Per serving: 146 cal., 12 g total fat (7 g sat. fat), 67 mg chol., 255 mg sodium, 3 g carbo., 0 g fiber, 7 g pro.
Dietary exchanges: 1 very lean meat, 2 fat.

Deviled Ham and Cheese Ball

From The Edible Palette, cookbook of the
Suffolk Art League, Suffolk, Virginia

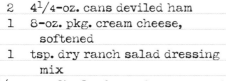

2	4¹/4-oz. cans deviled ham
1	8-oz. pkg. cream cheese, softened
1	tsp. dry ranch salad dressing mix
¹/2	cup finely chopped green sweet pepper
2	cups shredded cheddar cheese (8 oz.)

³/4 cup unsalted, dry-roasted
     sunflower seeds
     Assorted crackers or toasted
     baguette slices

Prep: 10 min. **Chill:** 2 hr.

1. In a medium bowl, combine all ingredients except sunflower seeds and crackers. Separate into two equal portions; refrigerate for 1 to 1¹/2 hours or until firm enough to handle. Form each portion into a ball; roll balls in sunflower seeds to coat. Cover and refrigerate for at least 1 hour before serving. Serve with assorted crackers or toasted baguette slices.

Makes 3 cups spread.
Per 2 tablespoons: 129 cal., 11 g total fat (5 g sat. fat), 26 mg chol., 231 mg sodium, 2 g carbo., 1 g fiber, 5 g pro. Dietary exchanges: 1 high-fat meat, ½ fat.

Party Pizza Appetizers

From Bonita Hellmich,
Greensburg, Indiana

1	lb. bulk pork sausage	1 1/2	tsp. dried oregano, crushed
1	14-oz. jar pizza sauce	1/4	tsp. garlic powder
1	cup chopped onion	3	cans refrigerated flaky biscuits (10 each can)
1/2	cup shredded sharp cheddar cheese (2 oz.)		
1/2	cup finely shredded Parmesan cheese (2 oz.)		**Prep:** 35 min. **Bake:** 8 min.

PERK UP YOUR PARTIES

Use bell peppers instead of bowls to hold dips or veggie sticks. Slice off pepper tops, scoop out seeds, and rinse with water before using. Pick from red, green, yellow, or orange peppers to add a burst of color to your party table. On your fresh veggie tray, include strips of crisp, peeled raw sweet potato and jicama. Jicama is a knobby root vegetable with a mild, sweet flavor and crunchy texture, much like celery.

1. In a medium skillet, cook, drain, and crumble sausage. In a medium bowl, combine sausage, pizza sauce, onion, cheeses, oregano, and garlic powder. Separate each biscuit into three rounds. Top each round with about 1 tablespoon sausage mixture. (To make ahead, place in single layer on baking sheets lined with waxed paper. Cover; freeze until firm. Transfer to freezer bags; seal and freeze.) Place on greased baking sheets. Bake in a 425°F oven for 8 to 10 minutes. Serve warm. Top with more shredded Parmesan cheese.

Makes 90 appetizers.

Per appetizer: 33 cal., 1 g total fat (0 g sat. fat), 3 mg chol., 128 mg sodium, 4 g carbo., 0 g fiber, 1 g pro. Dietary exchanges: ½ starch.

Sweet, Hot, and Sour Tennessee Whiskey Meatballs

From the Jack Daniel Distillery, Lynchburg, Tennessee

2 beaten eggs	3/4 cup apple jelly
1/2 cup fine dry bread crumbs	1/3 cup spicy brown mustard
1/2 cup finely chopped onion	1/3 cup whiskey or apple juice
1/4 cup milk	1 1/2 tsp. Worcestershire sauce
1/2 tsp. salt	Few dashes bottled hot pepper sauce
1/2 tsp. black pepper	
1 lb. bulk pork sausage	**Prep:** 20 min. **Bake:** 30 min.
1 lb. ground beef	

HERE'S A HOT IDEA
To keep hot dips or appetizers (such as these meatballs) hot, use a mini-crockery cooker, fondue pot, or chafing dish. Or pour dips into heatproof containers set on electric heating trays.

1. In a large bowl, combine eggs, bread crumbs, onion, milk, salt, and black pepper. Add sausage and beef; mix well. Shape into about forty-eight 1 1/4- to 1 1/2-inch meatballs. Place in a shallow baking pan. Bake, uncovered, in a 375°F oven about 30 minutes or until cooked through. Drain.

2. Meanwhile, in a large saucepan, stir together jelly, mustard, whiskey, Worcestershire sauce, and hot pepper sauce; heat and stir until jelly melts and mixture bubbles. Add meatballs, stirring gently to coat. Cook for 3 to 5 minutes or until sauce thickens slightly and meatballs are coated.

Makes about 48 meatballs.
Per meatball: 78 cal., 4 g total fat (2 g sat. fat), 20 mg chol., 115 mg sodium, 5 g carbo., 0 g fiber, 3 g pro. Dietary exchanges: 1 medium-fat meat.

Ozark Mountain Mulled Cider

From *Women Who Can Dish It Out*, cookbook of the
Junior League of Springfield, Missouri

8	cups apple cider or apple juice	Peel from 1 orange*
1/4	cup orange juice	Ground nutmeg
2	Tbsp. packed brown sugar	
3	inches stick cinnamon	**Prep:** 10 min. **Cook:** 30 min.
1	Tbsp. whole allspice	
1	tsp. whole cloves	
1	tsp. whole cardamom (optional)	

Ozarkian Myths Dispelled

The writers of *Women Who Can Dish It Out*, the newest cookbook by the Junior League of Springfield, Missouri, seasoned their recipes with some good humor:

Myth: A seven-course meal in the Ozarks consists of a pork fritter and a six-pack.

Myth: Formal dining in the Ozarks means everyone gets their own TV tray.

Myth: All five-star restaurants in the Ozarks end with "all you can eat."

1. In a large saucepan, combine cider, orange juice, and sugar.

2. Wrap whole spices and orange peel in 100-percent-cotton cheesecloth; add to saucepan. Bring to boiling; reduce heat. Cover and simmer about 30 minutes. Discard spice bag. Serve cider in mugs, sprinkled with nutmeg.

*Test Kitchen Tip: Use a vegetable peeler to peel the orange, making sure to get only the outer part and as little as possible of the bitter white layer under the orange skin.

Makes about eight (7-ounce) servings.
Per serving: 111 cal., 0 g total fat (0 g sat. fat), 0 mg chol., 1 mg sodium, 7 g carbo., 0 g fiber, 0 g pro. Dietary exchanges: 2 fruit.

Authentic Irish Coffee

From the St. James at Sag Bridge Church cookbook,
Lemont, Illinois

$1^1/2$	oz. Irish whiskey (3 Tbsp.)
1	Tbsp. brown sugar
1	cup brewed coffee
1	Tbsp. whipping cream, slightly whipped

Start to finish: 5 min.

1. Pour whiskey into a 10-ounce mug. Stir in brown sugar. Add coffee; stir until sugar is dissolved. With a spoon, carefully dollop whipped cream so it will float on the surface of the coffee.

Makes one (10-ounce) serving.

Per serving: 200 cal., 6 g total fat (3 g sat. fat), 21 mg chol., 14 mg sodium, 10 g carbo., 0 g fiber, 1 g pro. Dietary exchanges: 1 fat.

A Parish with a Purpose
St. James' earliest parishioners were primarily Irish, but German and Polish immigrants attended services too. They came to work in the limestone quarries and to build the Illinois & Michigan Canal, begun in 1836, that connected the Great Lakes to the Mississippi River. Some of their descendants still attend St. James at Sag Bridge Church.

Spiced Tea

From Southern Settings, a cookbook benefiting
Decatur General Hospital, Decatur, Alabama

2 cups water	3 cups orange juice
3 inches stick cinnamon	1/4 cup lemon juice
1/2 tsp. whole cloves	Ice (optional)
3 tea bags	
3/4 cup sugar	**Prep:** 15 min. **Chill:** 4 hr.
3 cups pineapple juice	

Good Medicine
When the idea to write a cookbook benefiting Decatur General Hospital was conceived in 1994, nurses, doctors, hospital supporters, and restaurateurs in this northern Alabama town pitched in with hundreds of recipes. One-and-a-half years later, Southern Settings was born. Proceeds from the sale of the book support hospital services, such as the nursery, and provide scholarships for employees to continue their education.

1. In a medium saucepan, combine water, cinnamon, and cloves. Bring to boiling; reduce heat. Cover; simmer for 5 minutes. Remove from heat; add tea bags. Let steep for 5 minutes. Remove tea bags and spices. Stir in sugar and juices. Cover and chill for at least 4 hours.

Makes eight (8-ounce) servings.
Per serving: 167 cal., 0 g total fat (0 g sat. fat), 0 mg chol., 5 mg sodium, 42 g carbo., 0 g fiber, 1 g pro. Dietary exchanges: 3 fruit.

Coffee Punch

From I'll Cook When Pigs Fly—And They Do in Cincinnati!
cookbook of the Junior League of Cincinnati, Ohio

1   qt. coffee ice cream
1   12-oz. can ginger ale, chilled
1   12-oz. can cream soda, chilled

Start to finish: 5 min.

1. Place ice cream in a punch bowl; stir to soften slightly. Slowly pour carbonated beverages down side of bowl, stirring into ice cream.

Note: The recipe doubles easily.

Makes 8 to 10 servings.
Per serving: 179 cal., 8 g total fat (5 g sat. fat), 25 mg chol., 44 mg sodium, 26 g carbo., 0 g fiber, 2 g pro. Dietary exchanges: 1 fat.

Around Town

Cincinnati (pop. 364,000) The city is surrounded by hills, graceful bridges, and the picturesque Ohio River. Each September, the city celebrates its German roots with the largest Oktoberfest outside Munich. Throughout the year, food lovers nosh on German specialties such as spareribs, kraut, and strudel. Another local favorite is Traditional Cincinnati Chili (see recipe, page 83).

Champagne Punch

From Gracious Goodness Christmas in Charleston, a cookbook benefiting
Bishop England High School, Charleston, South Carolina

SWEET OR DRY?
Technically, true Champagne comes only from the Champagne region of France. Champagne is just one kind of sparkling wine. You can use true Champagne for this recipe, or some other sparkling wine. The label on the bottle gives a hint to how sweet or dry it is. Brut is bone dry to nearly dry; extra sec or extra dry is slightly sweeter; sec is medium sweet; demi-sec is sweet; and doux is very sweet. Demi-sec and doux are considered dessert wines.

1	cup fresh strawberries
1	kiwi fruit, peeled and sliced
1	lemon, sliced and seeded
1	lime, sliced and seeded
1 1/2	cups sugar
1	20-oz. can pineapple chunks, drained
3/4	cup lemon juice

1	750-ml bottle Champagne, chilled
1	750-ml bottle dry white wine, chilled
	Additional lemon and/or lime slices (optional)

Prep: 25 min. **Freeze:** 8 hr.

1. Fill a 6-cup ring mold two-thirds full of water and freeze overnight. Remove from freezer; arrange strawberries, kiwi fruit, and seeded lemon and lime slices on top of ice. Fill mold with water to within 1/2 inch of top. (Fruit will not be completely covered.) Wrap mold with plastic wrap and refreeze.

2. Sprinkle 1/2 cup of the sugar on pineapple; set aside. Combine lemon juice and remaining sugar; stir until sugar dissolves. In a 3-quart punch bowl, combine the pineapple, lemon juice mixture, Champagne, and wine. Remove ice ring from mold; place gently in punch bowl with fruit side up. Float additional lemon and/or lime slices in punch bowl and cups when serving, if desired.

Make-ahead tip: Freeze ice ring up to 1 week before needed.

Makes about 2 quarts (sixteen 4-ounce servings).
Per serving: 161 cal., 0 g total fat (0 g sat. fat), 0 mg chol., 4 mg sodium, 27 g carbo., 1 g fiber, 1 g pro. Dietary exchanges: 2 fruit.

Cory's Health Shake

From *Family Favorites & Many More*, cookbook of the third-grade class at
Herbert Schenk Elementary School, Madison, Wisconsin

2	cups strawberries
1	large banana, cut up
1	cup milk
1	cup ice cubes
2	rounded Tbsp. creamy peanut butter
1	to 2 tsp. sugar (optional)

Start to finish: 10 min.

1. In a blender container, combine all ingredients. Cover and blend until smooth. Pour into glasses.

Makes four (6-ounce) servings.
Per serving: 157 cal., 8 g total fat (2 g sat. fat), 5 mg chol., 88 mg sodium, 19 g carbo., 3 g fiber, 6 g pro.
Dietary exchanges: 1½ fruit, ½ high-fat meat.

Cooking Class
Family Favorites & Many More grew out of a project of Mrs. Krizmanic's third-grade class at Herbert Schenk Elementary School in Madison, Wisconsin. As the class was studying the food pyramid and healthful eating, the children decided to ask their families, friends, school staff, and other students, as well as community and national celebrities, for their favorite recipes. The students were so pleased with the response that they compiled a class cookbook. It includes everything from snacks to main dishes to desserts, with notes and letters from celebrities in between.

Fruit Slush

From The Purple Pantry Cook Book, cookbook of the
University of Northern Iowa Alumni Association, Cedar Falls, Iowa

3 cups water	3 ripe medium bananas, mashed
2 cups sugar	12 cups ginger ale, chilled
1 46-oz. can unsweetened	
pineapple juice	**Prep:** 20 min. **Freeze:** 8 hr. **Stand:** 20 min.
1½ cups orange juice	
¼ cup lemon juice	

Purple Power

Located in quiet, picturesque Cedar Falls, the University of Northern Iowa is one of three state schools in Iowa. The students, staff, and alumni of UNI love purple! It's the school color and a symbol of school pride. That's why The Purple Pantry Cook Book boasts the color in its name and on its cover—and even uses purple type. Proceeds from this 300-plus-page, recipe-packed volume support activities and scholarships sponsored by the Alumni Association.

1. In a medium saucepan, combine water and sugar. Bring to boiling; remove from heat. Pour into a 13×9×2-inch baking pan. Stir in pineapple juice, orange juice, and lemon juice; add mashed bananas. Cover and freeze for 8 to 24 hours or until firm.

2. To serve, let mixture stand at room temperature for 20 to 30 minutes. For each serving, scrape a large spoon across frozen mixture to form slush (or break frozen mixture into small chunks); spoon about ½ cup slush into glass. Slowly pour about ½ cup of the ginger ale down side to fill glass; stir.

Makes twenty-four (8-ounce) servings.
Per serving: 149 cal., 0 g total fat (0 g sat. fat), 0 mg chol., 13 mg sodium, 38 g carbo., 1 g fiber, 0 g pro. Dietary exchanges: 2½ fruit.

2.

Breads and Spreads

Blueberry Gems

From Our Family Favorites, cookbook of the
Spring Valley Lutheran Church Sunday School, Spring Valley, Wisconsin

	Nonstick cooking spray		2	egg whites
1½	cups all-purpose flour		⅔	cup orange juice
¼	cup sugar		2	Tbsp. cooking oil
1½	tsp. baking powder		1	tsp. vanilla
¼	tsp. salt		1	cup fresh or frozen blueberries

Prep: 15 min. **Bake:** 15 min.

MUFFINS 101
Here are a few pointers to make your muffins the best they can be:
•After adding the liquid mixture to the flour mixture, stir just until moistened. If you try to stir out all the lumps, your muffins will have peaks, tunnels, and a tough texture.
•Bake the muffins as soon after mixing as possible. Batters that use baking powder and baking soda need to be baked immediately so the leavening power is not lost.
•Muffins are done when their tops are golden.
•To avoid soggy muffins, cool them in the baking pan only as long as directed in the recipe.

1. Lightly coat thirty-six 1¾-inch muffin cups with cooking spray; set aside.

2. In a medium bowl, stir together flour, sugar, baking powder, and salt. Make a well in center of flour mixture; set aside. In another bowl, stir together egg whites, orange juice, oil, and vanilla. Add egg white mixture all at once to flour mixture; stir just until moistened. Fold in blueberries.

3. Spoon into prepared muffin cups, filling each about two-thirds full. Bake in a 400°F oven for 15 to 18 minutes or until golden and toothpick inserted into centers comes out clean. Cool in pans on wire racks for 5 minutes; remove from pans. Serve warm.

Makes 36 muffins.
Per muffin: 35 cal., 1 g total fat (0 g sat. fat), 0 mg chol., 36 mg sodium, 6 g carbo., 0 g fiber, 1 g pro. Dietary exchanges: ½ starch.

Doughnut Muffins

From *Black Tie & Boots Optional*, cookbook of the
Colleyville Women's Club, Colleyville, Texas

1/3 cup shortening	1/2 cup milk
1/2 cup sugar	1/2 cup sugar
1 egg	1 tsp. ground cinnamon
1/2 tsp. orange extract or vanilla	1/4 cup butter or margarine, melted
1 1/2 cups all-purpose flour	
1 1/2 tsp. baking powder	**Prep:** 15 min. **Bake:** 20 min.
1/2 tsp. salt	

1. Grease twelve 2 1/2-inch muffin cups; set aside. In a large mixing bowl, beat shortening and 1/2 cup of the sugar with an electric mixer on medium to high speed until well combined. Add egg and orange extract; beat well. Combine flour, baking powder, and salt; add to egg mixture alternately with milk, beating well after each addition. Spoon batter into prepared muffin cups, filling each two-thirds full.

2. Bake in 350°F oven about 20 minutes or until a toothpick inserted in center comes out clean. Cool for 5 minutes; remove from pans. In a small bowl, combine the remaining 1/2 cup sugar and the cinnamon. While still warm, brush all sides of each muffin with melted butter and dip in the sugar-cinnamon mixture. Serve warm.

Makes 12 muffins.
Per muffin: 213 cal., 10 g total fat (4 g sat. fat), 29 mg chol., 199 mg sodium, 28 g carbo., 0 g fiber, 2 g pro. Dietary exchanges: 2 starch, 1 1/2 fat.

Gierek's Favorite Muffins

From the Greenfield Village School Cookbook,
Greenfield, New Hampshire

PAGE PHOTO APPEARS ON 36

2	cups all-purpose flour	1	cup milk
1	cup sugar	1/3	cup butter, melted
1/3	cup unsweetened cocoa powder	3/4	cup peanut butter-flavored baking pieces
1	Tbsp. baking powder		
1/2	tsp. salt		
1	slightly beaten egg		**Prep:** 15 min. **Bake:** 18 min.

Schoolhouse Favorites

When plans were announced to close the old Greenfield Village School, dedicated in 1886, Greenfield parents wanted to make sure the school—where a handheld bell still announced the start of each school day—would not be forgotten. A cookbook was proposed, and many town residents pitched in. Twelve-year-old Gierek Hoszkiewicz says this yummy chocolate-peanut butter muffin is his all-time favorite recipe.

1. Line eighteen 2½-inch muffin cups or six 3¼-inch jumbo muffin cups with paper bake cups (or grease muffin cups); set aside. In a medium bowl, stir together flour, sugar, cocoa powder, baking powder, and salt. Make a well in the center of the flour mixture.

2. In another bowl, combine egg, milk, and melted butter; add all at once to flour mixture. Stir just until moistened. Fold in peanut butter-flavored baking pieces.

3. Spoon batter into prepared muffin cups, filling each three-quarters full. Bake muffins until toothpick inserted in centers comes out clean. Bake regular muffins in a 400°F oven for 18 to 20 minutes; bake jumbo muffins in a 350°F oven about 30 minutes. Cool on wire rack for 5 minutes. Remove from cups; cool slightly.

Makes 18 regular muffins or 6 jumbo muffins.
Per regular muffin: 173 cal., 6 g total fat (2 g sat. fat), 23 mg chol., 188 mg sodium, 26 g carbo., 1 g fiber, 4 g pro. Dietary exchanges: 1½ starch, 1 fat.

Oatmeal Biscuits

From Delicious Developments, a cookbook benefiting Strong Memorial Hospital, Rochester, New York

2 cups all-purpose flour	1 cup milk
1 cup oat flour*	1/2 cup maple syrup
1 cup rolled oats	1 Tbsp. finely shredded orange peel
2 tsp. cream of tartar	
1 tsp. baking soda	
1 tsp. ground cinnamon	**Prep:** 15 min. **Bake:** 10 min.
2/3 cup butter	

1. Grease a very large cookie sheet; set it aside.

2. In a large bowl, combine the all-purpose flour, oat flour, rolled oats, cream of tartar, baking soda, and cinnamon. Using a pastry blender or two knives, cut in the butter until mixture resembles coarse crumbs. Combine the milk, maple syrup, and orange peel. Add to the flour mixture all at once; stir just until moistened.

3. For each biscuit, drop 1/4 cup dough onto prepared cookie sheet, dropping biscuits 2 inches apart. Bake in a 400°F oven for 10 to 12 minutes or until a toothpick comes out clean and bottoms are golden brown. Serve warm.

*Test Kitchen Tip: If you can't find oat flour at your supermarket, place 1 1/2 cups rolled oats in a blender container or food processor bowl. Cover and blend or process until finely ground. Measure 1 cup.

Makes 16 biscuits.
Per biscuit: 209 cal., 9 g total fat (5 g sat. fat), 23 mg chol., 171 mg sodium, 28 g carbo., 2 g fiber, 4 g pro. Dietary exchanges: 2 starch, 1 fat.

To Your Health
Nestled in upstate New York, Strong Memorial Hospital serves the Finger Lakes region that surrounds Rochester, providing much-needed health-care services and serving as the principal teaching hospital for the University of Rochester. The members of Friends of Strong, a volunteer group, support the hospital by donating their time and raising funds. Delicious Developments, a 272-page cookbook, is one way the organization helps support the hospital's trauma center.

Four Cheeses Baking Powder Biscuits

From Picnics, Potlucks & Prizewinners:
Celebrating Indiana Hospitality with 4-H Family and Friends

2 cups all-purpose flour	Monterey Jack, and American
1 Tbsp. baking powder	cheese, or 1 cup shredded
1/4 tsp. salt	four-cheese mix
1/4 cup butter, chilled	2/3 cup milk
1/4 cup each of shredded sharp cheddar, white cheddar,	

Prep: 15 min. **Bake:** 10 min.

Blue-Ribbon Biscuits

To Brandon Manier, 14, cooking is like a science experiment. He's always looking for new ways to perk up a standard biscuit recipe. His Four Cheeses Baking Powder Biscuits won him top 4-H honors at the Tipton County and Indiana state fairs.

1. In a medium bowl, stir together flour, baking powder, and salt. Cut in butter until the mixture resembles coarse crumbs.

2. Stir in cheeses. Add milk, stirring just until mixture is moistened. Turn out onto a lightly floured surface. Quickly knead dough by gently folding and pressing it 10 to 12 strokes or until nearly smooth. Pat or lightly roll dough to 1/2-inch thickness.

3. Cut dough with a floured 2 1/2-inch biscuit cutter. Place biscuits 1 inch apart on an ungreased baking sheet. Bake in a 450°F oven for 10 to 12 minutes or until bottoms are golden brown. Serve warm.

Makes 10 to 12 biscuits.

Per biscuit: 180 cal., 9 g total fat (6 g sat. fat), 26 mg chol., 306 mg sodium, 18 g carbo., 0 g fiber, 6 g pro. Dietary exchanges: 1 starch, 1 fat.

Grammer's Corn Bread

From Out of the Ordinary, cookbook of the
Hingham Historical Society, Hingham, Massachusetts

2	Tbsp. cooking oil		1	egg
2	cups stone-ground white cornmeal or cornmeal		1	cup buttermilk or sour milk*
1/2	cup all-purpose flour		1/2	cup water
1/4	cup sugar (optional)		1/4	cup bacon drippings or cooking oil
2 1/2	tsp. baking powder			
1	tsp. salt			
1/4	tsp. baking soda			

Prep: 20 min. **Bake:** 15 min.

THE COLORS OF CORNMEAL
Cornmeal can be white, yellow, or blue, depending on the type of corn that was dried and ground to make it. Cornmeal labeled "stone-ground" is slightly coarser than other cornmeal and has a slightly nuttier taste and crunch.

1. Pour 2 tablespoons oil into a 9- or 10-inch cast-iron skillet; place in oven and preheat oven to 450°F. (Or, to use a 9×9×2-inch baking pan, omit the 2 tablespoons oil and grease the bottom and 1/2 inch up the sides of the pan; set aside.)

2. Meanwhile, in a large bowl, combine cornmeal, flour, sugar (if desired), baking powder, salt, and baking soda. Make a well in the center of the cornmeal mixture; set aside.

3. In a medium bowl, combine egg, buttermilk, water, and bacon drippings or cooking oil. Add buttermilk mixture all at once to cornmeal mixture. Stir just until moistened.

4. Carefully and evenly spread batter into hot skillet (or prepared baking pan). Bake in the 450°F oven for 15 to 20 minutes or until golden. Serve warm.

*Note: To make 1 cup sour milk, place 1 tablespoon lemon juice or vinegar in a glass measuring cup. Add enough milk to make 1 cup total liquid; stir. Let the mixture stand for 5 minutes before using it in a recipe.

Makes 8 or 9 servings.
Per serving: 261 cal., 11 g total fat (3 g sat. fat), 34 mg chol., 497 mg sodium, 34 g carbo., 3 g fiber, 5 g pro. Dietary exchanges: 2 starch, 2 fat.

Overnight Coffee Cake

From Out of the Ordinary, cookbook of the
Hingham Historical Society, Hingham, Massachusetts

2	cups all-purpose flour		1	8-oz. carton dairy sour cream*
2	tsp. baking powder		3/4	cup packed brown sugar
1/2	tsp. baking soda		1	tsp. ground cinnamon
1/2	to 1 tsp. ground nutmeg		1/2	cup chopped nuts
1/2	tsp. salt			
3/4	cup butter, softened		**Prep:** 20 min. **Chill:** Overnight **Bake:** 30 min.
1	cup granulated sugar			
2	eggs			

Extraordinary Food

Now a 14-room museum, The Old Ordinary was built as a one-room home in 1680 and later became a tavern. It was frequented by Daniel Webster and other stagecoach travelers, who could get an "ordinary" meal there. Patrons drank their ale out of pint and quart tankards. If they overindulged, the owner would remind them to "watch your p's and q's." Proceeds from the sale of Out of the Ordinary help preserve and maintain the museum.

1. Grease and flour a 13×9×2-inch baking pan; set aside. In a medium bowl, combine flour, baking powder, baking soda, nutmeg, and salt; set aside.

2. In a large mixing bowl, beat butter with an electric mixer on medium to high speed for 30 seconds. Add granulated sugar; beat well. Add eggs and sour cream; beat until combined. Add flour mixture; beat on low speed just until combined. Spread batter into prepared pan. Stir together brown sugar, cinnamon, and nuts; sprinkle over batter. Cover; chill overnight.

3. Bake, uncovered, in a 350°F oven for 30 to 35 minutes or until toothpick inserted near the center comes out clean. Serve warm.

*Test Kitchen Tip: Reduced-fat sour cream should not be used in this recipe; this cake needs the extra fat to tenderize it.

Makes 12 servings.

Per serving: 378 cal., 20 g total fat (11 g sat. fat), 77 mg chol., 366 mg sodium, 46 g carbo., 1 g fiber, 5 g pro. Dietary exchanges: 3 fat.

Tennessee Whiskey Meatballs, p. 17

Jack's Party Pecans, p. 7

Oriental Cabbage Dip, p. 10

At your next party, try serving Jack's Party Pecans and Sweet, Hot, and Sour Tennessee Whiskey Meatballs, above left. The Jack Daniel Distillery in Lynchburg, Tennessee, above, offers free daily tours. For a bit of extra flair, line the serving bowl for Oriental Cabbage Dip, below left, with the outer leaves from heads of red and green cabbage.

Spiced Tea is tea with a twist—three kinds of fruit juice, cinnamon, and cloves. It's perfect for sipping on the front porch on a warm summer day.

Spiced Tea, p. 20

Party Pizza Appetizers, p. 16

MaMa's Dinner Rolls, p. 47

To be ready for drop-in company, assemble Party Pizza Appetizers, above left, then place in a single layer on a baking sheet lined with waxed paper and freeze until firm. Pop them in the oven for 10 minutes and they're done—hot, crusty, and covered with melted cheese. MaMa's Dinner Rolls, below left, are soft and buttery. They're just the thing for mopping up the delicious gravy that accompanies the Sunday dinner roast.

Gierek's Favorite Muffins, p. 28

Twelve-year-old Gierek Hoszkiewicz, standing left, of Greenfield, New Hampshire, says these chocolate-peanut butter muffins are his all-time favorite. He makes them at least once a week. He and his brother Krystian are developing a love of cooking, thanks to their parents.

Apple Bread, **p.** 41

Maple Oatmeal Bread, **p.** 44

Most quick breads are loaded with nuts, but not Apple Bread, above left. This way the sweet, fruity flavor of apple really comes through. Gail Foreman, pictured above with daughter Annie, has lived in Wenatchee, Washington, most of her life. As a teenager, she was an Apple Blossom Festival princess and worked in the area's apple orchards.
Try Maple Oatmeal Bread, left, toasted and spread with Maple Butter, for a breakfast that will get you out of bed.

Sour Cream Buns, p. 48

Apple-Pear Butter, p. 51

Cherry-Peach Jam, p. 52

Lori Hull, left, of Sacramento, California, created Cherry-Peach Jam when she began experimenting with combining different fruits in her jams and preserves. It remains one of her favorites.

Apple Bread

From Slices & Bites of the Wenatchee Valley,
cookbook of the Applarians, Wenatchee, Washington

PAGE PHOTO APPEARS NO. 37

3	cups all-purpose flour	3	cups shredded, peeled cooking apples (4 medium)*
1	tsp. baking soda	2	cups sugar
1	tsp. salt	2/3	cup cooking oil
1	tsp. ground cinnamon	1	tsp. vanilla
1/4	tsp. baking powder		
3	beaten eggs		

Prep: 30 min. **Bake:** 45 min.

APPLE APPEAL
Exposing the flesh of an apple to the air turns it brown. To help cut or shredded apples keep their pretty green-white color, toss them with just a few drops of lemon juice.

1. Grease and flour three 7$\frac{1}{2}$x3$\frac{1}{2}$x2-inch or two 8x4x2-inch loaf baking pans. Set aside. In a medium bowl, combine flour, soda, salt, cinnamon, and baking powder; set aside.

2. In a large bowl, combine eggs, apples, sugar, oil, and vanilla. Stir in flour mixture just until moistened. Pour batter into prepared pans. Bake in a 325°F oven for 45 to 55 minutes or until toothpick inserted in center comes out clean. Cool in pans on wire racks for 10 minutes. Remove from pans. Cool on wire racks. Wrap and store overnight before slicing.

*Note: Golden Delicious, Rome, Granny Smith, Jonathan, or Newtown pippin apples are good choices for this bread.

Makes 30 servings.
Per serving: 152 cal., 6 g total fat (1 g sat. fat), 21 mg chol., 129 mg sodium, 24 g carbo., 1 g fiber, 2 g pro. Dietary exchanges: ½ fruit, 1 starch, 1 fat.

Zucchini Nut Bread

From Perennial Palette, cookbook of the Southborough Gardeners, Southborough, Massachusetts

2	cups all-purpose flour
1	Tbsp. ground cinnamon
1½	tsp. baking powder
½	tsp. salt
¼	tsp. baking soda
3	slightly beaten eggs
2	cups finely shredded zucchini
1½	cups sugar

¾	cup cooking oil
2	tsp. vanilla
1	tsp. lemon extract
1	cup raisins
1	cup shelled sunflower seeds or chopped walnuts, toasted

Prep: 25 min. **Bake:** 55 min.

1. Grease bottoms and ½ inch up the sides of two 8×4×2-inch loaf pans; set aside. In a medium bowl, combine flour, cinnamon, baking powder, salt, and baking soda; set aside.

2. In a large bowl, combine eggs, zucchini, sugar, oil, vanilla, and lemon extract; mix well. Add flour mixture to zucchini mixture; stir just until moistened. (Batter will be lumpy.) Fold in raisins and sunflower seeds or nuts. Spoon batter into the prepared pans.

3. Bake in a 350°F oven about 55 minutes or until a toothpick inserted near the centers comes out clean. Cool in pans for 10 minutes. Remove from pans. Cool completely on wire racks.

Test Kitchen Tip: Most quick breads slice more easily if they are wrapped in foil and held overnight. However, this moist loaf slices nicely on the same day it's baked.

Makes 2 loaves (32 slices).
Per slice: 155 cal., 8 g total fat (1 g sat. fat), 20 mg chol., 72 mg sodium, 19 g carbo., 1 g fiber, 3 g pro. Dietary exchanges: 1½ starch, 1 fat.

Finnish Cardamom Bread

*From Treasured Recipes of the Shipwreck Coast, cookbook of the
Great Lakes Shipwreck Historical Society, Whitefish Point, Michigan*

4 to 4½ cups all-purpose flour	⅓ cup butter
1 pkg. active dry yeast	¼ cup water
½ to 1 tsp. ground cardamom	½ tsp. salt
¾ cup milk	2 eggs
½ cup sugar	

Prep: 20 min. **Rise:** 1 hr. + 30 min. **Bake:** 20 min.

Scandinavian Delights

The Finns, Swedes, and Norwegians who settled the 80-mile stretch of Lake Superior known as the Shipwreck Coast (two-thirds of the 550 ships that have gone down in Lake Superior met their fate here) brought their love of cardamom-laced baked goods with them from Scandinavia. Thanks to profits from the sale of Treasured Recipes of the Shipwreck Coast, tales of the ships that have braved the often-treacherous waters of the Great Lakes will continue to be told at the Shipwreck Museum.

1. In a large bowl, combine 2 cups of the flour, the yeast, and cardamom; set aside. In a medium saucepan, heat and stir milk, sugar, butter, water, and salt just until warm (120°F to 130°F) and butter almost melts. Add milk mixture and eggs to flour mixture. Beat with an electric mixer on low to medium speed for 30 seconds, scraping side of bowl constantly. Beat on high speed for 3 minutes. Stir in as much of the remaining flour as you can.

2. Turn dough out onto a lightly floured surface. Knead in enough of the remaining flour to make a moderately soft dough that is smooth and elastic (3 to 5 minutes). Shape dough into a ball. Place in a lightly greased bowl, turning once to grease surface of dough. Cover; let rise in a warm place until double in size (1 to 1¼ hours).

3. Punch dough down. Turn onto a lightly floured surface. Cover; let rest 10 minutes. Grease a baking sheet.

4. Divide dough into thirds. Shape each portion into a 15-inch rope. To shape, place the ropes 1 inch apart on prepared baking sheet. Loosely braid the ropes of dough, working from the center to each end. Press the ends together to seal and tuck under the loaf. Cover; let rise in a warm place until nearly double (about 30 minutes).

5. Bake in a 375°F oven for 20 to 25 minutes or until bread sounds hollow when tapped. (If necessary, cover loosely with foil for last 10 minutes of baking to prevent overbrowning.) Remove bread from baking sheet. Cool on a wire rack.

Makes 1 loaf (16 slices).
Per slice: 181 cal., 5 g total fat (3 g sat. fat), 38 mg chol., 128 mg sodium, 29 g carbo., 1 g fiber, 4 g pro. Dietary exchanges: 2 starch, ½ fat.

Maple Oatmeal Bread

*From Gretchen Grape of Holcombe, Wisconsin, winner of the
Wisconsin Maple Syrup Producers' third annual recipe contest*

PAGE PHOTO APPEARS ON 37

1	pkg. active dry yeast
1¼	cups warm water (105°F to 115°F)
⅓	cup maple syrup
1	Tbsp. cooking oil
1	tsp. salt
1	cup quick-cooking rolled oats

2¾ to 3¼ cups bread flour
Maple Butter (optional)

Prep: 15 min. **Rise:** 45 min. + 30 min. **Bake:** 35 min.

A Sticky Situation

Gretchen Grape knew she'd never win big money at the Wisconsin Maple Syrup Producers third annual recipe contest. She entered her yeast bread to support the event because she and her husband are fourth-generation maple syrup producers. "Whenever I can, I substitute maple syrup for granulated sugar," says Gretchen. "I'm always experimenting with new ways to sweeten with our homegrown product."

1. In a large bowl, sprinkle yeast over warm water; let stand 5 minutes. Stir in maple syrup, cooking oil, salt, and rolled oats. Stir in 2½ cups of the bread flour, a little at a time, until dough begins to form a ball.

2. Turn out onto a lightly floured surface. Knead in enough of the remaining bread flour to make a moderately stiff dough that is smooth and elastic (6 to 8 minutes).

3. Shape dough into a ball. Place in a lightly greased bowl, turning once to grease surface of dough. Cover; let rise in a warm place until double in size (45 to 60 minutes).

4. Punch dough down. Turn out onto a lightly floured surface. Divide dough in half. Cover; let dough rest for 10 minutes. Meanwhile, grease two 8×4×2-inch loaf pans.

5. To shape, gently pat and pinch each portion into a loaf shape, tucking edges beneath. Place into prepared pans. Sprinkle with quick-cooking rolled oats, if desired. Cover; let rise in a warm place until nearly double (30 to 40 minutes).

6. Bake in a 350°F oven for 35 to 40 minutes. Immediately remove from pans. Cool on wire racks. Serve with Maple Butter, if desired.

Maple Butter: Stir together 2 tablespoons maple syrup and ½ cup softened butter until smooth.

Makes 2 loaves (24 slices).
Per slice: 90 cal., 1 g total fat (0 g sat. fat), 0 mg chol., 98 mg sodium, 17 g carbo., 1 g fiber, 3 g pro. Dietary exchanges: 1 starch.

South-of-the-Border Bread

From Picnics, Potlucks & Prizewinners:
Celebrating Indiana Hospitality with 4-H Family and Friends

3	to 3½ cups all-purpose flour
1	pkg. active dry yeast
½	cup yellow cornmeal
¼	tsp. baking soda
½	cup buttermilk or sour milk*
⅓	cup finely chopped onion
¼	cup butter or margarine
¾	tsp. salt
½	cup shredded cheddar cheese (2 oz.)

1	egg
½	cup canned cream-style corn
⅓	cup chopped green sweet pepper
1	small fresh hot chile pepper, seeded and finely chopped
1	Tbsp. butter or margarine, melted

Prep: 40 min. **Rise:** 1 hr. + 30 min.
Bake: 30 min.

Taste of the State
The volunteers who worked on Picnics, Potlucks & Prizewinners: Celebrating Indiana Hospitality with 4-H Families and Friends gathered recipes to represent the diversity of Indiana agriculture and cooking. These folks, from all over the state, are loyal supporters of 4-H, a national organization that helps kids develop life skills through a variety of projects that range from baking biscuits or raising hogs to making model rockets or becoming computer savvy.

1. In a large bowl, combine 1¼ cups of the flour, yeast, cornmeal, and baking soda. In a small saucepan, combine the buttermilk, onion, the ¼ cup butter, and salt; heat and stir just until warm (120°F to 130°F) and butter almost melts. Add buttermilk mixture, cheese, egg, corn, sweet pepper, and hot chile pepper to flour mixture. Beat with an electric mixer on low speed for 30 seconds, scraping sides of bowl. Beat on high speed 3 minutes. Stir in as much remaining flour as you can.

2. Turn onto a lightly floured surface. Knead in enough remaining flour to make moderately stiff dough (6 to 8 minutes). Shape into a ball. Place in a greased bowl, turning to lightly grease surface. Cover; let rise until double in size (about 1 hour).

3. Grease a large baking sheet; set aside. Punch dough down; divide into thirds. Cover; let rest 10 minutes. Roll each third into a 14-inch rope. Place ropes on prepared baking sheet 1 inch apart. Starting in middle, loosely braid by bringing left rope under center rope. Bring right rope under new center rope. Repeat to end. On other end, braid by bringing alternate ropes over center rope to center.

4. Cover; let rise until nearly double (30 minutes). Bake in a 350°F oven for 30 minutes or until golden and bread sounds hollow when tapped. Brush with melted butter. Cool on wire rack.

*Note: To make sour milk, place 1½ teaspoons lemon juice or vinegar in a glass measuring cup. Add enough milk to make ½ cup total liquid; stir. Let stand for 5 minutes before using.

Makes 1 loaf (16 slices).
Per slice: 160 cal., 6 g total fat (3 g sat. fat), 28 mg chol., 225 mg sodium, 23 g carbo., 1 g fiber, 5 g pro. Dietary exchanges: 1½ starch, 1 fat.

Potato Bread with Caraway Seeds

From Beyond Burlap, cookbook of the
Boise Junior League, Boise, Idaho

1	medium potato
1	pkg. active dry yeast
1¼	cups warm water (105°F to 115°F)
3¾	to 4¼ cups all-purpose flour
1	tsp. salt
1	tsp. caraway seed

Prep: 1 hr. **Rise:** 45 min. + 35 min. **Bake:** 35 min.

Spud Country

In Boise, Idaho, members of the Junior League take their spuds seriously and with a grain of salt. Their cookbook, Beyond Burlap, is loaded with tater trivia, cooking tips, and folklore about Idaho's most famous crop. Junior League volunteers boiled, baked, mashed, and simmered 500 pounds of donated spuds to test 800 recipes. A total of 200 recipes—including some potato desserts—made the final cut.

1. In a small covered saucepan, cook potato in boiling salted water about 25 minutes or until tender. Drain; cool slightly; peel and mash. Measure ½ cup to use in recipe. Cool.

2. Meanwhile, in a large bowl, dissolve yeast in ½ cup of the warm water. Stir in 3 tablespoons of the flour. Let stand for 30 minutes. Stir in the remaining ¾ cup water, mashed potato, salt, and caraway seed. Stir in as much of the remaining flour as you can with a wooden spoon.

3. Turn out onto a lightly floured surface. Knead in enough remaining flour to make very stiff dough that is smooth and elastic (10 to 12 minutes). Shape dough into ball. Place dough in oiled bowl, turning once to coat the surface. Let rise in a warm place until double in size (45 to 60 minutes).

4. Punch dough down. Turn out onto lightly floured surface and knead until smooth (about 4 minutes), adding 1 to 2 tablespoons flour.

5. Butter a 10-inch cast-iron skillet; place dough in skillet. (Or form dough into a ball, tucking edges beneath. Place on greased baking sheet. Flatten slightly to circle 6 inches in diameter.) Cover; let rise until almost double (about 35 minutes).

6. Lightly brush dough with water; using a serrated knife, cut a ¼-inch-deep cross shape in center of loaf. Bake in a 400°F oven for 35 minutes or until golden. Remove from pan; cool completely on wire rack.

Makes 12 to 16 slices.

Per slice: 146 cal., 0 g total fat (0 g sat. fat), 0 mg chol., 180 mg sodium, 31 g carbo., 1 g fiber, 4 g pro. Dietary exchanges: 2 starch.

MaMa's Dinner Rolls

*From Bear-rif-ic Delights for All Appetites, cookbook of the
Church of the Living God, Chicago, Illinois*

1/4	cup warm water (105°F to 115°F)
2	pkgs. active dry yeast
1	cup milk
1	cup butter
1	cup sugar
1/2	tsp. salt

3	eggs
6	to 6 1/2 cups all-purpose flour
2	Tbsp. butter, melted

Prep: 40 min. **Rise:** 1 hr + 45 min. **Bake:** 20 min.

1. Stir together the warm water and yeast. Set aside.

2. In a medium saucepan, heat and stir milk, butter, sugar, and salt just until warm (120°F to 130°F) and butter almost melts. In a very large bowl, combine milk mixture, yeast mixture, and eggs. Stir in 4 1/2 cups of the flour. Cover bowl and let dough rise in a warm place until nearly double (1 to 1 1/2 hours). Stir dough down. Using a wooden spoon, stir in as much of the remaining flour as you can.

3. Turn the dough out onto a floured surface. Knead in enough of the remaining flour to make a moderately soft dough that is smooth and elastic (3 to 5 minutes). Cover and let rest for 10 minutes. (Dough will be soft.)

4. Brush three 9×1 1/2-inch round baking pans with some of the melted butter; set aside. On a lightly floured surface, roll dough to 1/2-inch thickness. Using a 2 1/2-inch round cutter, cut dough into about 30 rounds, rerolling dough as necessary. Brush rounds with remaining melted butter.

5. Fold each round nearly in half, buttered side inside, so that the top slightly overlaps the bottom. Divide rolls evenly among the prepared pans. Cover; let rise in a warm place until almost double (about 45 minutes).

6. Bake in a 350°F oven for about 20 minutes or until rolls are golden. Invert onto wire racks to cool slightly; serve warm.

Makes about 30 rolls.

Per roll: 182 cal., 8 g total fat (5 g sat. fat), 40 mg chol., 116 mg sodium, 25 g carbo., 1 g fiber, 4 g pro. Dietary exchanges: 1 1/2 starch, 1 1/2 fat.

Grandma's Good Cooking

Whenever Ronnie Hawkins wants to re-create a favorite dish from her childhood, she opens Bear-rif-ic Delights for All Appetites, a church cookbook filled with her grandmother's recipes. Because Ronnie's grandmother (Ronnie and her sister called her "MaMa") was the wife of the bishop of the Church of the Living God, she was expected to contribute. The congregation also expected it because she was a good cook. "Amen!" says Ronnie.

When the only grocer and café in the tiny town of Gove, Kansas, closed several years ago, residents faced a 20-mile round-trip to pick up necessities like a gallon of milk. So the hardworking residents of sparsely populated Gove County formed the Gove Community Improvement Association. They ultimately built a new grocery store and café. A community cookbook was proposed to help raise additional funds. Gove County Gleanings includes a chapter highlighting what local cooks are best known for: breads made from famous Kansas wheat.

Sour Cream Buns

From Gove County Gleanings, a cookbook benefiting the Gove Community Improvement Association, Gove County, Kansas

1	pkg. active dry yeast
1/4	cup warm water (105°F to 115°F)
1	8-oz. carton dairy sour cream
3	Tbsp. granulated sugar
2	Tbsp. shortening
1	tsp. salt
1/8	tsp. baking soda
1	egg

3	to 3 1/4 cups all-purpose flour
2	Tbsp. butter, softened
1/3	cup packed brown sugar
1	tsp. ground cinnamon
3/4	cup sifted powdered sugar
2	to 4 tsp. water

Prep: 35 min. **Rise:** 45 min. **Bake:** 15 min.

1. In a large bowl, dissolve yeast in warm water.

2. In a small saucepan, combine sour cream, granulated sugar, shortening, and salt. Heat and stir over medium-low heat until warm (120°F to 130°F) and shortening is almost melted. Stir in baking soda. Stir sour cream mixture and egg into yeast. Stir in as much of the flour as you can.

3. Turn dough out onto lightly floured surface; knead in enough of the remaining flour to make moderately soft dough (3 to 5 minutes total). Cover and let rest for 5 minutes.

4. Grease twelve 2 1/2-inch muffin cuts; set aside. On a lightly floured surface, roll dough into an 18×12-inch rectangle; spread with softened butter. Combine brown sugar and cinnamon; sprinkle evenly over the dough. Roll up, starting from the long side; seal seam. Slice into twelve 1 1/2-inch wide pieces. Place each bun, cut side down, in a prepared muffin cup. Cover and let rise in a warm place until 1/4 to 1/2 inch above tops of cups (45 minutes).

5. Bake in a 400°F oven about 15 minutes or until golden brown. Remove from pans. Combine powdered sugar and enough water to make an icing of drizzling consistency; drizzle over rolls. Serve warm.

Test Kitchen Tip: After baking, buns may be cooled, wrapped, labeled, and frozen for up to 3 weeks. To reheat, wrap buns in foil. Bake in a 325°F oven for 30 minutes. Prepare icing, and drizzle over warm rolls. Serve warm.

Makes 12 buns.

Per bun: 250 cal., 9 g total fat (4 g sat. fat), 32 mg chol., 246 mg sodium, 38 g carbo., 1 g fiber, 4 g pro. Dietary exchanges: 2 1/2 bread, 1 1/2 fat.

Cheddar-Corn Rolls

From *Savoring the Southwest Again*, cookbook of the
Roswell Symphony Guild, Roswell, New Mexico

4	to 4½ cups all-purpose flour
¾	cup cornmeal
2	pkg. active dry yeast
1¼	cups buttermilk or sour milk
¼	cup sugar
3	Tbsp. butter or cooking oil
3	Tbsp. Dijon-style mustard
2	tsp. salt
2	eggs

1 cup shredded sharp cheddar
cheese (4 oz.)

Prep: 45 min. **Rise:** 1½ hr. + 45 min.
Bake: 15 min.

1. In a large mixing bowl, combine 1½ cups of the flour, the cornmeal, and yeast; set aside.

2. In a medium saucepan, combine buttermilk, sugar, butter, mustard, and salt; heat and stir until mixture is lukewarm (120°F to 130°F). Add to flour mixture; add eggs and cheese.

3. Beat with an electric mixer on low to medium speed for 30 seconds, scraping side of bowl constantly. Beat 3 minutes on high speed. Stir in as much of the remaining flour as you can with a wooden spoon.

4. On a lightly floured surface, knead in enough of the remaining flour to make a moderately stiff dough that is smooth and elastic (6 to 8 minutes).

Place dough in a greased bowl; turn once to grease surface. Cover; let rise in a warm place until double (about 1½ hours).

5. Grease baking sheets; set aside. Punch dough down. Cover; let rest for 10 minutes. Divide into 18 equal portions. Shape each portion into a ball, pulling edges under to make a smooth top. Place balls, 1 inch apart, on prepared baking sheets. Press each down to flatten slightly. Cover and let rise in a warm place until nearly double (about 45 minutes). Bake in a 375°F oven for 15 to 18 minutes.

Makes 18 rolls.

Per roll: 202 cal., 5 g total fat (3 g sat. fat), 36 mg chol., 358 mg sodium, 31 g carbo., 1 g fiber, 7 g pro. Dietary exchanges: 2 starch, 1 fat.

A Symphony of Flavors
In Roswell, New Mexico, the orchestra never has to play for its supper. Instead, supper is served to the musicians—a buffet prepared by Roswell Symphony Guild members featuring recipes from their cookbook, *Savoring the Southwest Again.* Proceeds from the book keep the orchestra playing. Most of the musicians travel 200 miles or more to Roswell for the five performances each season.

Microwave Berry Jam

From *A Taste of Oregon*, cookbook of the
Junior League of Eugene, Oregon

1½	to 2¼ cups fresh or frozen boysenberries, strawberries, blueberries, or raspberries (enough for 1 cup mashed)
¾	cup sugar
2	tsp. lemon juice
¼	tsp. butter or margarine*

Prep: 10 min. **Cook:** 8 min.

Of Land and Sea

When settlers from back East first arrived in Oregon, they found a bountiful selection of fresh seafood and game, woods full of wild berries, and fertile land for farming and gardening. *A Taste of Oregon* illustrates how creative Oregon cooks are with native and homegrown ingredients. It features recipes of almost every type, including those that use fresh crab or salmon, pheasant or other wild game, and fruits and vegetables straight from the garden.

1. Thaw berries, if frozen; do not drain. Mash berries; measure 1 cup. In 2-quart microwave-safe casserole combine the mashed berries, sugar, lemon juice, and butter.

2. Microwave on 100 percent power (high) for 8 to 9 minutes or until mixture thickens and is reduced to about 1 cup, stirring every 2 minutes.** Cool. Cover and chill to store. (The mixture will thicken a little as it is cooled and chilled. If the consistency becomes too stiff, stir in water, 1 teaspoon at a time, to reach desired consistency.)

*Test Kitchen Tip: The ¼ teaspoon butter or margarine is just enough to prevent excess foaming.

**Note: If you prefer seedless jam, press the hot fruit mixture through a sieve to remove the seeds. The yield will be slightly less than 1 cup (sixteen 1-tablespoon servings).

Makes about 1 cup.
Per tablespoon: 42 cal., 0 g total fat (0 g sat. fat), 0 mg chol., 1 mg sodium, 11 g carbo., 0 g fiber, 0 g pro. Dietary exchanges: ½ fruit.

Apple-Pear Butter

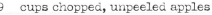

From Lori Hull,
Sacramento, California

9	cups chopped, unpeeled apples		1	tsp. ground cinnamon
3	cups chopped, unpeeled pears		1/2	tsp. ground cloves
3	cups water			
2	cups sugar		**Prep:** 30 min. **Cook:** 2 hr.
1	tsp. finely shredded lemon peel			

1. In a heavy 8- to 10-quart Dutch oven, combine apples, pears, and water. Bring to boiling; reduce heat. Cover and simmer for 30 minutes, stirring occasionally. Do not drain. Press mixture through a fine mesh sieve (you should have about 6 cups sieved mixture). Discard solids. Return sieved mixture to Dutch oven. Stir in sugar, lemon peel, cinnamon, and cloves. Bring to boiling; reduce heat. Simmer, uncovered, over low heat for 1¹/₂ hours or until very thick, stirring often.

2. Immediately ladle into hot, sterilized half-pint canning jars, leaving ¹/₄-inch headspace. Wipe jar rims; adjust lids. Process in boiling-water canner for 5 minutes (start timing when water boils). Remove jars and cool on racks.

Test Kitchen Tip: For good texture and flavor, choose fruit varieties that are best suited for canning. For apples, pick Granny Smith, Golden Delicious, or Rome Beauty. For pears, use ripe Bartletts.

Makes about four ¹/₂-pints.
Per tablespoon: 41 cal., 0 g total fat (0 g sat. fat), 0 mg chol., 0 mg sodium, 11 g carbo., 1 g fiber, 0 g pro. Dietary exchanges: ½ fruit.

Sweet on Jam
Lori Hull didn't grow up eating homemade jelly. But in 1990, she took a mother-and-daughter course with Loni on how to make freezer jam. It was a simple introduction and it paved the way for Lori to be named a Sacramento County Master Preserver in 1994 (a program offered through county extension offices). Canning became a way for Lori and Loni to spend time together. They donate many of their blue-ribbon winners to charities.

JAM BASICS

1. Bring the fruit mixture for jellies, jams, and conserves to a full, rolling boil. This means it bubbles vigorously and doesn't stop when stirred.

2. The hard boiling of the fruit can produce a white foam on the surface. Although it's harmless, canners often skim off the foam with a metal spoon before ladling the mixture into jars.

3. Food spills on the rim can prevent a perfect seal. Before topping with the lid and screw band, wipe rims with a clean, damp cloth.

4. Carefully add jars to boiling water in the canner. Jars shouldn't touch.

Cherry-Peach Jam

From Lori Hull.
Sacramento, California

3	cups finely chopped, pitted, peeled peaches (about 1½ lbs.)
2½	cups pitted tart red cherries, finely chopped (about 1¼ lbs.)
1	tsp. finely shredded lemon peel
1	Tbsp. lemon juice

1	1¾-oz. pkg. regular powdered fruit pectin
4	cups sugar

Prep: 35 min.

1. In a heavy 8- to 10-quart Dutch oven, combine chopped peaches, cherries, lemon peel, and lemon juice. Stir in powdered pectin. Bring fruit mixture to a full rolling boil, stirring constantly. Stir in sugar. Return to a full rolling boil, stirring constantly. Boil hard for 1 minute, stirring constantly with a wooden spoon. Remove from heat. Quickly skim off foam with a metal spoon.

2. Immediately ladle jam into hot, sterilized half-pint canning jars, leaving ¼-inch headspace. Wipe jar rims and adjust lids. Process jars in boiling-water canner for 5 minutes (start timing when water begins to boil). Remove jars and cool on racks.

Test Kitchen Tip: You can finely chop the peaches and cherries in a food processor. Use several on/off turns until fruit is finely chopped. Be careful not to overprocess the fruit, which will turn it into fruit puree.

Makes about five ½-pints.
Per tablespoon: 51 cal., 0 g total fat (0 g sat. fat), 0 mg chol., 1 mg sodium, 13 g carbo., 0 g fiber, 0 g pro. Dietary exchanges: ½ fruit.

3.

Beef, Pork, and Lamb

Braised Beef with Onions and Stout

From Cooking at the Irish Settlement, cookbook of
St. Patrick's Church, Cumming, Iowa

1	2-lb. boneless beef chuck pot roast		3	bay leaves
2	Tbsp. cooking oil		$1/2$	tsp. salt
1	large onion, sliced		$1/4$	tsp. black pepper
2	Tbsp. all-purpose flour		1	cup pitted dried plums
$3/4$	cup stout or other dark beer		2	to 3 Tbsp. hazelnuts (optional)
$3/4$	cup water		1	Tbsp. snipped fresh parsley
4	medium carrots, sliced 1 inch thick			

Prep: 20 min. **Bake:** 1 hr. 50 min.

1. In a 4-quart Dutch oven, brown meat in hot oil on both sides. Remove meat, reserving drippings in Dutch oven. Add onion; cook for 5 minutes. Remove from heat. Sprinkle flour over onion; stir to combine. Carefully stir in stout and water. Return the meat to the Dutch oven; add carrots, bay leaves, salt, and black pepper.

2. Bake, covered, in a 325°F oven for $1^{1}/2$ to $1^{3}/4$ hours or until meat is almost tender.

3. Stuff each dried plum with a hazelnut, if desired. Add dried plums and parsley to Dutch oven. Cover and bake for about 20 minutes more or until meat is tender. Discard bay leaves. Serve dried plums and onion-stout mixture with meat.

Makes 6 to 8 servings.
Per serving: 454 cal., 24 g total fat (8 g sat. fat), 97 mg chol., 303 mg sodium, 27 g carbo., 4 g fiber, 31 g pro. Dietary exchanges: 2 vegetable, 1½ fruit, 4 medium-fat meat, ½ fat.

PAGE 73 PHOTO APPEARS ON

Bloody Mary Pot Roast

From Savoring the Southwest Again, cookbook of the
Roswell Symphony Guild, Roswell, New Mexico

1	3- to 3½-lb. boneless beef bottom round roast
3	cloves garlic, thinly sliced
2	Tbsp. cooking oil
¾	cup Bloody Mary mix or hot-style tomato juice
¼	cup vodka or water
1	Tbsp. prepared horseradish
½	tsp. Worcestershire sauce

1	clove garlic, minced
2	Tbsp. vodka or water
4	tsp. cornstarch

Prep: 20 min. **Bake:** 2 hr.

1. Trim fat from roast. Cut slits in several places, making each slit about ½ inch long and 1 inch deep. Insert a small slice of garlic into each slit.

2. In a 4-quart Dutch oven, brown roast on all sides in hot oil. Remove from heat. Drain off fat. Combine Bloody Mary mix, the ¼ cup vodka, horseradish, Worcestershire sauce, and the minced garlic; carefully pour over roast. Bake covered, in a 325°F oven for 2 to 2½ hours or until very tender. Transfer to a platter, reserving juices in Dutch oven. Keep roast warm.

3. For gravy, measure cooking juices; skim off fat. If necessary, add enough water to measure 1½ cups. Return juices to Dutch oven. Combine the 2 tablespoons vodka and the cornstarch; stir into juices. Cook and stir over medium heat until bubbly; cook and stir for 1 minute more. Slice meat thinly across the grain; serve with gravy.

Makes 10 to 12 servings.
Per serving: 247 cal., 11 g total fat (3 g sat. fat), 87 mg chol., 145 mg sodium, 2 g carbo., 0 g fiber, 29 g pro. Dietary exchanges: 4 lean meat.

Around Town
Roswell, New Mexico (pop. 45,000) Located about 200 miles south of Albuquerque. Roswell is surrounded by pecan groves, chile pepper fields, and dairy farms. Home to the largest mozzarella cheese plant in the world, the town hosts the Chile Cheese Festival each fall, when more than 11 tons of chiles are roasted.

56

Brisket with Vegetables

From *A Taste of Tradition*, cookbook of Temple Emanu-El,
Providence, Rhode Island

1	4- to 4¼-lb. fresh beef brisket	2	lbs. potatoes, quartered (6 medium)
1	18-ounce bottle barbecue sauce	1	lb. carrots, cut into 2-inch pieces (6 medium)
1	cup ginger ale	2	medium onions, cut into wedges
1	envelope onion soup mix (half of a 2½-oz. box)	2	Tbsp. snipped parsley
2	cloves garlic, minced		
½	tsp. black pepper		
6	inches stick cinnamon		

Prep: 15 min. **Bake:** 3½ hr.

KEEP IT KOSHER
In the Jewish tradition, Passover meals include numerous traditional dishes, including Brisket with Vegetables. To make this recipe kosher for Passover, substitute catsup for the barbecue sauce. Serve it with steamed asparagus or red cabbage.

1. Trim excess fat from meat. Place meat in large, shallow roasting pan. Stir together barbecue sauce, ginger ale, dry soup mix, garlic, and black pepper. Pour over meat. Arrange cinnamon sticks around meat. Cover pan with foil.

2. Bake in a 325°F oven for 2 hours, turning meat once. Arrange potatoes, carrots, and onions around meat. Bake meat and vegetables, covered, about 1½ hours more or until tender.

3. Transfer meat and vegetables to a large serving platter. Discard cinnamon stick. Thinly slice the meat. Pour some of the sauce over the meat and vegetables. Sprinkle with parsley. Pass remaining sauce.

Make-ahead Tip: You can cook the meat and vegetables the day before, then cool and chill. Reheat before serving.

Makes 8 to 10 servings.
Per serving: 624 cal., 23 g total fat (8 g sat. fat), 157 mg chol., 1,082 mg sodium, 47 g carbo., 4 g fiber, 55 g pro. Dietary exchanges: 3 vegetable, 2 starch, 6 lean meat.

Italian Beef Sandwiches

From Ann Dehner,
Burlington, Iowa

1	4-lb. boneless beef sirloin or rolled rump roast, trimmed and cut into 2- to 3-inch pieces
½	cup water
1	0.7-ounce pkg. Italian salad dressing mix
2	tsp. Italian seasoning, crushed
½	to 1 tsp. crushed red pepper
½	tsp. garlic powder

10	to 12 Kaiser rolls or other sandwich rolls, split, or
1	loaf French bread, split Purchased roasted red pepper strips (optional)

Prep: 10 min. **Cook:** 5 or 10 hr.

1. Put beef in a 3½-, 4-, or 5-quart crockery cooker. Stir together water, salad dressing mix, Italian seasoning, crushed red pepper, and garlic powder; pour over beef. Cover and cook on low-heat setting for 10 to 12 hours. (Or cover and cook on high-heat setting for 5 to 6 hours.)

2. Remove meat with a slotted spoon. Using two forks, shred the beef. Serve beef on rolls. Top with roasted red pepper strips, if desired. Drizzle with some of the juices to moisten.

Makes 10 to 12 sandwiches.

Per sandwich: 396 cal., 10 g total fat (3 g sat. fat), 104 mg chol., 642 mg sodium, 31 g carbo., 1 g fiber, 41 g pro. Dietary exchanges: 2 starch, 5 lean meat.

58

Beef in Red Wine Gravy

From Irene Ellerton,
Ganaoque, Ontario, Canada

1½ lbs. beef stew meat, cut into 1-inch cubes	Salt
2 medium onions, cut up	Black pepper
2 beef bouillon cubes or half of a 2-oz. pkg. onion soup mix (1 envelope)	1½ cups dry red wine
	Hot cooked noodles (optional)
3 Tbsp. cornstarch	

Prep: 15 min. **Cook:** 5 or 10 hr.

WINE CHOICES
Choose a hearty red wine to make this aromatic stew—and to serve with it—such as a Cabernet Sauvignon, Merlot, Bordeaux, or Burgundy.

1. Place beef and onions in a 3½- or 4-quart crockery cooker. Add bouillon cubes. Sprinkle with cornstarch, salt, and black pepper. Pour wine over all.

2. Cover and cook on low-heat setting for 10 to 12 hours. (Or cover and cook on high-heat setting for 5 to 6 hours.) Serve over hot cooked noodles, if desired.

Makes 6 servings.
Per serving: 215 cal., 4 g total fat (1 g sat. fat), 64 mg chol., 405 mg sodium, 7 g carbo., 1 g fiber, 26 g pro. Dietary exchanges: ½ starch, 3 very lean meat.

Bogracs Gulyas (Kettle Goulash)

From Puttin' on the Peachtree, cookbook of the
Junior League of DeKalb County, Georgia

3	cups chopped onion		3	lbs. beef stew meat, cut into 1-inch cubes
1½	cups coarsely chopped green sweet pepper		1	6-oz. can tomato paste
3	cloves garlic, minced		½	cup cold water
2	Tbsp. bacon drippings or cooking oil		¼	tsp. salt
4	tsp. Hungarian paprika or regular paprika		¼	tsp. black pepper
				Hot cooked noodles
				Dairy sour cream

Prep: 30 min. **Bake:** 1½ hr.

1. In a 4- or 4½-quart Dutch oven, cook onion, sweet pepper, and garlic in hot bacon drippings about 5 minutes or until almost tender, stirring occasionally. Stir in paprika and cook for 2 minutes. Stir in beef cubes, tomato paste, water, salt, and black pepper.

2. Cover and bake in a 325°F oven for 1½ to 2 hours or until meat is tender. Serve over noodles; pass sour cream.

Makes 8 servings.
Per serving: 606 cal., 36 g total fat (14 g sat. fat), 147 mg chol., 186 mg sodium, 32 g carbo., 3 g fiber, 38 g pro. Dietary exchanges: 2 vegetable, 1½ starch, 4 medium-fat meat, 2 fat.

Puttin' on the Ritz, Southern Style

In Atlanta, it's a tradition that food shared with friends is cooked with love and served with style. According to the Junior League of DeKalb County, Georgia, the phrase that best describes this kind of cooking is "puttin' on the peachtree." To convey that its cookbook shows off the best of Atlanta cooking, the group used this catchy phrase as the book's title. This recipe came from the chapter on international fare.

Amy's Marinated Flank Steak

From *Just Peachey: Cooking Up a Cure,* cookbook of
Women Winning Against Breast Cancer, Warsaw, Indiana

1	1½-lbs. beef flank steak	2	Tbsp. tomato paste or catsup
½	cup light soy sauce	1	tsp. ground cumin
¼	cup orange juice	½	tsp. freshly ground black pepper
¼	cup dry red wine, dry sherry, or orange juice	2	small cloves garlic, minced
3	Tbsp. Dijon-style mustard		
3	Tbsp. olive oil or cooking oil		
2	Tbsp. grated fresh ginger or 1 tsp. ground ginger		

Prep: 15 min. **Marinate:** 4 hr. **Grill:** 12 min.

MAKE MINE MARINATED

A good soak is good for the soul—and it's good for your food too. Marinating is great in two ways. It adds flavor, and it tenderizes meats. Generally marinades are made with an acidic liquid (which has the tenderizing effect) such as wine, vinegar, or citrus juice, plus herbs and seasonings—and sometimes a little oil. The longer the meat spends luxuriating in the liquid, the more great flavor it will have.

1. Place flank steak in a large self-sealing plastic bag set in a shallow dish. For marinade, combine soy sauce, the ¼ cup orange juice, wine, mustard, oil, ginger, tomato paste, cumin, black pepper, and garlic. Pour marinade over steak in bag. Seal bag. Marinate in refrigerator for at least 4 hours or up to 8 hours.

2. Drain, discarding marinade. Grill steak on rack of uncovered grill directly over medium coals until desired doneness, turning once. (Allow 12 to 14 minutes for medium.) Slice meat thinly across the grain.

Makes 4 servings.
Per serving: 313 cal., 18 g total fat (7 g sat. fat), 87 mg chol., 255 mg sodium, 1 g carbo., 0 g fiber, 34 g pro. Dietary exchanges: 4½ lean meat, 1 fat.

Kansas City Strip Steaks

From The Kansas City Barbeque Society Cookbook.
Kansas City. Missouri

2	Tbsp. prepared horseradish		$^{1}/_{2}$	tsp. instant beef bouillon granules
2	Tbsp. lemon juice		4	8-oz. beef top loin steaks, cut 1 inch thick
4	cloves garlic, minced			
4	tsp. sugar			
2	tsp. paprika			
1	tsp. salt			
1	tsp. black pepper			

Prep: 10 min. **Chill:** 1 hr. **Grill:** 12 min.

1. Combine horseradish, lemon juice, garlic, sugar, paprika, salt, black pepper, and the bouillon granules. Trim fat from meat. Rub mixture on both sides of steaks. Cover; chill in refrigerator for 1 hour.

2. Grill on rack of uncovered grill directly over medium coals to desired doneness, turning once. (Allow 12 to 15 minutes for medium.)

Makes 8 servings.

Per serving: 276 cal., 19 g total fat (8 g sat. fat), 74 mg chol., 400 mg sodium, 8 g carbo., 0 g fiber, 22 g pro. Dietary exchanges: 3 lean meat, 2 fat.

A Judge's Oath
"I do solemnly swear to objectively and subjectively evaluate each barbecue meat that is presented to my eyes, my nose, and my palate. I accept my duty to be a judge so that truth, justice, excellence in barbecue, and the American way of life may be strengthened and preserved forever!"
—Ardie Davis (aka Remus Powers), author of The Kansas City Barbeque Society Cookbook

Rafter L Chicken-Fried Steak

From Dennis Dodson,
Poolville, Texas

1	beaten egg
1/2	cup buttermilk or sour milk
3/4	cup all-purpose flour
2	Tbsp. cornmeal
1/2	tsp. salt
1/2	tsp. black pepper

4	4- to 5-oz. beef cubed steaks
	Cooking oil
	Gravy (optional)

Prep: 15 min. **Cook:** 5 min. per batch

Come 'N' Get It! Serving hot, homemade biscuits is a sneaky way to give kids a history lesson—and an earful about moral values. But it seems to be working in Texas. In the past 10 years, Dennis Dodson of Poolville, Texas, has introduced thousands of Texas children to the history of Texas and its cowboy heritage. He's a chuck wagon cook, and the minute he pulls his rebuilt 1882 chuck wagon into a school yard, the lessons and cooking begin. His chuck wagon—and the smell of biscuits baking in a cast-iron Dutch oven—is just the ticket to keep kids listening.

1. In a shallow dish, combine egg and buttermilk. In another shallow dish, combine flour, cornmeal, salt, and black pepper. Dip meat into flour mixture to coat, then dip in egg mixture. Coat again with the flour mixture.

2. Pour oil into large skillet to a depth of 1/2 inch (about 1 3/4 cups oil). Heat oil until a bread cube dropped into the oil sizzles.

3. Cook steaks, two at a time, in hot oil for 5 to 8 minutes or until golden brown, turning once. (Keep first two cooked steaks warm in a 300°F oven while cooking remaining steaks.) Serve with your favorite gravy, if desired.

Makes 4 servings.
Per serving: 398 cal., 20 g total fat (4 g sat. fat), 119 mg chol., 394 mg sodium, 22 g carbo., 1 g fiber, 30 g pro. Dietary exchanges: 1½ starch, 3 lean meat, 2 fat.

Bill's Meat Loaf

From Bill Hurley Jr.
Salem, Oregon

3	eggs
3/4	cup seasoned fine dry bread crumbs
1	cup finely chopped fresh mushrooms
1/2	cup chopped onion
1/4	cup bottled barbecue sauce
1	Tbsp. Dijon-style mustard
1	Tbsp. Worcestershire sauce

1/2	tsp. garlic powder
1/2	tsp. bottled hot pepper sauce
1	lb. ground beef
1	lb. sweet Italian sausage (remove casings, if present)
1	lb. ground turkey
	Bottled barbecue sauce

Prep: 15 min. **Bake:** 1¼ hr. **Stand:** 10 min.

1. In a very large mixing bowl, stir together the eggs, bread crumbs, chopped mushrooms, onion, the ¼ cup barbecue sauce, mustard, Worcestershire sauce, garlic powder, and hot pepper sauce.

2. Add the beef, Italian sausage, and turkey; mix well. In a 3-quart rectangular baking dish, pat mixture into a loaf (about 11×5 inches).

3. Bake in a 350°F oven for 1¼ to 1½ hours or until center of the meat loaf is completely cooked, spooning additional barbecue sauce over loaf for the last 20 minutes of baking.

4. Let the meat loaf stand for 10 minutes. Using two spatulas, transfer loaf to a serving platter.

Makes 8 to 10 servings.

Per serving: 397 cal., 24 g total fat (8 g sat. fat), 169 mg chol., 870 mg sodium, 1˙ g carbo., 0 g fiber, 31 g pro. Dietary exchanges: 1 vegetable, ½ starch, 4 lean meat, 2 fat.

The Hero of Station No. 3

When Captain Bill Hurley Jr. yells, "Chow time!" his fellow firefighters race to the table as though they were answering a fire alarm. Cooking comes naturally to Bill, a fourth-generation firefighter from Salem, Oregon. His great-grandfather cooked in Minneapolis; his grandfather in Beverly Hills, California; and his dad in Culver City, California. There are no complaints from his coworkers. He nearly has to beat them off with a wooden spoon to prevent sampling before it's time to eat.

Caesar Salad Beef Burgers
on Garlic Crostini

From Jason Boulanger of Williston, Vermont.
$10,000 winner of the 1999 National Beef Cook-Off

PHOTO APPEARS ON PAGE 75

1½	lbs. ground beef			Olive oil
3	cloves garlic, minced		2	large cloves garlic, cut lengthwise into quarters
1	teaspoon salt		4	romaine lettuce leaves
½	teaspoon black pepper		¼	cup shredded Parmesan cheese
8	slices sourdough bread			

Start to finish: 30 min.

Hail Caesar!
When Jason Boulanger entered this recipe in the 1999 National Beef Cook-Off—hoping for the top $40,000 prize—he was studying wildlife biology at South Dakota State University. His garlicky dish was originally made with venison and 20-plus ingredients. Contest rules stipulate no more than six ingredients—and a start-to-finish time of 30 minutes or less. He whittled the recipe down to the six ingredients, with beef, of course.

1. Mix beef, minced garlic, salt, and black pepper. Shape into four ³/4-inch-thick patties, molding to fit the bread.
2. Grill burgers directly over medium coals, uncovered, for 13 to 15 minutes or until no longer pink, turning once. Season with additional salt and black pepper.
3. Meanwhile, brush both sides of bread with oil. Place bread around outer edge of grill. Grill a few minutes until lightly toasted, turning once; remove from grill. Rub both sides of each slice with a garlic quarter.
4. Place a lettuce leaf and a burger on four bread slices; sprinkle with cheese. Cover with remaining bread.

Makes 4 servings.
Per serving: 481 cal., 23 g total fat (7 g sat. fat), 112 mg chol., 984 mg sodium, 28 g carbo., 1 g fiber, 38 g pro. Dietary exchanges: 2 starch, 4½ lean meat, 1½ fat.

Bistro Beef "Steaks" with Wild Mushroom Sauce

From Helen Wolt of Colorado Springs, Colorado,

competitor in the 1999 National Beef Cook-Off

1	medium onion, cut in half
1¼	lbs. ground beef
¾	tsp. salt
	Black pepper
8	oz. sliced assorted fresh mushrooms, such as oyster, crimini, and shiitake (about 3 cups)

1½	cups (12 oz.) beer (preferably honey lager) or nonalcoholic beer
1	0.88-oz. pkg. brown gravy mix
2	tsp. chopped fresh thyme or ½ tsp. dried thyme, crushed

Start to finish: 30 min.

BEEF UP FAMILY MEALS

Half of the recipes in the National Beef Cook-Off show off new prepared meat products. Items such as heat-and-serve pot roast, prime rib, and beef stew can be fixed in the microwave oven in less than 10 minutes. Surprisingly, these refrigerated or frozen products don't have that warmed-over flavor often found in home-cooked leftovers. These quick-cooking meats cost more than if you bought the cuts and cooked them yourself, but when time is tight and you're craving beef, it's probably worth the price.

1. Finely shred half the onion. Thinly slice remaining onion; set aside.

2. Combine shredded onion, beef, and salt, mixing lightly but thoroughly. Lightly shape into four ½-inch-thick oval "steaks." Sprinkle tops of steaks with additional salt and black pepper, as desired.

3. Heat a large nonstick skillet over medium heat until hot. Place patties in skillet; cook 10 to 12 minutes to medium doneness (160°F) or until no longer pink in center, turning once. Remove from skillet; keep warm.

4. Add sliced onion, mushrooms, and ¼ cup of the beer to same skillet; cook over medium-high heat for 5 minutes or until vegetables are tender, stirring occasionally. Combine gravy mix with the remaining 1¼ cup beer, mixing until smooth; stir into mushroom mixture in skillet. Add half of the thyme; simmer for 1 minute or until thickened, stirring frequently. Spoon sauce over patties; sprinkle with remaining thyme.

Makes 4 servings.

Per serving: 351 cal., 18 g total fat (7 g sat. fat), 89 mg chol., 732 mg sodium, 12 g carbo., 1 g fiber, 29 g pro. Dietary exchanges: 2 vegetable, 3½ lean meat, 2 fat.

66

Norwegian Meatballs

From The Immanuel Lutheran Church Cookbook,
Story City, Iowa

2	eggs, beaten		$1/2$	tsp. ground nutmeg
$1/2$	cup milk		2	lbs. lean ground beef
$2/3$	cup crushed saltine crackers (about 18 crackers)		1	$10^3/4$-ounce can condensed cream of mushroom soup
$1/3$	cup finely chopped onion (1 small)		$3/4$	cup milk
$1/2$	tsp. celery salt			
$1/2$	tsp. black pepper			

Prep: 25 min. **Bake:** 30 min.

SCOOP 'EM UP
A number 16 scoop is the perfect size to shape these meatballs. If you don't have a scoop, use a $1/4$-cup measure, then roll the mixture between the palms of your hands to shape it into balls.

1. Grease a 3-quart rectangular baking dish; set aside.

2. In a large bowl, combine eggs and the $1/2$ cup milk. Stir in crushed crackers, onion, celery salt, black pepper, and $1/4$ teaspoon of the ground nutmeg. Add ground beef. Mix well. Shape mixture into 20 meatballs. Arrange meatballs in prepared baking dish. Bake, uncovered, in a 350°F oven for 30 minutes or until no pink remains.

3. In a medium saucepan, combine soup, the $3/4$ cup milk, and the remaining $1/4$ teaspoon nutmeg. Cook and stir over medium heat until heated through. To serve, transfer meatballs to a serving bowl or platter. Spoon sauce over meatballs.

Makes 5 or 6 servings.
Per serving: 469 cal., 26 g total fat (10 g sat. fat), 204 mg chol., 842 mg sodium, 17 g carbo., 1 g fiber, 39 g pro.
Dietary exchanges: 1 starch, 5 lean meat, 2 fat.

Stuffed Texas Onions Toluca

From Mesquite Country, cookbook of the
Hidalgo County Historical Museum, Edinburg, Texas.

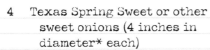

4	Texas Spring Sweet or other sweet onions (4 inches in diameter* each)	4	slices Muenster, Gruyère, or Mexican goat cheese (1 oz. each)
4	oz. chorizo or bulk hot Italian sausage	4	flour tortillas
4	oz. lean ground beef	1/3	cup picante sauce
1/4	tsp. salt	1/3	cup guacamole
1/4	tsp. black pepper		

Prep: 50 min. **Bake:** 12 min.

1. Remove a slice from top (stem end) of each onion so it sits flat. Starting at opposite end (root end), hollow each onion, leaving about a 1/2-inch-thick shell. Place onions in a steamer basket. Place in a Dutch oven over boiling water; cover and steam for 20 minutes. Remove; cool until easy to handle.

2. Meanwhile, for filling, in a medium saucepan, cook and stir chorizo, ground beef, salt, and black pepper for about 10 minutes or until meat is brown. Drain in colander.

3. Arrange onions in an 8×8×2-inch baking pan. Spoon sausage filling into onions. Top each onion with a cheese slice. Bake in a 350°F oven for 10 minutes. Wrap tortillas in foil and heat in the oven alongside onions for 10 minutes. Remove onions and tortillas from oven. Adjust oven rack so onions will be 5 to 6 inches from heat. Turn oven to broil. Broil onions for 2 to 3 minutes or until cheese begins to turn light brown. Place one tortilla on each plate. Top each tortilla with an onion. Serve with picante sauce and guacamole.

*Note: If onions are too large, peel off outer layers until they are 4 inches in diameter.

Makes 4 servings.
Per serving: 483 cal., 28 g total fat (13 g sat. fat), 69 mg chol., 1,149 mg sodium, 33 g carbo., 1 g fiber, 23 g pro. Dietary exchanges: 2 vegetable, 1½ starch, 2 high fat meat, 2 fat.

Grande Cuisine
On one side of the Rio Grande River, you'll find Mexico; on the other, the Rio Grande Valley of Texas. This balmy border region offers the beaches of South Padre, ranchlands and farms, and plenty of culture and history. The Hidalgo County Historical Museum helps preserve this history, and it created Mesquite Country to raise funds. It's filled with regional recipes such as this one.

Corn Pie in Ground Beef Crust

From Savoring the Southwest Again, cookbook of the
Roswell Symphony Guild, Roswell, New Mexico

1	cup chopped onion		1	tsp. ground cumin
1/2	cup chopped celery		1/2	tsp. crushed red pepper
1/2	cup chopped sweet pepper		1	lb. very lean ground beef
2	Tbsp. finely chopped, seeded jalapeño pepper		1/4	cup fine dry bread crumbs
1	Tbsp. minced garlic		2	slightly beaten eggs
1	Tbsp. olive oil		1/2	cup milk
1	14 1/2-ounce can diced tomatoes, drained		1	Tbsp. all-purpose flour
1/2	cup golden raisins		2 3/4	cups whole kernel corn
1	Tbsp. chili powder		2	green onions, thinly sliced

Prep: 40 min. **Bake:** 40 min. **Stand:** 10 min.

1. In a large skillet, cook onion, celery, sweet pepper, jalapeño pepper, and garlic in hot oil about 5 minutes or until tender, stirring occasionally. Remove from heat. Stir in drained tomatoes, raisins, chili powder, cumin, crushed red pepper, and 1/2 teaspoon salt. In a large bowl, combine ground beef, bread crumbs, and the onion-tomato mixture. Spread meat mixture evenly in an ungreased 2-quart square baking dish.

2. In same bowl, combine eggs, milk, flour, and 1/4 teaspoon salt; beat with a wire whisk until smooth. Stir in corn and green onions. Spoon evenly over meat layer. Bake, uncovered, in a 350°F oven about 40 minutes or until corn layer is just set and meat layer is no longer pink. Let stand for 10 minutes; cut into portions to serve.

Makes 6 servings.
Per serving: 325 cal., 9 g total fat (3 g sat. fat), 116 mg chol., 545 mg sodium, 45 g carbo., 5 g fiber, 23 g pro. Dietary exchanges: 4 vegetable, 1 1/2 starch, 1 1/2 lean meat, 1/2 fat.

Pastitsio

From The Heart of Pittsburgh, cookbook benefiting
Sacred Heart Elementary School, Pittsburgh, Pennsylvania

1	lb. lean ground beef
1	large onion, chopped
1	8-oz. can tomato sauce
1/4	cup dry white wine
1	4-inch-long piece stick cinnamon
8	oz. dried penne pasta
3/4	cup milk
2	slightly beaten eggs
2	Tbsp. butter, melted
2	Tbsp. butter

2	Tbsp. all-purpose flour
1/4	tsp. salt
1/8	tsp. black pepper
1 1/2	cups milk
3	slightly beaten eggs
1	cup shredded Kefalotiri, kasseri, or Romano cheese (4 oz.)*

Prep: 45 min. **Bake:** 35 min. **Stand:** 15 min.

1. For meat sauce, in a large skillet, cook ground beef and onion until meat is no longer pink. Drain off fat. Stir in tomato sauce, wine, and cinnamon stick. Bring to boiling; reduce heat. Cover and simmer for 30 minutes, stirring occasionally. Discard cinnamon stick.

2. Meanwhile, cook pasta according to package directions. Drain; rinse and drain again. In large bowl, toss pasta with the 3/4 cup milk, the 2 eggs, and the 2 tablespoons melted butter. Set pasta mixture aside.

3. For cream sauce, in a small saucepan, melt 2 tablespoons butter over medium heat. Stir in flour, salt, and black pepper until smooth. Gradually add the 1 1/2 cups milk. Cook and stir until mixture is thickened and bubbly. Gradually stir hot mixture into the 3 eggs. Set aside.

4. Grease a 3-quart rectangular baking dish. Layer half of the pasta mixture in prepared dish. Spread meat sauce over. Sprinkle with 1/3 cup of the cheese. Top with the remaining pasta; sprinkle with another 1/3 cup of the cheese. Pour cream sauce over all; sprinkle with remaining cheese.

5. Cover and bake in a 350°F oven for 20 minutes. Uncover and bake about 15 minutes more or until knife inserted in center comes out clean. Let stand for 15 minutes before serving.

*Test Kitchen Note: Kefalotiri and kasseri cheeses are both hard cheeses widely used in Greek cooking. They have sharp flavors that are similar to Romano cheese, which you may find more readily in your supermarket. Grated Parmesan cheese will work too.

Makes 8 servings.
Per serving: 553 cal., 30 g total fat (12 g sat. fat), 241 mg chol., 657 mg sodium, 31 g carbo., 2 g fiber, 36 g pro. Dietary exchanges: 1 milk, 1 starch, 3½ lean meat, 3½ fat.

A Heart for Learning
When the library at the 125-year-old Sacred Heart Elementary School needed high-tech updating, the Parent-Teacher Guild created a Sacred Heart cookbook as a means to raise money. The recipes these kids brought from home included Italian, Greek, Asian, African-American, Cajun, Polish, Jewish, and German dishes. This came as no surprise: Sacred Heart is a microcosm of Pittsburgh—a city of culturally diverse neighborhoods and cuisines.

Tacos in Pasta Shells

From Balancing Acts, cookbook of the
American Gold Gymnastics program, Fargo, North Dakota

18	dried jumbo pasta shells
1	Tbsp. butter
1¼	lbs. ground beef
1	8-oz. pkg. cream cheese, cut up
1	tsp. chili powder
1	16-oz. jar salsa

1	cup shredded cheddar cheese (4 oz.)
	Chopped fresh tomato (optional)
	Sliced ripe olives (optional)

Prep: 25 min. **Bake:** 30 min.

Go for the Gold
Almost 1,500 kids are involved in the American Gold Gymnastics program between sister cities Fargo, North Dakota, and Moorhead, Minnesota. Tired of selling pizza to make money, AGG parents decided a recipe collection would bring in the dollars needed to support travel to out-of-town gymnastic meets.

1. Cook pasta shells according to package directions; drain. Return to pan; toss with butter. Cool until easy to handle.

2. Meanwhile, in a large skillet, cook ground beef until brown, stirring to break up beef; drain off fat. Stir in cream cheese and chili powder until combined. Remove from heat; cool slightly. Divide beef mixture evenly among the pasta shells.

3. Spread about ½ cup of the salsa in a 2-quart rectangular baking dish. Arrange filled shells in dish. Spoon the remaining salsa over. Cover; bake in a 350°F oven for 15 minutes. Sprinkle with cheese. Bake, uncovered, for 15 minutes more. Sprinkle with chopped tomato and sliced ripe olives, if desired.

Makes 6 servings.
Per serving: 454 cal., 29 g total fat (13 g sat. fat), 100 mg chol., 758 mg sodium, 27 g carbo., 1 g fiber, 29 g pro. Dietary exchanges: 2 vegetable, 1 starch, 3 lean meat, 3 fat.

Hamburger, Potato, and Bean Casserole

From Bill Hurley Jr.,
Salem, Oregon

1	lb. lean ground beef
2	8-oz. cans tomato sauce
3	medium potatoes, peeled (if desired), halved lengthwise, and sliced 1/4 inch thick
1	medium onion, sliced
2	15 1/2-oz. cans dark red kidney beans, undrained

1	4 1/2-oz. can sliced mushrooms, drained
1	tsp. garlic powder
1/2	tsp. black pepper

Prep: 15 min. **Cook:** 3 hr.

1. In a large skillet, cook ground beef until no longer pink. Drain well.

2. Spoon 1/3 cup of the tomato sauce into the bottom of a 3 1/2- or 4-quart crockery cooker. Layer half of the potatoes, onion, undrained beans, beef, mushrooms, garlic powder, and black pepper. Repeat layers; pour the remaining tomato sauce over.

3. Cover and cook on high-heat setting for 3 to 3 1/2 hours or until the potatoes are tender. Stir mixture just before serving.

Makes 6 servings.

Per serving: 340 cal., 8 g total fat (3 g sat. fat), 48 mg chol., 815 mg sodium, 48 g carbo., 10 g fiber, 27 g pro. Dietary exchanges: 1 vegetable, 2 starch, 3 lean meat.

Potato Pan Burger

From the Carroll County 4-H Cookbook.
Carroll County, Ohio

SKINNY IT DOWN
To make a lower-fat version of this hearty dish, use reduced-fat cream of mushroom soup and light sour cream.

2	lbs. ground beef
1	envelope (half of a 2-oz. package) onion soup mix
1/4	cup all-purpose flour
1	10¾-oz. can condensed cream of mushroom soup
1	8-oz. carton dairy sour cream
3/4	cup water
1	Tbsp. catsup
1½	cups water

1/4	cup butter or margarine
1/2	tsp. salt
2	cups packaged instant mashed potato flakes
1/2	cup milk
2	eggs, beaten
1	cup all-purpose flour
2	tsp. baking powder

Prep: 30 min. **Bake:** 25 min.

1. In an extra-large skillet, cook ground beef until brown. Drain off fat. Stir in onion soup mix and the 1/4 cup flour. Stir in mushroom soup, sour cream, the 3/4 cup water, and the catsup. Cook until heated through, stirring occasionally.

2. Meanwhile, in a medium saucepan, combine the 1½ cups water, the butter, and salt; bring to boiling. Remove from heat. Add potato flakes and milk, stirring until combined. Stir in eggs, the 1 cup flour, and the baking powder.

3. Transfer beef mixture to a 3-quart rectangular baking dish; spoon potato mixture in mounds on top. Bake in a 425°F oven about 25 minutes or until potatoes are golden on top.

Makes 8 servings.
Per serving: 558 cal., 36 g total fat (16 g sat. fat), 831 mg chol., 831 mg sodium, 30 g carbo., 1 g fiber, 27 g pro. Dietary exchanges: 2 starch, 3 medium-fat meat, 4 fat.

Bloody Mary Pot Roast, p. 55

Put Bloody Mary Pot Roast in the oven on a chilly Saturday afternoon, then sit back and enjoy the aroma. Cookbook committee co-chairs Billie Michaud, left, and Patricia Eckert helped create *Savoring the Southwest Again*, a cookbook to benefit the Roswell Symphony of Roswell, New Mexico.

Kansas City Strip Steaks, p. 61

Bill's Meat Loaf, p. 63

Caesar Salad Beef Burgers on Garlic Crostini, p. 64

Cuts other than strip steaks will also benefit from the peppy seasoning that enlivens Kansas City Strip Steaks, opposite above. Captain Bill Hurley Jr. says his 3-pound meat loaf, opposite bottom, will feed five hungry firefighters. Most families could easily serve 8 to 10 from this flavorful loaf. Jason Boulanger, right, of Williston, Vermont, won $10,000 in the 1999 National Beef Cook-Off with his recipe for Caesar Salad Beef Burgers on Garlic Crostini, above.

Marcella Karwellis McGuire, above, of Pittsburgh, grew up in a Greek family where everything revolved around food. It's no wonder she's known throughout her neighborhood for cooking great classic Greek dishes such as Pastitsio, above right. Serve Tacos in Pasta Shells, right, with a crisp green salad, and dinner's on the table.

Pastitsio, p. 69

Tacos in Pasta Shells, p. 70

Zucchini Pork Chop Supper, p. 86

Volunteers who put together Taste of History to benefit the library in Hot Springs, South Dakota, admit there's no historical significance to Zucchini Pork Chop Supper, above left. But it's a hit with South Dakota cooks who like one-dish oven meals to keep them warm in the winter. There's a hint of cinnamon and cloves in the sweet jelly-based glaze used on Apple-Glazed Pork Kabobs, below left.

Apple-Glazed Pork Kabobs, p. 91

Apricot-Dijon Pork Salad, p. 92

Apple 'n' Sausage Breakfast Topper, p. 95

Italian Sausage and Spinach Pie, p. 98

Rich and robust Lamb Curry, above right, fragrant with spices and embellished with chutney, toasted coconut, and chopped fruits and nuts, is a meal in itself. Most backyard cooks stick to grilling pork, beef, or chicken. The Kansas City Barbeque Society Cookbook offers Lamb Chops Jalapeño, below, for a change of pace.

Lamb Curry, p. 99

Lamb Chops Jalapeño, p. 100

Pioneer Beans

From Taste of History, cookbook of
Friends of the Library, Hot Springs, South Dakota

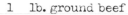

1	lb. ground beef
1/4	lb. sliced bacon, chopped
1	medium onion, chopped (1/2 cup)
1	15-oz. can red kidney beans, rinsed and drained
1	15-oz. can butter beans, rinsed and drained
1	15-oz. can pork and beans in tomato sauce

1	cup catsup
1/2	to 1 cup packed brown sugar
1/4	cup molasses
1	Tbsp. vinegar
1	Tbsp. prepared mustard

Prep: 15 min. **Bake:** 1 hr.

1. In a large skillet, cook ground beef, chopped bacon, and onion until meat is no longer pink and the onion is tender. Drain off fat.

2. Stir in drained kidney beans and butter beans, undrained pork and beans, catsup, brown sugar, molasses, vinegar, and mustard.

3. Transfer to a 2- to 2 1/2-quart casserole. Cover and bake in a 350°F oven for 30 minutes. Uncover casserole; bake for 30 minutes more.

Crockery cooker directions: Prepare beans as directed, except transfer meat and bean mixture to a 3 1/2- to 4-quart crockery cooker. Cover and cook on low-heat setting for 5 to 6 hours, or on high-heat setting for 2 1/2 to 3 hours.

Makes 12 servings.
Per serving: 256 cal., 7 g total fat (2 g sat. fat), 28 mg chol., 684 mg sodium, 38 g carbo., 4 g fiber, 15 g pro. Dietary exchanges: 2 1/2 starch, 1 lean meat, 1 fat.

For the Books

To raise money for a new library, volunteers in Hot Springs, South Dakota, compiled recipes, anecdotes, historic pictures, and artwork for their cookbook, Taste of History. In the process, they discovered that the book was a way to record local recipes and memories that would be lost if not written down. Preserving the past is important in this community, which flourished at the turn of the 20th century, thanks to visitors who flocked here seeking the curative powers of the town's namesake springs.

Beef-and-Bean Medley

From the Carroll County 4-H Cookbook.
Carroll County, Ohio

1	lb. ground beef
1	cup chopped onion (1 large)
6	slices bacon, crisp-cooked, drained, and crumbled
2	16-oz. cans baked beans
1	15-oz. can butter beans, rinsed and drained
1	15-oz. can red kidney beans, rinsed and drained
1	cup catsup
1/2	cup water

1/4	cup packed brown sugar
3	Tbsp. vinegar
1/8	tsp. black pepper
1	8- to 10-oz. bag corn chips or tortilla chips
2	cups shredded cheddar cheese (8 oz.)
1/2	cup sliced green onions

Prep: 25 min. **Cook:** 4 hr. on low heat; 2 hr. on high heat

1. In a large skillet, cook ground beef and onion until beef is brown. Drain off fat. Transfer beef mixture to a 3½- or 4-quart crockery cooker. Add crumbled bacon, baked beans, butter beans, and kidney beans. In a small bowl, combine catsup, water, brown sugar, vinegar, and black pepper. Add catsup mixture to crockery cooker. Stir to combine. Cover and cook on low-heat setting for 4 to 6 hours or on high-heat setting for 2 to 3 hours.

2. Serve over or with corn or tortilla chips. Sprinkle with shredded cheese and green onions.

Makes 8 to 10 servings.

Per serving: 664 cal., 32 g total fat (12 g sat. fat), 74 mg chol., 1,505 mg sodium, 65 g carbo., 8 g fiber, 31 g pro. Dietary exchanges: 4 starch, 3 medium-fat meat, 2½ fat.

Traditional Cincinnati Chili

From I'll Cook When Pigs Fly—And They Do in Cincinnati!,

cookbook of the Junior League of Cincinnati, Ohio

5	bay leaves		1	15- to 15½-oz. can red kidney beans, rinsed and drained
1	tsp. whole allspice		1	8-oz. can tomato sauce
2	lbs. lean ground beef		1	Tbsp. vinegar
2	cups chopped onion		1	tsp. Worcestershire sauce
1	clove garlic, minced		½	tsp. salt
2	Tbsp. chili powder		¼	tsp. black pepper
1	tsp. ground cinnamon			Hot cooked spaghetti (optional)
½	tsp. ground red pepper			
4	cups water			

Prep: 25 min. **Cook:** 45 min.

1. For spice bag, place bay leaves and allspice on a square of double-thickness 100 percent cotton cheesecloth. Bring up corners and tie with clean kitchen string; set aside.

2. In a Dutch oven, cook beef, onion, and garlic until the meat is no longer pink; drain well. Stir in chili powder, cinnamon, and red pepper. Cook and stir for 1 minute. Stir in water, beans, tomato sauce, vinegar, Worcestershire sauce, salt, and black pepper. Add spice bag. Bring to boiling; reduce heat. Cover and simmer for 30 minutes. Uncover; simmer for 15 to 20 minutes more or until of desired consistency. Remove spice bag; discard. Serve chili over spaghetti, if desired.

Makes 8 servings.

Per serving: 256 cal., 11 g total fat (4 g sat. fat), 71 mg chol., 435 mg sodium, 15 g carbo., 5 g fiber, 25 g pro. Dietary exchanges: 1½ vegetable, ½ starch, 2½ lean meat, ½ fat.

Chili Town

Cincy's first chili parlor was opened in 1922 on Vine Street by the Bulgarian Kiradjieff family, who called it Empress, after the Empress Theater next door. Today the city's chili parlors are a beloved institution, and residents enjoy chili on everything from French fries and eggs to appetizers, sandwiches, and pizza.

Cranberry Pork Roast

From Recipes of Yesterday & Today, cookbook of the
Agency United Methodist Church, Agency, Iowa

4	medium potatoes, peeled and cubed	1/2	cup snipped dried apricots
1	3-lb. boneless pork top loin roast (single loin)	2	Tbsp. sugar
1	16-oz. can whole cranberry sauce	1	tsp. dry mustard
1	15-oz. can apricot halves, drained	1/4	tsp. ground red pepper
1	medium onion, chopped	1	Tbsp. cornstarch
		1	Tbsp. cold water

Prep: 20 min. **Cook:** 5 1/2 to 6 1/2 hr.

1. Place potatoes in bottom of a 5- or 6-quart crockery cooker. Place meat on top of potatoes; set aside. In a blender container or food processor bowl, combine cranberry sauce, drained apricots, onion, dried apricots, sugar, mustard, and ground red pepper. Cover and blend or process until nearly smooth.

2. Pour fruit mixture over pork. Cover and cook on low-heat setting for 5 1/2 to 6 1/2 hours. Remove roast and potatoes from cooker to platter. Cover and keep warm.

3. For sauce, transfer cooking juices from cooker to a 4-cup glass measure. Skim off fat. Measure 2 cups juices; discard remaining juices. Pour juices into a medium saucepan. Stir together cornstarch and water. Add to saucepan, stirring to combine. Cook and stir over medium heat until thickened and bubbly; cook and stir for 2 minutes more. Slice roast. Serve sauce with potatoes and roast.

Makes 12 servings.
Per serving: 307 cal., 6 g total fat (2 g sat. fat), 67 mg chol., 75 mg sodium, 36 g carbo., 2 g fiber, 26 g pro. Dietary exchanges: 1 fruit, 1 starch, 3 lean meat.

Pork Chops with Caramelized Onions

From Savoring the Southwest Again, cookbook of the
Roswell Symphony Guild, Roswell, New Mexico

2	Tbsp. all-purpose flour
4	boneless pork loin chops, cut ¾ inch thick (about 1 lb.)
2	Tbsp. butter
2	large onions, cut into ½-inch wedges
2	cloves garlic, minced
1	tsp. snipped fresh rosemary

¼	tsp. salt (optional)
¼	tsp. black pepper
⅓	cup dry white wine or beef broth
⅓	cup beef broth

Start to finish: 30 min.

SWEET TREAT Caramelized onions add a scrumptious sweetness to lots of dishes. All vegetables and fruits contain natural sugars. When heated, these sugars brown and caramelize, becoming more intense in flavor. Onions are great candidates for caramelizing because they contain plenty of natural sugars. Onions are caramelized by cooking them slowly in butter or oil.

1. Place flour in shallow dish. Dip pork chops in flour, coating both sides. In heavy, large skillet, melt butter over medium-high heat; add chops and brown on both sides. Remove chops from heat. Reduce heat to medium. Add onions, garlic, rosemary, salt (if desired), and black pepper to skillet. Cover and cook for 5 minutes, stirring twice. Uncover and cook for 5 minutes more or until onions are browned, stirring occasionally.

2. Add wine; boil gently until wine is reduced by half. Stir in beef broth. Return chops to skillet. Cover and simmer for 8 to 10 minutes more or until chops are slightly pink in centers and juices run clear (instant-read thermometer inserted into center of chop registers 170°F). Remove chops to platter; cover and keep warm.

3. For sauce, gently boil juices and onions for 2 to 4 minutes or until slightly thickened, stirring constantly. Spoon onions and sauce over chops.

Makes 4 servings.
Per serving: 265 cal., 12 g total fat (6 g sat. fat), 78 mg chol., 174 mg sodium, 9 g carbo., 1 g fiber, 26 g pro. Dietary exchanges: ½ starch, 3 lean meat, ½ fat.

PAGE PHOTO APPEARS ON NO. 77

Zucchini Pork Chop Supper

From Taste of History, cookbook of
Friends of the Library, Hot Springs, South Dakota

1	14-oz. pkg. herb-seasoned stuffing croutons (about 9½ cups)
¼	cup butter or margarine, melted
4	cups coarsely chopped zucchini
1	10¾-oz. can condensed cream of celery soup
1	8-oz. carton light dairy sour cream
¾	cup milk
½	cup shredded carrot
1	Tbsp. snipped fresh parsley or 1 tsp. dried parsley
¼	to ½ tsp. black pepper
6	pork loin chops, cut ¾ inch thick (about 2¼ lbs. total)

Prep: 25 min. **Bake:** 50 min.

1. In a large mixing bowl, stir together 7½ cups of the croutons and the melted butter or margarine; toss to combine. Place half of the buttered croutons in a greased 3-quart rectangular baking dish.

2. In another large bowl, stir together zucchini, condensed soup, light sour cream, ½ cup of the milk, the carrot, parsley, and black pepper. Spoon over croutons in the baking dish. Sprinkle the remaining buttered croutons on top of the zucchini mixture.

3. Coarsely crush the remaining stuffing croutons and place in a shallow dish. Place the remaining ¼ cup milk in another shallow dish. Dip the pork chops in milk and then in crushed stuffing to coat.

4. Place pork chops on top of stuffing in baking dish. Sprinkle with any remaining crushed stuffing.

5. Bake, uncovered, in a 350°F oven for 50 to 60 minutes or until the chops are slightly pink in the center and the juices run clear.

Makes 6 servings.

Per serving: 639 cal., 24 g total fat (10 g sat. fat), 130 mg chol., 1,417 mg sodium, 57 g carbo., 4 g fiber, 46 g pro. Dietary exchanges: 1 milk, 2 vegetable, 2 starch, 4 medium-fat meat.

Rosemary Pork Chops

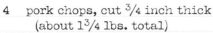

From I'll Cook When Pigs Fly—And They Do in Cincinnati!,

cookbook of the Junior League of Cincinnati, Ohio

4	pork chops, cut ³/4 inch thick (about 1³/4 lbs. total)		4	tsp. snipped fresh rosemary or 1 tsp. dried rosemary, crushed
2	Tbsp. Dijon-style mustard		¹/2	tsp. salt
2	Tbsp. balsamic vinegar		¹/2	tsp. black pepper
2	Tbsp. lemon juice			
2	Tbsp. olive oil			
3	cloves garlic, minced			

Prep: 10 min. **Marinate:** 2 hr. **Grill:** 20 min.

1. Place meat in a self-sealing plastic bag set in a shallow dish. For marinade, in a small bowl, whisk together remaining ingredients. Pour marinade over meat. Seal bag. Marinate in the refrigerator for at least 2 hours or up to 4 hours. Turn frequently.

2. Drain meat; discard marinade. In a grill with a cover, arrange medium-hot coals around a drip pan. Test for medium heat above pan. Place chops on rack over drip pan.

3. Cover and grill for 20 to 24 minutes or until meat juices run clear.

Makes 4 servings.
Per serving: 300 cal., 14 g total fat (4 g sat. fat), 105 mg chol., 244 mg sodium, 2 g carbo., 0 g fiber, 39 g pro. Dietary exchanges: 5½ lean meat.

Prominent Pigs
The title I'll Cook When Pigs Fly—And They Do in Cincinnati! might lead you to believe that this is a cookbook by and for people who don't like to cook. The reference is actually to Cincinnati's famous statues of four winged pigs on smokestacks towering over Sawyer Point Park. The statues' significance? Cincinnati was the pork-packing capital of the world in the early to mid-1800s.

Pork and Green Chile Casserole

From the Greenfield Village School Cookbook,
Greenfield, New Hampshire

Around Town
Greenfield, New Hampshire (pop. 1,500) Incorporated in 1791 and situated in the middle of southern New Hampshire, the town is a haven to many professionals who commute to Boston. Families savor a peaceful, quiet lifestyle. Highways 136 and 31 are busiest in the fall, when visitors come here to enjoy New Hampshire's colors, which peak late September to mid-October.

$1^1/2$	lbs. boneless pork		$^1/4$	cup water
1	Tbps. cooking oil		2	to 3 Tbsp. salsa
1	15-oz. can black beans, rinsed and drained		$^1/2$	cup shredded cheddar cheese (2 oz.)
1	14$^1/2$-oz. can diced tomatoes			
1	10$^3/4$-oz. condensed cream of chicken soup			
2	4$^1/2$-oz. cans chopped green chiles			
1	cup quick-cooking brown rice			

Prep: 20 min. **Bake:** 30 min. **Stand:** 10 min.

1. Trim fat from pork. Cut pork into $^1/2$-inch cubes. In a large skillet, brown pork, half at a time, in hot oil. Drain off fat. Return pork to the skillet.

2. Stir in black beans, tomatoes, condensed soup, chiles, brown rice, water, and salsa. Bring mixture to boiling. Carefully pour into a 2-quart square baking dish. Bake, uncovered, in a 350°F oven for 30 minutes.

Sprinkle with cheese; let stand for 10 minutes before serving.

Makes 8 servings.
Per serving: 271 cal., 13 g total fat (4 g sat. fat), 49 mg chol., 717 mg sodium, 22 g carbo., 4 g fiber, 20 g pro. Dietary exchanges: 1 vegetable, 1 starch, 2 lean meat, 1 fat.

Grilled Pork Tenderloin and Pineapple

From Just Peachey: Cooking Up a Cure, cookbook of
Women Winning Against Breast Cancer, Warsaw, Indiana

2   ¾- to 1-lb. pork tenderloins
3   Tbsp. soy sauce
2   Tbsp. lime juice
2   Tbsp. orange juice
2   Tbsp. cooking oil
½   tsp. dry mustard
¼   tsp. garlic powder

1   fresh medium pineapple, peeled, cored, and cut crosswise into 8 slices

Prep: 20 min. **Grill:** 30 min. **Marinate:** 8 hr.

PERFECT PINEAPPLE
To make cutting a pineapple easier, use a large, sharp knife to slice off the bottom stem and the green top. Stand the pineapple on one cut end and slice off the skin in wide strips, from top to bottom. To remove the eyes, cut diagonally around the fruit, following the pattern of the eyes and making narrow wedge-shaped grooves into the pineapple as you cut away the eyes. When trimming, cut away as little of the fruit as possible.

1. Trim fat from pork, if necessary; place pork in a self-sealing plastic bag set in a shallow dish. For marinade, combine soy sauce, lime juice, orange juice, oil, dry mustard, and garlic powder. Pour marinade over pork in bag. Seal bag. Marinate in refrigerator for at least 8 hours or up to 24 hours, turning bag occasionally.

2. Drain, reserving marinade. In a grill with a cover, arrange medium-hot coals around a drip pan*. Test for medium heat above pan. Place pork on grill rack over drip pan. Cover and grill for 30 to 45 minutes or until meat is slightly pink in center (meat thermometer registers 160°F) and juices run clear. Brush occasionally with marinade during the first 20 minutes of grilling. Discard remaining marinade. Add pineapple slices to grill directly over coals for the last 5 minutes of grilling; turn slices once.

Note: To grill on gas grill, preheat grill. Reduce heat to medium. Adjust for indirect cooking. Grill as above, except place meat on a rack in a roasting pan.

Makes 8 servings.
Per serving: 189 cal., 5 g total fat (1 g sat. fat), 50 mg chol., 383 mg sodium, 12 g carbo., 1 g fiber, 22 g pro. Dietary exchanges: 1 fruit, 3 lean meat.

Country Boy Pork Tenderloins

From The Kansas City Barbeque Society Cookbook,
Kansas City, Missouri

1	cup apple butter		1/4	tsp. black pepper
1/2	cup white vinegar		1/4	tsp. paprika
1	Tbsp. sugar			Few dashes bottled hot pepper
1	Tbsp. Worcestershire sauce			sauce
1	Tbsp. brandy		2	1-lb. pork tenderloins
1	Tbsp. soy sauce			
1/2	tsp. dry mustard			
1/2	tsp. salt			

Prep: 10 min. **Marinate:** 2 hr. **Grill:** 45 min.

KANSAS CITY BARBEQUE SOCIETY TIP
Direct heat is obtained by distributing the coals evenly over the bottom of the grill. It's great for hot dogs, hamburgers, sausage, steaks, and chicken pieces.
Indirect heat is obtained by moving coals to each side and placing a foil drip pan under the meat between the coals. Indirect heat cooks slower and is best for thick or large pieces of meat such as ribs, roasts, and whole chicken or turkey.

1. In a medium bowl, stir together apple butter, vinegar, sugar, Worcestershire sauce, brandy, soy sauce, dry mustard, salt, black pepper, paprika, and hot pepper sauce.

2. Place the tenderloins in a large plastic bag set in a shallow dish. Pour the apple butter mixture over meat. Seal bag; marinate in the refrigerator for 2 to 8 hours. Drain meat, reserving the marinade.

3. In a grill with a cover, arrange medium-hot coals around the drip pan. Test for medium heat above drip pan.

Place tenderloins on grill rack over drip pan.

4. Cover; grill for 45 to 55 minutes or until thermometer inserted in center of meat registers 160°F, brushing occasionally with marinade during the first 20 minutes of grilling. Discard any remaining marinade.

5. For a gas grill, preheat grill. Reduce heat to medium. Adjust for indirect cooking. Grill as above.

Makes 6 to 8 servings.
Per serving: 459 cal., 3 g total fat (1 g sat. fat), 89 mg chol., 442 mg sodium, 64 g carbo., 2 g fiber, 37 g pro. Dietary exchanges: 4 starch, 3½ lean meat.

PAGE 77 PHOTO APPEARS ON

Apple-Glazed Pork Kabobs

From The Kansas City Barbeque Society Cookbook,
Kansas City, Missouri

1	cup apple jelly
2	Tbsp. honey
2	Tbsp. lemon juice
2	Tbsp. butter or margarine
1	tsp. ground cinnamon
1/4	tsp. ground cloves
1	lb. boneless pork loin, cut into 1-inch cubes
1	tsp. garlic powder
1/2	tsp. celery salt

1/2	to 1 tsp. black pepper
1	large onion, cut into 1-inch pieces
2	large green sweet peppers, cut into 1-inch pieces
1	Tbsp. olive oil
	Sliced green onion (optional)
	Hot cooked couscous

Prep: 20 min. **Grill:** 12 min.

1. In a shallow dish, soak eight 12-inch-long bamboo skewers in water for 30 minutes. In a saucepan, combine jelly, honey, lemon juice, butter, cinnamon, and cloves. Bring to boiling; reduce heat. Simmer, uncovered, for 4 to 5 minutes or until of glaze consistency; stir frequently.

2. Sprinkle pork with garlic powder, celery salt, and black pepper. Thread pork, onion, and sweet peppers alternately onto skewers. Drizzle with oil. Grill, uncovered, directly over medium coals for 12 to 15 minutes or until pork is barely pink in center and vegetables are tender. Turn frequently and brush with glaze after 6 minutes. If desired, stir sliced green onion into couscous; serve with kabobs.

Makes 4 servings.
Per serving: 521 cal., 15 g total fat (6 g sat. fat), 83 mg chol., 266 mg sodium, 73 g carbo., 3 g fiber, 26 g pro. Dietary exchanges: 4 vegetable, 2 starch, 2 medium-fat meat, 1 fat.

Around Town
Kansas City, Missouri (pop. 1.6 million) Kansas City is a barbecue-lover's heaven. Given its more than 60 barbecue restaurants, you'll need more than a long weekend to eat your way through this town.

Apricot-Dijon Pork Salad

From Patricia Schroedl of Jefferson, Wisconsin,
winner of the top prize at the National Pork Producers Council contest

1	cup apricot preserves
1/4	cup white wine vinegar
2	Tbsp. Dijon-style mustard
1/2	tsp. ground ginger
1	lb. pork tenderloin
1	10-oz. pkg. torn mixed salad greens
1	15 1/4-oz. can apricot halves, drained and sliced

1/2	cup dried tart cherries
8	green onions, cut into 1/2-inch pieces
1/4	cup toasted pecan pieces
2	oz. provolone cheese, shredded

Prep: 20 min. **Grill:** 12 min.

A $5,000 Dollar Salad
Patricia Schroedl entered her first cooking contest at her county's "dairy day" celebration when she was 13 years old. She's been creating and experimenting ever since. She showcased two Wisconsin specialties—cherries and cheese—and her homemade apricot preserves in this recipe.

1. Snip large pieces of preserves. Combine preserves, vinegar, mustard, and ginger. Reserve 1/3 cup for brushing on pork; set aside remaining amount for dressing.
2. Cut tenderloin in half lengthwise almost to opposite side; open and lay flat. Place on a grill rack directly over medium-hot coals. Grill for 4 minutes. Turn meat over and grill for 4 minutes more. Brush top of meat with some of the 1/3 cup apricot mixture; grill for 2 minutes. Turn meat over again and brush top with remaining apricot mixture. Grill for 2 to 4 minutes more or until juices run clear.
3. Meanwhile, combine greens, apricots, cherries, onions, and pecans. Divide among four plates. Slice pork 1/2 inch thick. Arrange on top of greens mixture; drizzle with remaining apricot mixture. Sprinkle with cheese.

Makes 4 servings.
Per serving: 604 cal., 12 g total fat, (4 g sat. fat), 76 mg chol., 259 mg sodium, 94 g carbo., 6 g fiber, 35 g pro. Dietary exchanges: 4 vegetable, 5 fruit, 4 lean meat.

Hawaiian Spareribs

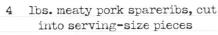

From Angel Food, cookbook of

St. Michael's Episcopal Church, Brigham City, Utah

4	lbs. meaty pork spareribs, cut into serving-size pieces	1	8-oz. can crushed pineapple, undrained
1	cup packed brown sugar	1/2	cup finely chopped onion
3	Tbsp. cornstarch	3	Tbsp. soy sauce
1	cup vinegar	1	Tbsp. yellow mustard
3/4	cup chili sauce		
3/4	cup water		

Prep: 15 min. **Bake:** 1½ hr.

EASY CLEANUP
These may be the messiest (and most delicious) ribs you'll ever eat, but lining the roasting pan with foil minimizes the cleanup.

1. Line a 15×10×2-inch roasting pan with foil. Arrange ribs, meaty side down, in a single layer in pan. Cover and bake in a 350°F oven 45 minutes.

2. Meanwhile, for the sauce, in a 2-quart saucepan, stir together brown sugar and cornstarch. Stir in vinegar, chili sauce, water, undrained pineapple, onion, soy sauce, and mustard. Cook and stir over medium heat until thickened and bubbly; cook and stir for 2 minutes more.

3. Remove roasting pan from oven. Drain fat from ribs. Turn ribs, meaty side up. Spoon 2 cups of the sauce over the ribs. Reserve remaining sauce in saucepan. Cover ribs and bake about 45 minutes more or until ribs are tender. Remove ribs to a serving platter. Heat sauce in saucepan; serve with ribs.

Makes 6 to 8 servings.
Per serving: 558 cal., 19 g total fat (7 g sat. fat), 89 mg chol., 992 mg sodium, 57 g carbo., 2 g fiber, 39 g pro. Dietary exchanges: 4 starch, 4½ medium-fat meat.

Barbecued Baby Back Ribs

From The Kansas City Barbeque Society Cookbook,
Kansas City, Missouri

KANSAS CITY BARBEQUE SOCIETY TIP
Coals should be at least 80 percent ashed over before grilling. If a fire is too cool, knock off some of the ashes and add charcoal.

$3^{1}/_2$	to 4 lbs. pork loin back ribs		$^1/_2$	tsp. celery seed
1	Tbsp. paprika		$^1/_4$	tsp. ground red pepper
$1^{1}/_2$	tsp. garlic salt		$^1/_2$	cup apple juice
1	tsp. onion powder			
1	tsp. dried sage, crushed			

Prep: 15 min. **Grill:** $1^1/_4$ hr.

1. Trim fat from ribs. Combine all ingredients except apple juice. Rub mixture over both sides of the ribs.

2. For a charcoal grill with cover, arrange medium-hot coals around drip pan. Test for medium heat above drip pan. Place ribs on grill rack over drip pan. Cover; grill for $1^1/_4$ to $1^1/_2$ hours or until ribs are tender and no pink remains, brushing occasionally with apple juice after the first 45 minutes of cooking.

3. For a gas grill, preheat grill. Reduce heat to medium. Adjust for indirect cooking. Grill as above.

Makes 8 servings.
Per serving: 324 cal., 14 g total fat (5 g sat. fat), 94 mg chol., 253 mg sodium, 3 g carbo., 0 g fiber, 43 g pro. Dietary exchanges: 6 lean meat.

Apple 'n' Sausage Breakfast Topper

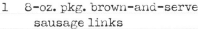

From Slices & Bites of the Wenatchee Valley,
cookbook of the Applarians, Wenatchee, Washington

1	8-oz. pkg. brown-and-serve sausage links
4½	tsp. cornstarch
½	tsp. ground cinnamon
1½	cups apple juice
¼	cup packed brown sugar

2	cups thinly sliced apples
½	cup raisins (optional)
	Hot waffles, pancakes, or French toast

Prep: 15 min. **Cook:** 4 min.

1. Slice the sausage links ½ inch thick and set aside.

2. In a medium saucepan, combine cornstarch and cinnamon. Stir in apple juice and brown sugar. Cook and stir until thickened.

3. Stir in sausage, apples, and, if desired, raisins. Cover; simmer for 4 to 5 minutes or until sausage is heated through. Serve over waffles, pancakes, or French toast.

Makes 3½ cups.
Per ½-cup topper: 119 cal., 4 g total fat (1 g sat. fat), 11 mg chol., 174 mg sodium, 18 g carbo., 1 g fiber, 3 g pro. Dietary exchanges: 1 fruit, ½ high-fat meat.

Apple Appeal
Most of America's apples are grown in Washington state. To celebrate that fact, Wenatchee sponsors a 10-day Apple Blossom Festival each April. One of the festival's highlights is the selection of a queen and her court to promote Washington apples in the upcoming year. The queen earns a $5,000 scholarship. The Wenatchee royalty have the Applarians, a group that promotes the festival, to thank for cookbook sales that support the scholarships.

Biscuits and Sausage Gravy

From Bill Hurley Jr.,
Salem, Oregon

1	lb. sweet Italian sausage (remove casings, if present)
4	oz. fresh mushrooms, chopped (about 1½ cups)
½	cup chopped onion
1	to 2 fresh jalapeño peppers, finely chopped
¼	cup all-purpose flour
1	tsp. sugar

½	tsp. garlic powder
⅛	tsp. ground cloves
2	cups milk
¼	cup snipped fresh basil
	Bottled hot pepper sauce
8	biscuits (homemade or purchased)

Start to finish: 25 min.

1. In a large skillet, cook Italian sausage, mushrooms, onion, and jalapeño peppers until sausage is brown. Drain off fat, reserving ¼ cup of the drippings.

2. Return the reserved drippings and the drained sausage mixture to skillet. Stir in flour, sugar, garlic powder, and cloves.

3. Add milk all at once. Cook and stir over medium heat until mixture is thickened and bubbly. Cook and stir for 1 minute more. Stir in basil; season to taste with hot pepper sauce. Heat through. Serve over hot biscuits.

Makes 8 servings.
Per serving: 293 cal., 17 g total fat (6 g sat. fat), 37 mg chol., 589 mg sodium, 22 g carbo., 1 g fiber, 13 g pro. Dietary exchanges: ½ milk, 1 starch, 1 high-fat meat, 1 fat.

Potato Sausage Tart

*From Beyond Burlap, cookbook of the
Boise Junior League, Boise, Idaho*

1	recipe Pastry for Single-Crust Pie (see recipe, below)		2	eggs
2	large baking potatoes (about 1 lb. total)		1/2	cup dairy sour cream
1/4	tsp. salt		1	tsp. dried oregano, crushed
1/8	tsp. black pepper		2	Tbsp. butter or margarine, melted
1	lb. mild Italian sausage or turkey Italian sausage		3/4	cup shredded cheddar cheese (3 oz.)
2	cups cream-style cottage cheese			

Prep: 25 min. **Bake:** 40 min. **Stand:** 10 min.

THE BEST BAKED POTATO
Idaho cooks are adamant that the best baked potatoes come out of a conventional oven. And don't wrap them in foil. If you like, butter or oil potatoes before baking for a crisper crust. Bake on the oven rack in a 425° oven for 45 to 60 minutes. To serve, "blossom" the potato by pricking an "X" on the top. Push gently from each end to reveal the fluffy, dry meat.

1. Prepare pastry for a 10-inch deep-dish pie plate. Line pastry shell with double thickness of foil. Bake in a 450°F oven 8 minutes. Remove foil. Bake 5 minutes more or until dry. Set aside. Reduce oven temperature to 350°F.

2. Peel and quarter potatoes. Cook in boiling lightly salted water for 20 to 25 minutes or until tender; drain. Mash with potato masher or beat with an electric mixer until smooth. Stir in salt and black pepper. Measure 2 cups.

3. Remove sausage casings, if present. In a large skillet, cook sausage until no longer pink; drain. In blender or food processor, combine cottage cheese and eggs. Cover; blend or process until smooth. Transfer to a large bowl. Using electric mixer, beat in mashed potatoes, sour cream, and oregano.

4. Place sausage in bottom of pastry shell. Spoon potato mixture over sausage. Drizzle with melted butter. Sprinkle with cheese.

5. Bake in a 350°F oven for 40 to 45 minutes or until heated through. Let stand 10 minutes before serving.

Pastry for Single-Crust Pie: Combine 1 1/4 cups all-purpose flour and 1/4 teaspoon salt. Using pastry blender, cut in 1/3 cup shortening until pieces are pea-size. Sprinkle 4 to 5 tablespoons cold water, 1 tablespoon at a time, over mixture. Gently toss with fork just until all dough is moistened. Form into ball. On lightly floured surface, roll dough into a 12-inch circle. Transfer to a 9-inch pie plate or a 10-inch deep-dish pie plate. Trim to 1/2 inch beyond edge of plate. Fold under extra pastry; crimp.

Makes 8 servings.
Per serving: 515 cal., 34 g total fat (15 g sat. fat), 124 mg chol., 790 mg sodium, 25 g carbo., 2 g fiber, 23 g pro. Dietary exchanges: 2 starch, 2 high-fat meat, 2 fat.

Italian Sausage and Spinach Pie

*From The Heart of Pittsburgh, a cookbook benefiting
Sacred Heart Elementary School, Pittsburgh, Pennsylvania*

1	lb. bulk Italian sausage
1	medium onion, chopped (½ cup)
5	eggs
1	egg white
1	10-oz. pkg. frozen chopped spinach, thawed and well drained
2	cups shredded mozzarella cheese (8 oz.)

½	of a 15-oz. carton part-skim ricotta cheese (about 1 cup)
½	tsp. garlic powder
	Pastry for a double-crust 9- or 10-inch pie
1	beaten egg yolk
1	Tbsp. water

Prep: 45 min. **Bake:** 50 min. **Stand:** 10 min.

1. In a large skillet, cook Italian sausage and chopped onion for 10 to 15 minutes or until sausage is no longer pink and onion is tender. Drain off excess fat from meat.

2. In a large mixing bowl, beat together whole eggs and egg white. Stir in the drained spinach, mozzarella, ricotta cheese, garlic powder, and the meat mixture.

3. Line a 9- or 10-inch pie plate with half of the pastry. Spread filling evenly in pastry-lined plate. Trim pastry to edge of pie plate. Top with remaining pastry. Seal and crimp edge as desired. Brush top of pastry with a mixture of egg yolk and the water. Cut slits in the top of the pastry to allow steam to escape.

4. Bake in a 375°F oven for 50 to 55 minutes or until top is golden. Cover edge with foil, if necessary, to prevent overbrowning. Let stand 10 minutes. Cut into wedges to serve.

Makes 10 servings.
Per serving: 459 cal., 32 g total fat (11 g sat. fat), 178 mg chol., 578 mg sodium, 22 g carbo., 1 g fiber, 20 g pro. Dietary exchanges: 1½ starch, 2 high-fat meat, 3 fat.

Lamb Curry

From West of the Rockies, cookbook of the
Junior Service League of Grand Junction, Colorado

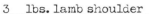

3	lbs. lamb shoulder
3	Tbsp. olive oil or cooking oil
1	medium onion, chopped
2	Tbsp. all-purpose flour
2	Tbsp. curry powder
2	cups chicken broth
2	cups peeled, diced celery root
4	medium tomatoes, coarsely chopped (3 cups)
1	cup whipping cream

2	medium cooking apples (such as Golden Delicious), peeled, cored, and coarsely chopped
	Hot cooked rice
	Desired condiments (such as chutney, toasted shredded coconut, or chopped apples or nuts)

Prep: 20 min. **Cook:** 1½ hr.

1. Trim fat from lamb. Cut lamb into 1-inch cubes, discarding bone.
2. In a large saucepan or Dutch oven, brown lamb, one-third at a time, in hot oil, cooking onion with last portion of lamb. Stir in flour; cook for 7 minutes, stirring frequently. Stir in curry powder; stir in chicken broth. Add celery root and three of the tomatoes. Bring to boiling; reduce heat. Cover and simmer about 1½ hours or until meat is tender.
3. Stir in whipping cream. Simmer, uncovered, for 2 minutes more. Stir in the apples and the remaining tomato. Heat through. Serve with rice and desired condiments.

Makes 8 servings.
Per serving: 434 cal., 25 g total fat (10 g sat. fat), 99 mg chol., 298 mg sodium, 32 g carbo., 3 g fiber, 22 g pro. Dietary exchanges: 2 vegetable, ½ fruit, 1 starch, 2 lean meat, 3 fat.

Around Town
Grand Junction, Colorado (pop. 110,000) Grand Junction is a paradise for outdoor lovers. Visitors can hike in the Colorado National Monument (a mini Grand Canyon), paddle down the Colorado River, ski at Powderhorn Ski Resort, or visit vineyards, and peach, apricot, apple, or cherry orchards in nearby Palisade.

Lamb Chops Jalapeño

From the Kansas City Barbeque Society Cookbook,
Kansas City, Missouri

8	lamb rib or loin chops, cut 1 inch thick (about 2½ lbs.)		1/3	to ½ cup jalapeño jelly
½	tsp. salt		1/4	cup lemon juice
½	tsp. black pepper		2	tsp. yellow mustard
½	tsp. ground cinnamon			Couscous with peas and shredded carrot (optional)
1	8-oz. can crushed pineapple (juice pack), undrained			

Prep: 15 min. **Grill:** 10 min.

1. Trim fat from meat. Combine salt, black pepper, and cinnamon; rub mixture onto both sides of meat. Set aside.

2. For glaze, in a medium saucepan, combine undrained pineapple, jalapeño jelly, lemon juice, and mustard. Bring to boiling; reduce heat. Simmer, uncovered, for 10 minutes. Stir occasionally.

3. Grill meat on rack of uncovered grill directly over medium coals to desired doneness, turning once. (Allow 10 to 14 minutes for medium rare; 14 to 16 minutes for medium.) Set aside 1 cup of glaze. Brush with remaining glaze during last 5 minutes of grilling. Serve meat with reserved glaze. Serve with couscous, if desired.

Makes 4 servings.
Per serving: 430 cal., 16 g total fat (6 g sat. fat), 139 mg chol., 437 mg sodium, 29 g carbo., 1 g fiber, 43 g pro. Dietary exchanges: 1 starch, 5 lean meat.

4.

Poultry

St. Michael's Church's Famous Fried Chicken

From Angel Food, cookbook of
St. Michael's Episcopal Church, Brigham City, Utah

1	3-lb. whole chicken, cut up, or 3 lbs. meaty chicken pieces (breasts, thighs, and drumsticks)
4	cups buttermilk or sour milk*
1½	cups all-purpose flour
2	tsp. garlic salt

2	tsp. paprika
	Salt
	Black pepper
½	cup cooking oil

Prep: 30 min. **Chill:** 3 hr. **Marinate:** 8 hr. **Bake:** 35 min.

1. Place chicken in an extra-large bowl. Cover with lightly salted water. Cover and chill in the refrigerator for 3 hours. Drain. Place chicken pieces in a self-sealing plastic bag set in a large bowl. Pour buttermilk over chicken. Close bag. Marinate in the refrigerator for at least 8 hours or overnight. Drain chicken, discarding the buttermilk.

2. In a shallow dish, combine flour, garlic salt, and paprika. Generously coat the chicken pieces with the flour mixture. Sprinkle chicken pieces with salt and black pepper.

3. In a large skillet, heat the oil over medium-high heat. Fry the chicken pieces, half at a time, in the hot oil for 2 to 4 minutes, turning to brown evenly. Transfer browned chicken pieces to a 3-quart rectangular baking dish.

4. Bake in a 375°F oven for 35 to 45 minutes or until chicken is tender and no longer pink (an instant-read thermometer should register 170°F in breast pieces and 180°F in chicken thighs and legs).

*Note: To make 4 cups sour milk, place ¼ cup lemon juice or vinegar in a 4-cup glass measure. Add enough milk to make 4 cups liquid; stir. Let the mixture stand for 5 minutes before using it.

Makes 6 to 8 servings.
Per serving: 426 cal., 22 g total fat (5 g sat. fat), 81 mg chol., 458 mg sodium, 25 g carbo., 1 g fiber, 30 g pro. Dietary exchanges: 1½ starch, 3½ medium-fat meat, 1 fat.

Chicken Old Ladies on a Bus

From Atlanta Cooknotes, 80th-anniversary cookbook of the Atlanta Junior League, Atlanta, Georgia

2	lbs. meaty chicken pieces
1/3	cup orange marmalade
1/3	cup bottled barbecue sauce
2	Tbsp. Worcestershire sauce
2	Tbsp. lemon juice

Prep: 10 min. **Bake:** 1 hr.

Tasty Talk

Atlanta Cooknotes was created by the Atlanta Junior League in honor of its 80th birthday. This sweet and tangy glazed chicken was developed from a conversation overheard between two elderly ladies on a city bus.

1. Skin chicken, if desired. Arrange chicken in a foil-lined 13×9×2-inch baking pan; set aside. In a small bowl combine marmalade, barbecue sauce, Worcestershire sauce, and lemon juice; pour over chicken.

2. Bake, uncovered, in 350°F oven for 45 minutes, spooning sauce over chicken occasionally. Increase oven temperature to 400°F. Bake for 15 minutes more or until chicken is tender and no longer pink.

Makes 4 to 6 servings.
Per serving: 282 cal., 8 g total fat (2 g sat. fat), 92 mg chol., 336 mg sodium, 22 g carbo., 0 g fiber, 30 g pro. Dietary exchanges: 1½ starch, 3½ very lean meat, ½ fat.

Southern Baked Chicken with Fruit "Salsa"

From Diane Halferty of Corpus Christi, Texas,
first-place winner in the Kretschmer's Wheat Germ Contest

PAGE PHOTO APPEARS ON 113

2	cups chopped fresh rhubarb (cut into 1-inch pieces)
1/2	cup sugar
1/2	cup dried cranberries
1/4	cup cider vinegar
1	tsp. finely chopped ginger
1	cup coarsely chopped strawberries
6	medium boneless, skinless chicken breast halves

1	cup buttermilk
1/2	cup toasted wheat germ
1/3	cup plain dry bread crumbs
3	Tbsp. all-purpose flour
1 1/2	tsp. freshly ground black pepper
3/4	tsp. salt
3	Tbsp. cooking oil

Prep: 35 min. **Bake:** 10 min.

Germ of an Idea
Diane Halferty's main dish won first place in the Kretschmer's Wheat Germ Contest, but she gives her husband some of the credit for her creation. He likes strawberry-rhubarb pie, she says, and she thought those flavors would go well with chicken. She chose to bake—rather than fry—the chicken, a technique she learned in spa-style cooking classes.

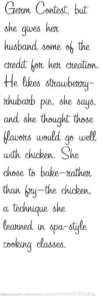

1. For salsa, in a medium saucepan, combine rhubarb, sugar, cranberries, vinegar, and ginger. Bring to boiling, stirring occasionally. Reduce heat; simmer, uncovered, for 25 minutes or until rhubarb is tender. Remove from heat. Stir in strawberries; cool.

2. Meanwhile, place chicken in a large bowl. Pour buttermilk over; let stand for 15 minutes. Meanwhile, in a shallow dish combine wheat germ, bread crumbs, flour, black pepper, and salt. Dip chicken in crumb mixture to coat.

3. In a large skillet, heat half of the oil. Add half of the chicken in a single layer. Brown chicken about 2 minutes on each side. Carefully transfer to a 13×9×2-inch baking pan. Repeat with remaining chicken and oil. Bake in a 400°F oven 10 minutes or until chicken is no longer pink. Serve with salsa.

Makes 6 servings.
Per serving: 390 cal., 11 g total fat (2 g sat. fat), 69 mg chol., 440 mg sodium, 42 g carbo., 4 g fiber, 32 g pro. Dietary exchanges: 2 fruit, 1 starch, 4 very lean meat, 1 fat.

Chicken Paprikash

From Favorite Recipes of Sokol Greater Cleveland,
Cleveland, Ohio

3 slices bacon, chopped	Salt
1 cup chopped onion (1 large)	Black pepper
1 cup chopped carrot (2 medium)	1 8-oz. carton dairy sour cream
1 cup chopped celery (2 stalks)	1/3 cup all-purpose flour
1 tsp. paprika	1 1/3 cups water
1/8 tsp. black pepper	1/2 tsp. finely shredded
Dash ground cloves	lemon peel
1 bay leaf	Hot cooked noodles or rice
3 to 3 1/2 lbs. meaty chicken pieces (breasts, thighs, and drumsticks)	

Prep: 30 min. **Bake:** 55 min.

SPICE NOTES
Paprika is made from grinding sweet red pepper pods. Its color can range from bright orange-red to deep blood-red, and its flavor ranges from mild to fiery. Most of the paprika you find on your supermarket shelves comes from Spain, South America, California, and Hungary. The Hungarian type is considered to be the best. Store paprika in a cool, dark place for up to 6 months.

1. In a large skillet, cook bacon until almost crisp. Remove bacon, reserving drippings in skillet. Drain bacon on paper towels. In the same skillet, cook onion, carrot, and celery in reserved drippings over medium heat for 5 minutes. Stir in paprika, the 1/8 teaspoon black pepper, the cloves, and bay leaf. Stir in cooked bacon.

2. Arrange vegetable mixture in the bottom of a 13×9×2-inch baking pan. Arrange chicken pieces on top of vegetable mixture. Sprinkle chicken lightly with salt and black pepper. Bake in a 375°F oven for 45 to 55 minutes or until chicken is tender and no longer pink and an instant-read thermometer registers 170°F when inserted in center of chicken breast or 180°F when inserted in thigh or drumstick.

3. Meanwhile, stir together sour cream and flour until smooth. Gradually whisk in water until smooth.

4. Remove chicken from baking pan. Cover chicken; keep warm. For sauce, stir sour cream mixture into vegetable mixture in pan. Stir in lemon peel. Bake, uncovered, about 10 minutes more or until thickened and bubbly around the edges. Discard bay leaf. Transfer sauce to a large serving dish. Arrange chicken in serving dish with sauce. Serve with hot cooked noodles or rice.

Makes 6 servings.
Per serving: 634 cal., 32 g total fat (12 g sat. fat), 195 mg chol., 349 mg sodium, 39 g carbo., 3 g fiber, 47 g pro. Dietary exchanges: 1 vegetable, 2 starch, 6 medium-fat meat.

Angel Chicken

From Sher Garfield,
Bellevue, Washington

6	skinless boneless chicken breast halves (about 1½ lbs.)
¼	cup butter
1	0.7-oz. pkg. Italian salad dressing mix
1	10¾-oz. can condensed golden mushroom soup

½	cup dry white wine
½	of an 8-oz. tub cream cheese with chives and onion
	Hot cooked angel-hair pasta
	Snipped fresh chives (optional)

Prep: 15 min. **Cook:** 4 hr.

1. Place chicken in a 3½- or 4-quart crockery cooker. In a medium saucepan, melt the butter. Stir in the dry salad dressing mix. Stir in soup, wine, and cream cheese until combined. Pour over the chicken. Cover and cook on low-heat setting for 4 to 5 hours.

2. Serve chicken and sauce over hot cooked pasta. Sprinkle with fresh chives, if desired.

Makes 6 servings.
Per serving: 405 cal., 17 g total fat (9 g sat. fat), 110 mg chol., 1,043 mg sodium, 26 g carbo., 1 g fiber, 32 g pro. Dietary exchanges: 1½ starch, 3 very lean meat, 3 fat.

Easy Orange Chicken

From *Savoring the Southwest Again*, cookbook of the
Roswell Symphony Guild, Roswell, New Mexico

1/4 cup all-purpose flour	2 Tbsp. cooking oil
1/2 tsp. salt	3 oranges
1/2 tsp. curry powder	1 tsp. sugar (optional)
1/2 tsp. chili powder	Hot cooked rice (optional)
1/4 tsp. garlic powder	
1/4 tsp. black pepper	**Prep:** 20 min. **Bake:** 20 min.
6 medium skinless, boneless chicken breast halves (about 1 1/2 lbs.)	

1. In a large plastic bag, combine flour, salt, curry powder, chili powder, garlic powder, and black pepper; add chicken and shake to coat, reserving any extra flour mixture. In a large skillet, heat 1 tablespoon of the oil over medium-high heat. Add half of the chicken breasts and cook about 5 minutes or until lightly browned, turning once. Transfer chicken to a 2-quart rectangular baking dish. Repeat with remaining chicken and oil. Stir any remaining flour mixture into pan drippings in skillet. Remove skillet from heat.

2. Squeeze juice from oranges (you should have 1 cup). Stir juice into flour mixture in skillet; add sugar, if desired, and stir until smooth. Pour juice mixture over chicken.

3. Bake, uncovered, in a 350°F oven for 20 to 25 minutes or until chicken is tender and no longer pink. Serve over hot cooked rice, if desired.

Makes 6 servings.
Per serving: 202 cal., 6 g total fat (1 g sat. fat), 66 mg chol., 256 mg sodium, 8 g carbo., 0 g fiber, 27 g pro. Dietary exchanges: 1/2 fruit, 4 very lean meat, 1/2 fat.

Busy Day El Rancho Chicken

From Celebrate San Antonio, cookbook of the
San Antonio Junior Forum, San Antonio, Texas

1	10¾-oz. can reduced-sodium condensed cream of mushroom soup
1	10¾-oz. can reduced-sodium condensed cream of chicken soup
1	10-oz. can diced tomatoes with green chiles
1	medium green sweet pepper, chopped (¾ cup)
1	medium onion, chopped (½ cup)

1½	tsp. chili powder
¼	tsp. black pepper
12	6- or 7-inch corn tortillas, cut into thin, bite-size strips
3	cups cubed cooked chicken
1	8-oz. pkg. (2 cups) shredded cheddar cheese
	Sliced tomatoes (optional)
	Sliced green onions (optional)

Prep: 20 min. **Bake:** 48 min. **Stand:** 10 min.

1. Combine soups, undrained tomatoes with chiles, sweet pepper, onion, chili powder, and black pepper. Set aside.

2. To assemble, sprinkle about one-third of the tortilla strips over bottom of an ungreased 3-quart rectangular baking dish. Layer half of the chicken over tortilla strips; spoon half of soup mixture on top. Sprinkle half of the cheese and another one-third of the tortilla strips over the soup mixture. Layer with the remaining chicken, soup mixture, and tortilla strips.

3. Bake, uncovered, in a 350°F oven about 45 minutes or until bubbly around edges and center is hot. Uncover; sprinkle with the remaining cheese. Bake for 3 to 4 minutes more or until cheese is melted. Top with sliced tomatoes and green onions, if desired. Let stand 10 minutes before serving.

Makes 8 servings.
Per serving: 365 cal., 16 g total fat (7 g sat. fat), 85 mg chol., 752 mg sodium, 28 g carbo., 1 g fiber, 27 g pro. Dietary exchanges: 1 vegetable, 1½ starch, 3 lean meat, 1 fat.

Hurley's Mucho Gusto Enchiladas

From Bill Hurley Jr.,
Salem, Oregon

1½	lbs. skinless, boneless chicken breast halves
1	large onion, chopped (1 cup)
½	cup loosely packed cilantro
1	tsp. crushed red pepper
2	fresh jalapeño peppers, seeded and chopped
2	tsp. chili powder
1	clove garlic, minced
1	Tbsp. cooking oil
1	19-oz. can enchilada sauce

1	Tbsp. diced green chile peppers
1	cup cooking oil
10	6-inch corn tortillas
1	cup shredded Monterey Jack cheese
1	cup shredded cheddar cheese
1	2¼-oz. can sliced pitted ripe olives
3	green onions, thinly sliced

Prep: 1 hr. **Bake:** 22 min.

1. In a large saucepan, combine chicken, ⅔ cup of the onion, cilantro, ½ teaspoon of the red pepper, half the jalapeño peppers, the chili powder, and garlic. Add enough water to cover chicken. Bring to boiling; reduce heat.

2. Simmer, covered, 15 to 20 minutes or until chicken is no longer pink. Remove chicken; shred. Discard cooking liquid.

3. In a large skillet, heat the 1 tablespoon oil over medium-high heat. Add the remaining onion, remaining red pepper, and remaining jalapeño peppers. Add shredded chicken, ½ cup of the enchilada sauce, and green chile peppers. Bring to boiling; reduce heat.

4. Simmer the chicken mixture, covered, for 15 minutes, stirring occasionally. Keep warm.

5. In a medium skillet, heat the 1 cup oil. Working quickly, fry tortillas, one at a time, in hot oil for 10 to 15 seconds or until tortilla is hot but not crisp. Pat dry between paper towels.

6. Immediately place about ⅓ cup chicken mixture onto each tortilla near an edge; roll up. Place filled tortillas, seam sides down, in a lightly greased 2-quart rectangular baking dish. Pour the remaining enchilada sauce over. Cover with foil.

7. Bake in a 350°F oven for 20 to 25 minutes or until heated through. Uncover; sprinkle cheeses over. Return to oven and bake for 2 to 3 minutes more or until cheeses are melted. To serve, sprinkle with olives and green onions. Serve with sour cream and guacamole, if desired.

Makes 5 servings.

Per serving: 599 cal., 30 g total fat (11 g sat. fat), 115 mg chol., 924 mg sodium, 42 g carbo., 4 g fiber, 42 g pro. Dietary exchanges: 2 vegetable, 2 starch, 4½ very lean meat, 2 fat.

Mucho, Mucho! Captain Bill Hurley Jr.'s version of this recipe in the National Firefighters Recipe Book calls for 30 tortillas, 4 cans of enchilada sauce, and 2 pounds of cheese. And he recommends you have an assistant! These scaled-down portions make this a family casserole.

Pineapple-Lemon Chicken

From Nancy Rinehart,
Chicago, Illinois

2	whole medium chicken breasts (about 2 lb. total)
1	20-oz. can crushed pineapple (juice pack)
1	small lemon, very thinly sliced
1/3	cup catsup
1/3	cup honey
1	Tbsp. Worcestershire sauce

2	cloves garlic, minced
1	tsp. salt
1/4	tsp. dried rosemary, crushed
1	tsp. cornstarch
	Hot cooked rice

Prep: 30 min. **Marinate:** 2 hr. **Grill:** 50 min.

1. Cut chicken breasts in half. Place in a self-sealing plastic bag set in a large bowl; set aside. Drain pineapple, reserving 1/4 cup juice. Combine pineapple, reserved juice, lemon slices, catsup, honey, Worcestershire sauce, garlic, salt, and rosemary. Pour over chicken. Seal bag. Marinate in refrigerator for at least 2 hours or up to 24 hours. Drain chicken, reserving the marinade.

2. In a grill with a cover, arrange medium-hot coals around a drip pan. Test for medium heat above pan. Place chicken, bone side down, on rack over pan. Brush with some of the reserved marinade. Cover; grill for 50 to 60 minutes or until chicken is tender and no longer pink. Turn and brush with about 1/4 cup of the reserved marinade halfway through grilling.

3. In a medium saucepan, combine remaining reserved marinade and cornstarch. Cook and stir over medium heat until thickened and bubbly. Cook 2 minutes more. To serve, spoon sauce over chicken and rice.

Makes 4 servings.
Per serving: 426 cal., 2 g total fat (0 g sat. fat), 66 mg chol., 949 mg sodium, 74 g carbo., 2 g fiber, 29 g pro. Dietary exchanges: 1½ fruit, 3 starch, 3 very lean meat.

Pigall's Fusion Chicken

From I'll Cook When Pigs Fly—And They Do in Cincinnati!,
cookbook of the Junior League of Cincinnati, Ohio

2	medium whole chicken breasts (about 2 lbs. total)	¹⁄₂	tsp. grated fresh ginger
1	cup dry red wine	¹⁄₂	tsp. five-spice powder
¹⁄₄	cup hoisin sauce	¹⁄₄	tsp. crushed red pepper
¹⁄₄	cup chopped onion		Wild rice pilaf (optional)
1	Tbsp. soy sauce		
1	tsp. bottled minced garlic		

Prep: 15 min. **Grill:** 50 min. **Marinate:** 1 hr.

1. Cut chicken breasts in half (leave skin on). Place in a self-sealing plastic bag set in a shallow dish. For marinade, combine remaining ingredients (except rice pilaf). Pour over chicken. Seal bag. Marinate in the refrigerator for 1 to 2 hours.

2. Drain chicken, reserving marinade. In a grill with a cover, arrange medium-hot coals around drip pan. Test for medium heat above pan. Place chicken, bone sides down, on rack over pan. Cover; grill 50 to 60 minutes or until chicken is no longer pink, turning once.

3. Meanwhile, place reserved marinade in a small saucepan. Bring to boiling; reduce heat. Simmer, uncovered, for 10 minutes. Strain, if desired. Serve chicken with rice pilaf, if desired. Drizzle hot marinade over chicken.

Makes 4 servings.
Per serving: 333 cal., 12 g total fat (4 g sat. fat), 90 mg chol., 620 mg sodium, 12 g carbo., 0 g fiber, 30 g pro. Dietary exchanges: 1 starch, 4 lean meat.

TWO STYLES, ONE GREAT TASTE
The term "fusion cuisine" refers to the coming together of East and West—generally Asian flavors and Western cooking techniques. Hoisin sauce is a sweet, spicy Chinese sauce made from soybeans, garlic, chile peppers, and spices that can be used straight out of the jar like a barbecue sauce. Five-spice powder is a pungent mixture of cinnamon, cloves, fennel seed, star anise, and Szechwan peppercorns that is used generously in Chinese cooking.

Miss Mary's Famous Chicken with Pastry

From Miss Mary Bobo's Boarding House.
Lynchburg, Tennessee

1	3- to 3½-lb. whole broiler-fryer chicken	¼	tsp. black pepper	
3	cups water	1	cup all-purpose flour	
1	medium onion, cut into wedges	¼	tsp. salt	
½	cup sliced celery (1 stalk)	⅓	cup shortening	
1	tsp. salt	3	to 4 Tbsp. cold water	
½	cup all-purpose flour		Milk	
½	cup water			

Prep: 45 min. **Cook:** 1 hr. **Bake:** 20 min.

Room and Board
The dinner bell rings promptly at noon at Miss Mary Bobo's Boarding House. Miss Mary's is the place to go in Lynchburg, Tennessee, for traditional Southern cooking. This homey chicken casserole is one of the restaurant's most popular recipes. Desserts are different every day and often include Jack Daniel's whiskey, made in Lynchburg.

1. In a Dutch oven, combine chicken, the 3 cups water, the onion, celery, and the 1 teaspoon salt. Bring to boiling; reduce heat. Cover and simmer for 1 to 1¼ hours or until chicken is no longer pink. Drain, reserving 3 cups broth. Discard vegetables. Set chicken aside. When cool enough to handle, remove skin and bones from chicken; discard skin and bones. Coarsely chop chicken (you should have about 3 cups total). Place chicken in 2-quart rectangular baking dish; set aside.

2. In same Dutch oven, combine the ½ cup flour, the ½ cup water, and the black pepper. Gradually stir reserved broth into flour mixture. Cook and stir over medium heat until thickened and bubbly. Pour evenly over chicken.

3. For pastry, in medium bowl, combine the 1 cup flour and the ¼ teaspoon salt. Cut in shortening until pieces are pea-size. Sprinkle 1 tablespoon of the cold water over the mixture; gently toss with a fork. Push moistened dough to side of bowl. Repeat moistening dough, using 1 tablespoon of the water at a time, until all dough is moistened. Form dough into a ball. On a lightly floured surface, roll dough into an 11×6-inch rectangle. Cut lengthwise into twelve ½-inch-wide strips. Brush strips with milk. Place six of the strips lengthwise across chicken mixture. Cut the remaining strips in half crosswise. Place shorter strips crosswise over longer strips in dish.

4. Bake in a 450°F oven for 20 to 25 minutes or until pastry is golden and filling is bubbly.

Makes 6 servings.
Per serving: 440 cal., 17 g total fat (4 g sat. fat), 62 mg chol., 551 mg sodium, 22 g carbo., 1 g fiber, 23 g pro. Dietary exchanges: 1½ starch, 2½ very lean meat, 1½ fat.

Southern Baked Chicken with Fruit "Salsa," p. 104

Hurley's Mucho Gusto Enchiladas, p. 109

Honey-Dijon Barbecued Chicken, p. 123

Grilled Garlic Turkey Sausage, p. 125

Hudson's Chicken Burgers, p. 124

Renata Stanko, above, of Lebanon, Oregon, won $500 in the Gilroy Garlic Festival Recipe Contest in Gilroy, California, for Grilled Garlic Turkey Sausage with Garlic Cranberry Sauce, above left. Consider making the sauce to serve with a Thanksgiving turkey. Recipe contributor Gail Hudson of Minneapolis says these lean chicken burgers, below left, are a summertime staple. She serves them with fresh corn on the cob from the vegetable stand just down the street from her house.

Fried Whitefish, p. 128

Bertha Endress Rollo, left, lived with her grandparents, mother, and brother in the lighthousekeeper's quarters at Whitefish Point, Michigan, from 1910 to 1931. Her grandfather was the lighthousekeeper for 28 years. Bertha's recollections fill Treasured Recipes of the Shipwreck Coast.

The Ozarks meet the south of France in this dish that uses fresh fish native to the area around Springfield, Missouri. The recipe originated with the French uncle of Marcel Bonetti, chef of Hemingway's Blue Water Cafe, a popular Ozarks-area restaurant.

Ozark Trout Doria, p. 130

Shrimp Gravy, p. 133

Small, historic Trinity Episcopal Church, left, is one of 30 churches on Edisto Island, South Carolina. For his version of an Edisto favorite, recipe contributor Tom Kapp started with a recipe he obtained from an area tugboat captain and added a few of his own twists. Tom likes serving the dish over grits. "Grits are a real Southern tradition," he says. "For us, they're like eating rice or potatoes."

A crab boil out on the family dock, inset, is a way of life on Edisto Island, South Carolina. Sweet, creamy Crab Quiche is just the kind of dish you'd expect on a picnic table on Edisto.

Crab Quiche, p. 137

Batter-Dipped Fried Clams, p. 138

Crunchy Ranch Fingers

From Balancing Acts, cookbook of the
American Gold Gymnastics program, Fargo, North Dakota

	Nonstick cooking spray
1	cup cornflake crumbs
1	Tbsp. snipped fresh parsley
1/4	tsp. salt
1/8	tsp. black pepper
1/3	cup buttermilk ranch salad dressing
1	Tbsp. water

3/4	lb. skinless, boneless chicken breast halves, cut into bite-size strips
	Buttermilk ranch salad dressing

Start to finish: 22 min.

A CRUMB-Y TIP
The best way to make the cornflake crumbs needed for this recipe is to put cornflakes in a plastic bag, then lay the bag flat on the countertop. Roll over the bag gently with a rolling pin. Repeat until you've created enough crumbs to make 1 cup.

1. Coat a 15×10×1-inch baking pan with cooking spray; set aside.

2. Combine cornflake crumbs, parsley, salt, and black pepper. Stir together salad dressing and water. Dip chicken strips into the dressing mixture, allowing excess to drip off; dip into crumb mixture to coat. Arrange strips in prepared pan. Bake in a 425°F oven for 12 to 15 minutes or until chicken is no longer pink. Serve strips with more salad dressing.

Makes 4 servings.
Per serving: 208 cal., 10 g total fat (2 g sat. fat), 50 mg chol., 444 mg sodium, 11 g carbo., 1 g fiber, 18 g pro. Dietary exchanges: ½ starch, 2 lean meat, 1 fat.

HOW TO MAKE A SCALOPPINE

A thin, quick-cooking piece of meat—like the chicken in this recipe—is called a scaloppine (think of a "scallop") in Italian cooking terms. The best tool for making a scaloppine is the flat side of a metal meat tenderizer. You can use the same technique on veal, pork, or beef. Just be sure to pound gently; if you pound too hard, you'll shred the meat, causing it to fall apart.

Lemon Butter Chicken Breasts

From Atlanta Cooknotes, 80th anniversary cookbook of the
Atlanta Junior League, Atlanta, Georgia

6	medium boneless skinless chicken breast halves (1½ lbs.)		⅓	cup butter
½	cup all-purpose flour		2	Tbsp. lemon juice
½	tsp. salt			Hot cooked rice or pilaf (optional)
2	tsp. lemon pepper seasoning			

Prep: 15 min. **Cook:** 17 min.

1. Place each chicken breast half between two pieces of plastic wrap. Pound lightly into a rectangle about ¼ to ⅛ inch thick. Remove plastic wrap. In a shallow bowl, combine the flour and salt. Coat chicken breasts with flour mixture. Sprinkle chicken breasts with lemon pepper seasoning.

2. In a 12-inch skillet, cook the chicken breasts in hot butter, half at a time, over medium-high heat for about 3 minutes on each side or until brown and no longer pink. Return all of the chicken to the skillet, overlapping chicken breasts slightly. Drizzle lemon juice over the chicken breasts. Cook for 2 to 3 minutes more or until pan juices are slightly reduced. Serve chicken and pan juices over hot cooked rice or pilaf, if desired.

Makes 6 servings.

Per serving: 258 cal., 12 g total fat (7 g sat. fat), 95 mg chol., 725 mg sodium, 8 g carbo., 0 g fiber, 27 g pro. Dietary exchanges: 2 starch, 3 very lean meat, 2 fat.

Honey-Dijon Barbecued Chicken

From The Kansas City Barbeque Society Cookbook.
Kansas City, Missouri

PHOTO APPEARS ON PAGE 114

1	3-lb. broiler-fryer chicken, quartered		1	clove garlic, minced
¼	cup olive oil		½	tsp. black pepper
¼	cup white Zinfandel wine		¼	tsp. salt
2	Tbsp. honey			
2	Tbsp. Dijon-style mustard			

Prep: 15 min. **Marinate:** 2 hr. **Grill:** 45 min.

1. Place chicken in a plastic bag set in large bowl. For marinade, combine oil, wine, honey, mustard, garlic, black pepper, and salt. Pour marinade over chicken; close bag. Marinate in the refrigerator for 2 to 4 hours, turning bag occasionally. Drain chicken, reserving marinade.

2. In a grill with a cover, arrange medium-hot coals around drip pan. Test for medium heat above the pan. Place chicken, bone sides down, on grill rack over drip pan. Cover and grill for 45 to 55 minutes or until chicken is tender and no longer pink, brushing with reserved marinade after 30 minutes. Discard any remaining marinade.

Makes 4 servings.
Per serving: 380 cal., 23 g total fat (6 g sat. fat), 118 mg chol., 171 mg sodium, 3 g carbo., 0 g fiber, 37 g pro. Dietary exchanges: 3 medium fat meat.

The Royal 'Que
Each fall, Kansas City, Missouri, plays host to the American Royal Barbecue, a contest sanctioned by the Kansas City Barbeque Society. About 375 teams from around the world vie for top barbecue honors.

Hudson's Chicken Burgers

From Gail Hudson,
Minneapolis, Minnesota

PAGE PHOTO APPEARS ON 115

1	lb. uncooked ground chicken
1/4	cup snipped fresh basil
1/4	cup fine dry bread crumbs
4	tsp. Worcestershire sauce
1/8	tsp. salt
1/8	tsp. black pepper
8	slices toasted French bread, or four kaiser rolls or

hamburger buns, split and toasted
Assorted accompaniments, such as lettuce leaves, sliced tomato, or sliced onion (optional)

Prep: 15 min. **Grill:** 8 min.

A LEANER BURGER
If you want a really lean chicken burger, ask the butcher to grind only the chicken breast, and save yourself about 45 calories and 8 grams of fat per sandwich. Most ground chicken contains both light and dark meat and sometimes some of the skin, so it's not as diet-wise as you'd expect. Ground chicken breast is sometimes available in the self-serve meat case too, often labeled "diet lean."

1. In a medium bowl, combine ground chicken, basil, bread crumbs, Worcestershire sauce, salt, and black pepper. Shape the chicken mixture into four 1/2-inch-thick patties. (The mixture may be sticky. If necessary, wet hands to shape patties.)

2. Grill patties on the rack of an uncovered grill directly over medium coals for 8 to 10 minutes or until chicken is no longer pink, turning halfway through grilling. Serve patties on toasted French bread, rolls, or buns with, if desired, lettuce leaves, tomato, and onion slices.

Makes 4 servings.
Per serving: 342 cal., 12 g total fat (0 g sat. fat), 0 mg chol., 544 mg sodium, 32 g carbo., 2 g fiber, 24 g pro. Dietary exchanges: 2 starch, 2½ lean meat, 1 fat.

Grilled Garlic Turkey Sausage with Garlic Cranberry Sauce

From Renata Stanko of Lebanon, Oregon, winner of the Gilroy Garlic Festival Recipe Contest

PAGE PHOTO APPEARS ON 115

1	16-oz. can whole berry cranberry sauce
1	Tbsp. finely shredded orange peel
1/4	cup orange juice
4	cloves garlic, minced
1 1/4	lbs. ground turkey
1/4	lb. ground pork sausage
10	cloves garlic, minced
1	Tbsp. snipped fresh marjoram or

	1 tsp. dried marjoram, crushed
1	Tbsp. snipped fresh oregano or
	1 tsp. dried oregano, crushed
1	Tbsp. snipped fresh parsley
1	tsp. salt
1/4	tsp. freshly ground black pepper
	Dash ground red pepper

Prep: 20 min. **Grill:** 15 min.

1. For sauce, combine cranberry sauce, the orange peel, orange juice, and the 4 cloves garlic. Reserve 1/4 cup; cover and chill remainder.

2. For sausage, in a large bowl, combine turkey, pork, the 10 cloves garlic, the marjoram, oregano, parsley, salt, and black and red pepper. Divide mixture into six portions. Shape each portion around a metal skewer, forming a log about 5 inches long.

3. Grill on the rack of an uncovered grill directly over medium coals for 15 to 18 minutes or until no longer pink and juices run clear. Turn to brown evenly and brush with reserved sauce mixture halfway through cooking. Serve with remaining sauce.

Makes 6 servings.
Per serving: 350 cal., 15 g total fat (5 g sat. fat), 87 mg chol., 620 mg sodium, 34 g carbo., 2 g fiber, 19 g pro. Dietary exchanges: 2 fruit, 2½ very lean meat, 2½ fat.

Fourteen Cloves!
Renata Stanko, inspired by a friend who had previously won the Gilroy Garlic Festival Recipe Contest, decided to enter for herself. Tired of grilling ordinary burgers, Renata created a garlic-laden turkey sausage and cranberry sauce. The recipe made her a $500 winner. Renata took her daughters with her to the northern California community to watch crafters, listen to music and sample lots of garlic creations.

Sweet Berry Turkey Loaf

From Helen Conwell of Fairhope, Alaska, winner of the
Butterball One-Dish Meals Contest

1/2	cup vegetable juice cocktail		2	cups thinly sliced onion
2	eggs		2	15- to 17-oz. cans sweet potatoes, drained
2 1/4	cups corn bread stuffing mix		1/2	tsp. salt
1	cup dried cranberries		1/4	tsp. black pepper
1	cup finely chopped onion		2	Tbsp. butter, melted (optional)
1	tsp. poultry seasoning			
2	lbs. ground turkey			
2	Tbsp. butter or margarine			

Prep: 30 min. **Bake:** 1 hr. 15 min. **Stand:** 10 min.

Beyond Meat and Potatoes

Helen Conwell makes meat loaf when she can't think of anything else to fix for dinner, using whatever ground meat is on hand. To win first place in the Butterball One-Dish Meals Contest, she combined ground turkey with stuffing mix. The sweet potatoes on the side reflect her Southern roots. The onion and cranberry addition was borrowed from a favorite pork loin recipe. Helen has been entering recipe contests for about 10 years. As a finalist in the Paul Newman sauces contest, she had her biggest win—$10,000, which she donated to charity.

1. Combine vegetable juice cocktail, eggs, 2 cups of the stuffing mix, 1/2 cup of the cranberries, the chopped onion, and poultry seasoning; add turkey. Mix well. Form into a 10×4-inch loaf in a 3-quart rectangular baking dish. Bake, uncovered, in a 350°F oven for 45 minutes or until a meat thermometer registers 140°F.

2. Meanwhile, in a large skillet, melt the 2 tablespoons butter and add the sliced onion. Cook and stir over medium heat until the onion is tender and begins to brown, about 15 minutes. Stir in the remaining cranberries; set aside.

3. Arrange sweet potatoes around partially cooked loaf. Sprinkle potatoes with salt and black pepper. Spoon onion mixture atop loaf. Crush remaining stuffing mix; sprinkle over potatoes. If desired, drizzle melted butter over potatoes.

4. Bake for 30 minutes more or until meat thermometer registers 170°F. Let stand for 10 minutes before serving.

Makes 8 to 10 servings.
Per serving: 446 cal., 16 g total fat (5 g sat. fat), 151 mg chol., 668 mg sodium, 51 g carbo., 5 g fiber, 26 g pro. Dietary exchanges: 3 1/2 starch, 2 very lean meat, 2 fat.

5.

Fish and Seafood

Fried Whitefish

From *Treasured Recipes of the Shipwreck Coast*, cookbook of the
Great Lakes Shipwreck Historical Society, Whitefish Point, Michigan

PHOTO APPEARS ON PAGE 116

1	cup all-purpose breading mix (about half of a 10-oz. pkg.)
1	cup packaged biscuit mix
1/3	cup grated Parmesan cheese
1	Tbsp. onion soup mix
1 1/2	tsp. paprika
1 1/2	tsp. dried Italian seasoning, crushed
1 1/2	tsp. dried parsley flakes
1/2	tsp. garlic powder
1	to 1 1/4 lb. fresh or frozen whitefish, haddock, or other firm-textured fish fillets
	Shortening or cooking oil

Start to finish: 25 min.

To the Lighthouse

The lighthouse at Whitefish Point, Michigan, serves as a beacon to ships and to the tourists who come here to see Lake Superior's first light station, built in 1849. Visitors can tour the renovated lightkeepers' quarters and the Shipwreck Museum. Like the Chippewa Indians who occupied Whitefish Point before them, the keepers of the lighthouse feasted on the abundant whitefish.

1. Stir together the breading mix, biscuit mix, Parmesan cheese, onion soup mix, paprika, Italian seasoning, parsley, and garlic powder. Place half of the mixture in a shallow dish. (Place remaining mixture in a jar or self-sealing plastic bag. Cover or seal. Store in refrigerator for up to 3 weeks. Stir or shake mixture before using.)

2. Thaw fish, if frozen. Rinse and pat dry. Cut into four pieces. Measure thickness of fish. Dip into breading mixture, turning to coat both sides.

3. In a large skillet, heat 1/4 inch melted shortening over medium heat. Add fish in a single layer. (If fillets have skin, fry skin side last.) Fry on one side until golden brown. Allow 3 to 4 minutes per side for 1/2-inch-thick fillets (5 to 6 minutes per side for 1-inch-thick fillets). Turn carefully. Fry until fish flakes easily when tested with a fork. Drain on paper towels. Keep warm in a 300°F oven while frying remaining fish.

Makes 4 servings.
Per serving: 352 cal., 17 g total fat (4 g sat. fat), 69 mg chol., 795 mg sodium, 21 g carbo., 0 g fiber, 25 g pro. Dietary exchanges: 1 1/2 starch, 3 very lean meat, 2 1/2 fat.

Glazed Salmon

From *Rave Reviews*, cookbook of the Friends of the
Ogunquit Playhouse, Ogunquit, Maine

4	6-oz. fresh or frozen skinless salmon fillets
3	Tbsp. snipped fresh mint
2	Tbsp. soy sauce
1	Tbsp. brown sugar
2	tsp. finely shredded lime peel
2	Tbsp. lime juice
1	tsp. olive oil

1/2	tsp. freshly ground black pepper
	Lime wedges

Prep: 15 min. **Marinate:** 2 hr. **Broil:** 8 min.

1. Thaw salmon, if frozen. In a small bowl, combine mint, soy sauce, brown sugar, lime peel, lime juice, oil, and black pepper. Place salmon in a self-sealing plastic bag. Set in bowl; pour mint mixture over, turning to coat. Seal bag; marinate in the refrigerator for 2 hours, turning occasionally.

2. Drain salmon, reserving marinade. Measure thickness of salmon. Place salmon, skin side down, on unheated rack of broiler pan; tuck under any thin edges. Spoon reserved marinade over. Broil 4 inches from heat until fish flakes easily when tested with a fork. (Allow 4 to 6 minutes per 1/2-inch thickness. If fish is 1 inch or more thick, turn it over halfway through broiling.) Serve with lime wedges.

Makes 4 servings.
Per serving: 224 cal., 7 g total fat (1 g sat. fat), 88 mg chol., 575 mg sodium, 3 g carbo., 0 g fiber, 35 g pro. Dietary exchanges: 4½ lean meat.

Around Town

Ogunquit, Maine (pop. 900) Ogunquit is an Algonquin Indian word for "beautiful place by the sea," and many people agree that this southern Maine town is indeed a special place. In summer, it swells to almost 30,000 residents from the United States, Canada, and around the world. Vistors love the town's 3-plus miles of sandy beaches; its art museums, galleries, fine seafood; and, of course, the town's ultimate catch of the day: a lively play at the esteemed Ogunquit Playhouse, where, since 1933, some of Broadway's best talent has performed.

130

Ozark Trout Doria

From Women Who Can Dish It Out, cookbook of the
Junior League of Springfield, Missouri

PHOTO APPEARS ON PAGE 117

Around Town

Springfield, Missouri (pop. 156,000) Known as the "Gateway to Ozark Mountain Country," Springfield is 35 miles north of Branson, America's music-show capital. While in Springfield, stop at one of the many Asian restaurants for a taste of Cashew Chicken, a beloved Ozarks version of Chinese chicken and gravy. At Lambert's Cafe, look out for a throwed roll (literally, a roll that is thrown by the waiter).

1	small lemon
2	8- to 10-oz. boneless trout or 1 lb. fresh or frozen fish fillets, ½ to 1 inch thick
3	Tbsp. all-purpose flour
¼	tsp. salt
¼	tsp. black pepper
1 or 2	Tbsp. cooking oil
⅓	cup fish broth or chicken broth
2	Tbsp. dry white wine
¼	cup sliced fresh mushrooms
¼	cup chopped, seeded, peeled cucumber
1	tsp. finely chopped shallot
¼	cup diced, seeded, peeled tomato
2	Tbsp. snipped fresh parsley
2	Tbsp. sliced almonds, toasted

Start to finish: 30 min.

1. Peel and section lemon, discarding seeds. Chop sections; set aside. Rinse fish; pat dry. Spread trout open; discard heads and tails, if present. In shallow bowl, combine flour, salt, and black pepper; dip fish in flour mixture to coat both sides.

2. In a large nonstick skillet, heat half of the oil over medium heat. Add 1 trout (spread open) or half of the fish fillets. Cook for 3 to 4 minutes or until fish flakes easily when tested with a fork, turning with a wide metal spatula halfway through cooking. (Reduce heat if necessary to prevent overbrowning.) Remove fish; keep warm. Repeat with the remaining oil and fish.

3. Carefully add broth and wine to skillet. Cook for 1 minute, scraping up browned bits. Add mushrooms, cucumber, shallot, and chopped lemon. Cook, uncovered, for 3 to 4 minutes. Add tomato and parsley; heat through. Spoon sauce over fish; sprinkle with almonds.

Makes 2 to 4 servings.
Per serving: 465 cal., 19 g total fat (3 g sat. fat), 130 mg chol., 464 mg sodium, 16 g carbo., 2 g fiber, 51 g pro. Dietary exchanges: 3 vegetable, 6 very lean meat, 2½ fat.

New England Stuffed Sole

From Out of the Ordinary, cookbook of the
Hingham Historical Society, Hingham, Massachusetts

8	large or 12 small fresh or frozen sole or flounder fillets (1½ lbs. total)	1¼	tsp. dried sage, crushed
1½	cups soft bread crumbs	¼	tsp. salt
1	medium onion, finely chopped (½ cup)	⅛	tsp. black pepper
¼	cup butter, melted	2	Tbsp. butter, melted
1	Tbsp. lemon juice		Snipped fresh parsley
1	Tbsp. snipped fresh parsley		Lemon wedges
1	tsp. soy sauce		

Prep: 20 min. **Bake:** 30 min.

1. Thaw fish, if frozen; set aside. In a small bowl, stir together the bread crumbs, onion, the ¼ cup melted butter, the lemon juice, the 1 tablespoon parsley, soy sauce, sage, salt, and black pepper. Spoon 1 to 2 tablespoons of the bread crumb mixture onto each fish fillet. Roll up fish around stuffing; secure with wooden toothpicks, if necessary. Arrange in a 3-quart rectangular baking dish. Drizzle with the 2 tablespoons melted butter.

2. Bake in a 350°F oven about 30 minutes or until fish just flakes easily when tested with a fork and stuffing is heated through. Sprinkle with additional parsley and serve with lemon wedges.

Makes 4 to 6 servings.
Per serving: 291 cal., 29 g total fat (13 g sat. fat), 151 mg chol., 563 mg sodium, 8 g carbo., 1 g fiber, 34 g pro. Dietary exchanges: ½ starch, 4½ very lean meat, 2 fat.

Around Town

Hingham, Massachusetts (pop. 20,000) Incorporated in 1635 as part of the Massachusetts Bay Colony, this coastal community is about 15 miles from Boston. Out of the Ordinary not only includes local dishes but also recounts the town's history. In 1637, a young weaver by the name of Samuel Lincoln arrived from Hingham, England. He is famous for being the first American ancestor of Abraham Lincoln.

Edisto Breakfast Shrimp

From 'Pon Top Edisto: Cookin' 'Tweenst the Rivers, cookbook of
Trinity Episcopal Church, Edisto Island, South Carolina

½	lb. fresh or frozen medium shrimp
1	Tbsp. lemon juice
⅛	tsp. ground red pepper
2	Tbsp. bacon drippings*, butter, or margarine
¼	cup finely chopped onion
¼	cup finely chopped red or green sweet pepper

2	Tbsp. all-purpose flour
¾	cup chicken broth
	Salt
	Ground black pepper
	Hot cooked hominy grits or biscuits

Start to finish: 30 min.

1. Thaw shrimp, if frozen. Peel and devein shrimp. Rinse shrimp; pat dry. In small bowl, combine shrimp, lemon juice, and ground red pepper; let stand while cooking vegetables.

2. In a medium skillet, heat bacon drippings or butter over medium heat for 30 seconds. Add onion and sweet pepper; cook for 4 to 5 minutes or until vegetables are tender. Stir in flour. Cook and stir about 2 minutes or until golden. Carefully stir in broth; add shrimp. Cook and stir over medium heat for 1 to 2 minutes or until mixture is thickened and bubbly. Cook for 1 to 2 minutes more or until shrimp turn opaque. Season to taste with salt and black pepper. Serve over hominy grits or biscuits.

*Note: If using bacon drippings, cook 3 to 4 slices bacon to yield 2 tablespoons bacon drippings. Crumble cooked bacon over or serve strips alongside shrimp, if desired.

Makes 2 or 3 servings.
Per serving: 308 cal., 14 g total fat (5 g sat. fat), 143 mg chol., 779 mg sodium, 25 g carbo., 1 g fiber, 19 g pro. Dietary exchanges: ½ vegetable, 1½ starch, 5 very lean meat, 2½ fat.

Shrimp Gravy

From 'Pon Top Edisto: Cookin' 'Tweenst the Rivers, cookbook of Trinity Episcopal Church, Edisto Island, South Carolina

1½ lbs. fresh or frozen medium shrimp
5   slices bacon
1   cup thinly sliced green onion
1   medium green sweet pepper, chopped (¾ cup)
4   cloves garlic, minced
1   Tbsp. all-purpose flour

¼   tsp. garlic salt
¼   tsp. black pepper
12   oz. fresh mushrooms, sliced (4½ cups)
3   cups hot cooked grits

Start to finish: 20 min.

1. Thaw shrimp, if frozen. Peel and devein shrimp. Rinse shrimp; pat dry. Set aside.

2. In a large skillet, cook bacon until crisp. Remove bacon from skillet; drain on paper towels. Reserve 2 tablespoons drippings in the skillet. Crumble bacon and set aside.

3. Heat reserved bacon drippings over medium heat. Add green onion, sweet pepper, and garlic; cook until tender. Stir in flour, garlic salt, and black pepper. Stir in mushrooms and shrimp. Cover and cook about 5 minutes or until shrimp turn pink and mushrooms are tender, stirring mixture occasionally.

4. Serve immediately with hot cooked grits. Top with crumbled bacon.

Makes 4 to 6 servings.
Per serving: 353 cal., 12 g total fat (4 g sat. fat), 209 mg chol., 887 mg sodium, 32 g carbo., 2 g fiber, 29 g pro. Dietary exchanges: 3 vegetable, 1 starch, 3 very lean meat, 1½ fat.

Paradise Found
A love for seafood comes naturally to the residents of Edisto Island, South Carolina, a piece of heaven an hour south of Charleston. It's no surprise that 'Pon Top Edisto: Cookin' 'Tweenst the Rivers from Trinity Episcopal Church includes some of the best seafood recipes around. Where does the book title come from? It's a local expression for "up on top of Edisto," which might be how an Edisto resident would answer the question "Where do you live?"

Tradd Street Shrimp

From Gracious Goodness . . . Charleston!, a cookbook benefiting
Bishop England High School, Charleston, South Carolina

SOUP SUBSTITUTE
To trim the fat and sodium in this cheesy shrimp-and-rice dish, use reduced-fat and reduced-sodium condensed cream of mushroom soup in place of the regular soup.

1	6-oz. pkg. long grain and wild rice mix
1	cup chopped green sweet pepper (1 large)
1	cup chopped celery
1	cup chopped onion (1 large)
1/4	cup butter
1	10³/4-oz. can condensed cream of mushroom soup
1	cup shredded cheddar cheese (4 oz.)

1	cup shredded Swiss cheese (4 oz.)
1	to 1¹/2 lbs. cooked, peeled, and deveined shrimp
1/4	tsp. ground black pepper
2	lemons, very thinly sliced

Prep: 25 min. **Bake:** 40 min. **Stand:** 10 min.

1. Prepare rice mix according to package directions. Meanwhile, in a medium saucepan, cook and stir sweet pepper, celery, and onion in hot butter about 5 minutes or just until tender.
2. In a very large bowl, combine the cooked rice, cooked vegetable mixture, condensed soup, cheddar cheese, and Swiss cheese. Stir in shrimp. Spoon mixture into a 3-quart rectangular baking dish. Sprinkle with half of the black pepper. Arrange lemon slices over shrimp mixture. Sprinkle with the remaining black pepper. Bake, covered, in a 375°F oven about 40 minutes or until heated through. Let stand 10 minutes before serving.

Makes 6 servings.
Per serving: 488 cal., 26 g total fat (14 g sat. fat), 207 mg chol., 1,313 mg sodium, 33 g carbo., 2 g fiber, 31 g pro. Dietary exchanges: 2 starch, 3 very lean meat, 4 fat.

Bayside Enchiladas

From Savoring Cape Cod, cookbook of the Massachusetts Audubon Society, benefiting Wellfleet Bay Wildlife Sanctuary

½	lb. fresh or frozen medium shrimp
½	lb. fresh or frozen bay scallops
1	8-oz. carton dairy sour cream
½	cup salsa
2	cups shredded Monterey Jack cheese (8 oz.)
6	7- to 8-inch flour tortillas
¼	cup cottage cheese

¼	cup milk
2	Tbsp. grated Parmesan cheese
¼	cup chopped green onions
¼	cup sliced ripe olives

Prep: 30 min. **Bake:** 30 min.

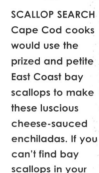

SCALLOP SEARCH Cape Cod cooks would use the prized and petite East Coast bay scallops to make these luscious cheese-sauced enchiladas. If you can't find bay scallops in your area, use quartered sea scallops instead.

1. Thaw shrimp and scallops, if frozen. Peel and devein shrimp. Rinse shrimp and scallops; pat dry with paper towels. Set aside.

2. In a small bowl, combine sour cream and salsa. Stir in shrimp, scallops, and 1 cup of the Monterey Jack cheese. Spread about ⅓ cup of the shrimp mixture onto each tortilla near an edge; roll up. Place filled tortillas, seam sides down, in a 3-quart rectangular baking dish; set aside.

3. In a blender container or food processor bowl, combine cottage cheese, milk, and Parmesan cheese. Cover and blend or process until almost smooth. Spoon mixture over prepared enchiladas. Sprinkle with green onions and olives. Bake, uncovered, in a 350°F oven for 25 minutes. Sprinkle with the remaining 1 cup Monterey Jack cheese. Bake about 5 minutes more or until cheese melts.

Makes 6 servings.
Per serving: 401 cal., 24 g total fat (13 g sat. fat), 105 mg chol., 674 mg sodium, 20 g carbo., 1 g fiber, 25 g pro. Dietary exchanges: 1½ starch, 3 very lean meat, 3½ fat.

Dungeness Crab Fritters

From A Taste of Oregon, cookbook of the
Junior League of Eugene, Oregon

½	lb. fresh or frozen lump crabmeat		2	tsp. baking powder
2	eggs, beaten		⅛	tsp. salt
2	Tbsp. chopped green onion		3	Tbsp. butter
2	Tbsp. chopped tomato			Lemon wedges (optional)
1	Tbsp. chopped green sweet pepper			
1	Tbsp. snipped fresh parsley			
1	tsp. Worcestershire sauce			
¼	cup all-purpose flour			

Start to finish: 30 min.

GET CRABBY
Hefty Dungeness crabs (they can range in size from 1 to almost 4 pounds) are found all the way from Alaska to Mexico. Their flesh is particularly succulent and sweet. Though an Oregonian may make these light, puffy fritters from Dungeness crab meat, other types of crab work just as well. Be sure you buy lump crabmeat, which comes from the body of the crab, rather than meat from the claw or flaked meat.

1. Thaw crabmeat, if frozen. In a medium bowl combine crabmeat, eggs, green onion, tomato, sweet pepper, parsley, and Worcestershire sauce. In a small bowl, stir together flour, baking powder, and salt. Add flour mixture all at once to crab mixture; stir to combine.

2. In a large nonstick skillet, melt butter over medium-high heat. Drop 4 or 5 rounded tablespoonfuls of the crab mixture into hot butter. Cook for 1 minute on each side (if fritters brown too quickly, reduce heat to medium). Keep warm in oven while frying remaining fritters. Serve with lemon wedges, if desired.

Makes 4 to 6 servings.
Per serving: 203 cal., 13 g total fat (7 g sat. fat), 161 mg chol., 1,020 mg sodium, 7 g carbo., 0 g fiber, 15 g pro. Dietary exchanges: ½ starch, 2 very lean meat, 2 fat.

Crab Quiche

From 'Pon Top Edisto: Cookin' 'Tweenst the Rivers, cookbook of
Trinity Episcopal Church, Edisto Island, South Carolina

PAGE 119 PHOTO APPEARS ON

1	recipe Baked Pastry Shell (see recipe, below)
3	Tbsp. finely chopped green onion
1	Tbsp. butter or margarine
3	eggs
1/2	lb. cooked crabmeat (2 cups) or one 6- to 8-oz. pkg. flake-style imitation crabmeat (see tip, page 12)

1	cup half-and-half, light cream, or milk
3	Tbsp. dry vermouth (optional)
1	Tbsp. tomato paste
1	tsp. salt
1/4	tsp. black pepper
1/2	cup shredded Swiss cheese (2 oz.)

Prep: 10 min. **Bake:** 30 min. **Stand:** 10 min.

1. Prepare Baked Pastry Shell as directed; set aside. In a small skillet, cook green onion in hot butter until tender. Remove from heat.

2. In a medium bowl, beat eggs slightly with a fork. Stir in crabmeat, half-and-half, vermouth (if using), tomato paste, salt, and black pepper. Stir in onion mixture. Pour egg mixture into pastry shell. Sprinkle with shredded Swiss cheese.

3. Bake the quiche in a 375°F oven about 30 minutes or until a knife inserted near the center comes out clean. Let stand for 10 minutes before serving. Cut into wedges to serve.

Baked Pastry Shell: Stir together 1 1/4 cups all-purpose flour and 1/4 teaspoon salt. Cut in 1/3 cup shortening. Moisten dough with 4 to 5 tablespoons cold water total, adding 1 tablespoon at a time and tossing with a fork. On a lightly floured surface, roll dough into a 12-inch circle. Ease pastry into a 9-inch pie plate. Trim pastry to 1/2 inch beyond edge of pie plate. Fold under extra pastry. Crimp edge. Prick bottom and side of pastry. Line pastry with a double thickness of foil. Bake in a 450°F oven for 8 minutes. Remove foil. Bake for 5 to 6 minutes more or until golden brown. Cool on wire rack.

Test Kitchen Tip: You may want to cut the salt in the quiche filling to 1/2 teaspoon if using imitation crabmeat, which is high in sodium.

Makes 8 servings.
Per serving: 279 cal., 18 g total fat (7 g sat. fat), 130 mg chol., 498 mg sodium, 16 g carbo., 1 g fiber, 13 g pro. Dietary exchanges: 1 starch, 1 1/2 very lean meat, 3 fat.

Around Town
Edisto Island, South Carolina (pop 2,200) This haven is located 40 miles south of Charleston. In addition to its twisting saltwater creeks and inlets, sandy beaches, and historic homes and churches, the lush island boasts more species of plants than in all of Europe. Winning the hearts of residents and visitors alike are the island's massive live oak trees—hundreds of years old and dramatically draped with Spanish moss.

Batter-Dipped Fried Clams

From the Yarmouth Clam Festival,
Yarmouth, Maine

½	cup milk
1	egg yolk
1	Tbsp. butter, melted and cooled
¼	tsp. salt
½	cup all-purpose flour
1	egg white

1 pint shucked clams, rinsed and
well drained
Cooking oil for deep frying
Tartar Sauce (see recipe, below)

Prep: 10 min. **Cook:** 1½ min. per batch

Clam Up!

Dig into plenty of coastal specialties at the Yarmouth Clam Festival in the postcard-perfect New England town of Yarmouth, Maine. For one weekend each July, fried, steamed, stuffed, and raw clams are featured along with clam cakes and clam chowder. You can also try other seafood specialties—and strawberry shortcake. At the 1999 Maine Clam Shucking Championship, the winner shucked 25 clams in one minute!

1. In a medium bowl, combine milk, egg yolk, melted butter, and salt. Sift flour over milk mixture; stir until smooth. In a small mixing bowl, beat egg white to soft peaks with an electric mixer. Fold the beaten egg white into milk mixture.

2. In a deep-fat fryer or large saucepan, heat oil to 375°F. Poke each clam with a fork. Dip clams into batter. Fry a few at a time about 1½ minutes or until golden brown, turning once. Remove with slotted spoon; drain on paper towels. Keep warm in a 300°F oven while frying remaining clams. Serve with Tartar Sauce.

Tartar Sauce: Combine 1 cup mayonnaise; ¼ cup finely chopped sweet pickle relish; 1 tablespoon each finely chopped onion, snipped parsley, and diced pimiento; and 1 teaspoon lemon juice.

Makes 8 appetizer servings.
Per serving: 219 cal., 17 g total fat (3 g sat. fat), 51 mg chol., 135 mg sodium, 8 g carbo., 0 g fiber, 9 g pro.
Dietary exchanges: ½ starch, 1 medium-fat meat, 2 fat.

6.

Eggs and Cheese

Garlic-Cheese-Grits Casserole

From Southern Settings, a cookbook benefiting
Decatur General Hospital, Decatur, Alabama

3	cups water		2	slightly beaten eggs
1	tsp. salt		1½	cups shredded cheddar cheese
¾	cup quick-cooking grits			(6 oz.)
1	or 2 cloves garlic, minced			
⅛	tsp. ground red pepper			
¼	cup butter, cut up			

Prep: 25 min. **Bake:** 30 min.

CAN'T GET ENOUGH GARLIC? If you love garlic, try roasting some. It's great for stirring into mashed potatoes, for spreading on toasted bread, or for mixing into mayonnaise for a sandwich spread or salad dressing. To roast garlic, peel away the outer skin from a head of garlic. Cut off the pointed top portion with a knife. The cloves will be exposed, but the bulb will be intact. Place in a small baking dish. Drizzle with olive oil. Bake, covered, in a 425°F oven for 25 to 30 minutes. When cloves are cool enough to handle, press to remove the paste. Use immediately or refrigerate, covered, for 1 to 2 days.

1. Grease a 1½-quart casserole; set aside. In a medium saucepan, bring water and salt to boiling. Stir in the grits, garlic, and red pepper; reduce heat. Cover and simmer for 5 to 7 minutes or until thickened, stirring occasionally. Stir in butter until melted. Gradually stir about 1 cup of the hot mixture into the eggs. Stir egg mixture into mixture in saucepan. Add cheese, stirring until melted.

2. Transfer mixture to the prepared casserole. Bake, covered, in a 350°F oven for 15 minutes. Uncover; bake for 15 to 20 minutes more or until casserole is golden brown and bubbly. Serve immediately.

Makes 8 servings.
Per serving: 209 cal., 14 g total fat (8 g sat. fat), 91 mg chol., 475 mg sodium, 12 g carbo., 0 g fiber, 8 g pro. Dietary exchanges: 1 starch, 1 medium-fat meat, 1½ fat.

Sausage-Cheese-Grits Casserole

From Southern Settings, a cookbook benefiting
Decatur General Hospital, Decatur, Alabama

3½	cups water		2	Tbsp. butter
1	cup quick-cooking white (hominy) grits		¾	lb. bulk pork sausage
¼	tsp. salt		½	cup milk
1	cup shredded sharp cheddar cheese (4 oz.)		4	beaten eggs

Prep: 20 min. **Bake:** 35 min. **Stand:** 10 min.

1. Grease a 2-quart rectangular baking dish; set aside.

2. In a large saucepan, bring water to boiling. Stir in grits and salt. Reduce heat to medium-low. Cover and cook for 15 minutes or until thick, stirring occasionally. Remove from heat. Stir in ½ cup of the cheddar cheese and the butter until melted. Set aside.

3. In a large skillet, cook sausage until thoroughly cooked; drain off fat. Stir cooked sausage, milk, and eggs into grits mixture. Spoon into prepared dish.

4. Bake, uncovered, in a 350°F oven about 30 minutes or just until set. Sprinkle with the remaining ½ cup cheddar cheese. Bake, uncovered, about 5 minutes more or until cheese melts. Let stand 10 minutes before serving.

Makes 8 servings.
Per serving: 347 cal., 23 g total fat (11 g sat. fat), 155 mg chol., 446 mg sodium, 17 g carbo., 0 g fiber, 14 g pro. Dietary exchanges: 1 starch, 1½ medium-fat meat, 3 fat.

PHOTO APPEARS ON PAGE 153

Killer Omelet

From The Heart of Pittsburgh, a cookbook benefiting
Sacred Heart Elementary School, Pittsburgh, Pennsylvania

⅓ cup chopped green sweet pepper	¼ cup whipping cream
⅓ cup chopped red sweet pepper	¼ cup shredded cheddar cheese (1 oz.)
1 fresh jalapeño pepper, seeded and finely chopped	¼ cup shredded Swiss cheese (1 oz.)
Bacon drippings or olive oil	
1 medium tomato, seeded and chopped	**Start to finish:** 30 min.
6 eggs	

THE PERFECT OMELET
Follow these tips and you'll be filling and folding an omelet like a chef in no time:
• Use a nonstick pan with sloped sides. It helps you slide out the finished omelet.
• Coat the omelet pan with nonstick cooking spray or melt butter in the pan. Heat the pan until a drop of water sizzles.
• Cook the omelet over medium heat. As the eggs set, lift their edges with a spatula to let the uncooked egg on top flow underneath.

1. In a 10-inch nonstick skillet with flared sides, cook sweet peppers and jalapeño pepper in 1 tablespoon bacon drippings or oil over medium heat for 2 to 3 minutes or until tender. Stir in tomato. Remove vegetable mixture from skillet; set aside.

2. In a medium mixing bowl, lightly beat the eggs and whipping cream. In same skillet, heat 1 teaspoon bacon drippings or oil over medium heat. Add half of the egg mixture. As eggs set, run a spatula around the edge of the skillet, lifting cooked eggs so uncooked portion flows underneath.

3. When eggs are set but still shiny, spoon half of the vegetable mixture across the center of the omelet. Sprinkle filling with half of the cheddar cheese and half of the Swiss cheese. Fold sides over. Heat for 1 to 2 minutes more to melt the cheese. Transfer omelet to a serving plate; keep warm.

4. Repeat with another 1 teaspoon bacon drippings or oil and remaining egg mixture, vegetable mixture, and cheeses.

Makes 4 serving.
Per serving: 280 cal., 23 g total fat (11 g sat. fat), 359 mg chol., 166 mg sodium, 5 g carbo., 0 g fiber, 14 g pro. Dietary exchanges: 2 vegetable, 2 high-fat meat, 1 fat.

Bacon Potato Frittata

From Betty Nichols of Eugene, Oregon,
runner-up in the National Potato Board contest

4	slices bacon, cut into $1/2$-inch pieces
$3/4$	lb. (about 2 medium) potatoes, cut into $1/4$-inch-thick slices
6	large slightly beaten eggs
$1/4$	cup milk
$1/2$	tsp. black pepper
$1/4$	tsp. salt
$1 1/2$	cups grated Parmesan cheese

$1/2$	cup thinly sliced green onions
2	Tbsp. finely snipped fresh basil or 2 tsp. dried basil, crushed
	Salsa and/or dairy sour cream (optional)

Prep: 15 min. **Cook:** 27 min.

1. In a large nonstick skillet, cook bacon pieces until crisp, stirring occasionally. With slotted spoon, remove bacon to paper towels. Drain off all but 2 tablespoons drippings from pan. (If necessary, add vegetable oil to make 2 tablespoons fat.) Add potato slices to skillet. Cover; cook over medium heat for 12 to 15 minutes or until tender and lightly browned, turning potatoes over occasionally and lowering heat, if necessary, to prevent overbrowning.

2. Meanwhile, in a medium bowl, beat eggs, milk, black pepper, and salt until combined. Stir in Parmesan cheese, green onions, and basil; set aside.

3. Spread potatoes in an even layer in a skillet; sprinkle with bacon. Pour in egg mixture. Cover; reduce heat to medium-low. Cook for 15 to 20 minutes or until top surface of the egg is just set. (Decrease heat to low, if necessary, to allow center to cook through without overcooking edges.) Loosen edges of frittata from pan; carefully invert onto large serving plate. Cut into wedges to serve. Pass salsa and/or sour cream, if desired.

Makes 4 to 6 servings.
Per serving: 324 cal., 20 g total fat (8 g sat. fat), 342 mg chol., 588 mg sodium, 16 g carbo., 2 g fiber, 20 g pro. Dietary exchanges: 1 starch, 1½ medium-fat meat, 1 fat.

One Potato, Two
Betty Nichols, an amateur artist, finds cooking as expressive as creating a work of art. Because she loves Italian foods, she entered this "spudtacular" version of a frittata (an Italian omelet that isn't folded and flipped) in a contest sponsored by the National Potato Board. As a runner-up, she won a gift certificate to an Internet shopping site, where she bought a new electric mixer. Betty has been entering recipe contests for 40 years and has been a finalist at some of America's biggest competitions.

Herbed Egg and Cheese Casserole

From Celebrate San Antonio, cookbook of the
San Antonio Junior Forum, San Antonio, Texas

PAGE PHOTO APPEARS ON 154

HOMETOWN Tip

HOW TO COOK A HARD-BOILED EGG
Place eggs in a single layer in a saucepan. Add enough cold water to come 1 inch above the eggs. Bring to boiling over high heat. Reduce heat so water is just below simmering; cover. Cook for 15 minutes; drain. Run cold water over the eggs or place them in ice water until cool enough to handle.

1/4	cup butter or margarine
1/4	cup all-purpose flour
1/4	tsp. dried thyme, crushed
1/4	tsp. dried basil, crushed
1/4	tsp. dried marjoram, crushed
1	12-oz. can evaporated milk or 1 1/3 cups half-and-half or light cream
2/3	cup milk
2	cups shredded sharp cheddar cheese (8 oz.)

18	eggs, hard cooked and thinly sliced
1/2	lb. bacon, crisp-cooked, drained, and crumbled
1/4	cup finely snipped fresh parsley
1	cup fine dry bread crumbs
1/4	cup butter or margarine, melted

Prep: 20 min. **Bake:** 25 min.

1. In a medium saucepan, melt 1/4 cup butter. Stir in flour, thyme, basil, and marjoram. Stir in evaporated milk and milk all at once. Cook and stir over medium heat until thickened and bubbly. Remove from heat. Gradually add cheddar cheese to sauce. Stir after each addition until cheese is melted. Set aside.

2. Lightly grease a 3-quart rectangular baking dish. Layer half of the sliced eggs, bacon, and parsley in dish. Pour half of the sauce over all. Repeat layers, ending with sauce.

3. In a small bowl, stir together bread crumbs and the 1/4 cup melted butter; sprinkle over casserole. Bake in a 350°F oven for 25 to 30 minutes or until heated through.

Note: You can shave a few grams of fat from each serving without sacrificing the rich flavor by using fat-free evaporated milk, reduced-fat cheddar cheese, and turkey bacon.

Makes 12 servings.
Per serving: 372 cal., 27 g total fat (13 g sat. fat), 374 mg chol., 472 mg sodium, 13 g carbo., 0 g fiber, 20 g pro. Dietary exchanges: 1 milk, 2 medium-fat meat, 3 fat.

Mock Cheese Soufflé

From Monte Claire Carpenter,
Lynnville, Tennessee

8	slices white bread, cubed (6 cups)		$1^1/2$	cups milk
$1^1/2$	cups shredded sharp cheddar cheese or Monterey Jack cheese with jalapeño peppers		2	tsp. Worcestershire sauce
4	eggs		$1/2$	tsp. salt

Prep: 20 min. **Chill:** 2 hr. **Bake:** 45 min.

1. In a $1^1/2$-quart ungreased soufflé dish, layer half of the bread cubes. Top with half of the cheese. Repeat layers with the remaining bread and cheese; press lightly.

2. In a medium bowl, combine eggs, milk, Worcestershire sauce, and salt. Pour mixture over layers in dish. Cover and refrigerate for 2 hours or overnight.

3. Bake, uncovered, in a 350°F oven for 45 to 50 minutes or until a knife inserted near the center comes out clean. Serve the soufflé immediately.

Makes 6 servings.
Per serving: 284 cal., 15 g total fat (8 g sat. fat), 176 mg chol., 639 mg sodium, 21 g carbo., 1 g fiber, 16 g pro. Dietary exchanges: $1^1/2$ s-arch, $1^1/2$ medium-fat meat, 1 fat.

Cooking for Her Community Monte Claire Carpenter of Lynnville, Tennessee, was the unofficial chef of First National Bank in Pulaski, where she worked for 40 years. After the bank became a dinner theater in 1985, she cooked 50,000 meals in the 11 years the theater operated. She even cooked while appearing in the starring role of "Driving Miss Daisy." If she hadn't, she says, she would have worried about the buffet line.

Breakfast Casserole

From Bully's Best Bites, cookbook of the
Junior Auxiliary of Starkville, Mississippi

1½	lb. bulk pork sausage or bulk Italian sausage	¾	tsp. dry mustard
	Nonstick cooking spray	1	10¾-oz. can condensed cream of mushroom soup
2½	cups seasoned croutons	½	cup milk
2	cups shredded cheddar cheese (8 oz.)		
2½	cups milk		
4	beaten eggs		

Prep: 25 min. **Chill:** 2 hr. **Bake:** 50 min.
Stand: 10 min.

REDUCED-FAT CASSEROLE
Use 1½ pounds turkey breakfast sausge or turkey Italian sausage links (with casings removed), in place of the pork sausage. Substitute 2 cups shredded reduced-fat cheddar cheese for regular cheese; 1 cup refrigerated or thawed frozen egg product for the eggs; fat-free milk for regular milk; and reduced-fat condensed cream of mushroom soup for the regular soup. Savings: About 170 calories and 20 grams of fat per serving.

1. In a large skillet, cook and stir sausage over medium heat until no pink remains; drain.

2. Meanwhile, lightly coat a 3-quart rectangular baking dish with cooking spray. Spread croutons evenly in bottom of prepared dish. Sprinkle 1 cup of the cheese over croutons. Top with sausage. In a large bowl, combine the 2½ cups milk, the beaten eggs, and the dry mustard. Pour over layers in baking dish. Stir together soup and the ½ cup milk. Spoon soup mixture evenly over mixture in baking dish. Cover and chill in the refrigerator for at least 2 hours or up to 24 hours.

3. Bake, uncovered, in a 325°F oven for 45 minutes. Sprinkle the remaining 1 cup cheese over casserole. Bake for 5 to 10 minutes more or until a knife inserted near the center comes out clean. Let stand for 10 minutes before serving.

Makes 10 servings.
Per serving: 472 cal., 35 g total fat (15 g sat. fat), 154 mg chol., 883 mg sodium, 14 g carbo., 1 g fiber, 20 g pro. Dietary exchanges: 1 starch, 2½ high-fat meat, 3 fat.

Asparagus-Cheese Puff

*From A Taste of Heaven, cookbook of the
First Baptist Church choir, Richmond, Virginia*

	Nonstick cooking spray		1½	cups milk
1	lb. asparagus		3	slightly beaten eggs
1	Tbsp. butter		½	tsp. salt
½	cup chopped onion		⅛	tsp. black pepper
1	tsp. curry powder			
4	slices white or wheat bread			
1	cup shredded sharp cheddar cheese (4 oz.)			

Prep: 15 min. **Bake:** 15 min. **Stand:** 5 min.

1. Lightly coat a 2-quart rectangular baking dish with nonstick cooking spray; set aside.

2. Snap off and discard woody bases of asparagus. Cut asparagus into 1- to 2-inch pieces (about 2 cups total); set aside. In a medium skillet, melt butter over medium heat. Add onion; cook for 3 minutes, stirring occasionally. Add asparagus and curry powder. Cook and stir for 2 to 3 minutes more or until onion and asparagus are just tender.

3. Arrange bread slices in bottom of prepared baking dish, cutting bread to fit, if needed. Spoon asparagus mixture evenly over bread. Sprinkle cheddar cheese over top. In a medium mixing bowl, combine milk, eggs, salt, and black pepper. Pour over cheese. Bake in a 450°F oven for 15 to 20 minutes or until a knife inserted near the center comes out clean. Let stand for 5 to 10 minutes before serving.

Makes 6 servings.

Per serving: 221 cal., 13 g total fat (7 g sat. fat), 136 mg chol., 485 mg sodium, 14 g carbo., 2 g fiber, 13 g pro. Dietary exchanges: 1½ vegetable, ½ starch, 1 medium-fat meot, 1½ fat.

Maple-Bacon Oven Pancake

From Diane Dunn,
Daytona Beach, Florida

1 1/2	cups packaged biscuit mix
1	cup shredded cheddar cheese (4 oz.)
2	eggs
3/4	cup milk
1/4	cup maple-flavored syrup

5	slices bacon, crisp-cooked and crumbled
	Maple-flavored syrup (optional)

Prep: 15 min. **Bake:** 13 min.

WHY AN A.M. MEAL?
A morning meal helps provide the 40-plus nutrients that our bodies need each day. Kids especially need breakfast. Children who eat after waking perform better at school and at play. Several studies show that with food in their stomachs, kids (and adults) have increased problem-solving ability, memory, verbal fluency, and creativity.

1. In a mixing bowl, combine biscuit mix, 1/2 cup of the cheddar cheese, the eggs, milk, and 1/4 cup syrup; beat until nearly smooth. Spread in greased and floured 13×9×2-inch baking pan. Bake in a 425°F oven for 10 to 12 minutes or until toothpick inserted near center comes out clean. Sprinkle with the remaining 1/2 cup cheese and bacon; bake for 3 minutes more. Cut into squares and serve with additional syrup, if desired.

Makes 12 servings.
Per serving: 150 cal., 8 g total fat (3 g sat. fat), 49 mg chol., 294 mg sodium, 15 g carbo., 0 g fiber, 6 g pro.
Dietary exchanges: 1 starch, 1/2 medium-fat meat, 1 fat.

7.

Pasta, **Rice**, and Beans

150

White Beans with Tomato, Basil, and Parmesan

From *Gatherings*, cookbook of the
Des Moines Junior Women's Club, Des Moines, Iowa

8 oz. dried bow-tie pasta	1/4 cup snipped fresh basil or
1 Tbsp. olive oil	2 tsp. dried basil, crushed
3 cloves garlic, minced	1 Tbsp. lemon juice
3 cups cooked Great Northern or cannellini beans or two 15-oz. cans Great Northern or cannellini beans, rinsed and drained	1/4 tsp. salt (optional)
	1/2 cup grated Parmesan cheese
	Freshly ground black pepper
	Fresh basil leaves
2 large tomatoes, chopped (3 cups)	**Start to finish:** 30 min.

GIVE 'EM A SQUEEZE

You'll get more flavor out of dried herbs if you crush them before using them in recipes. Empty the correct amount in your hand. Crush the herb with the fingers of your other hand to release the herb's flavor, and add it to the specified ingredients. Some dried herbs, such as rosemary and thyme, are more easily crushed with a mortar and pestle—but if you don't have one, crush them with a wooden spoon against the inside of a bowl.

1. Cook pasta according to package directions; drain and keep warm. In a large nonstick skillet, heat the oil over medium-low heat. Add the garlic; cook, stirring occasionally, for 1 to 2 minutes or until golden. Stir in the beans, tomatoes, and basil. Cook, uncovered, for 5 minutes. Stir in lemon juice and, if desired, salt. Serve over hot cooked pasta. Sprinkle with Parmesan cheese and freshly ground black pepper. Garnish with basil leaves.

Makes 4 servings.
Per serving: 480 cal., 9 g total fat (3 g sat. fat), 10 mg chol., 247 mg sodium, 77 g carbo., 12 g fiber, 25 g pro. Dietary exchanges: 1 vegetable, 4½ starch, 1 lean meat, ½ fat.

Pasta with Chickpeas

From *Women Who Can Dish It Out*, cookbook of the
Junior League of Springfield, Missouri

3/4 cup finely chopped onion	1/4 tsp. black pepper
2 cloves garlic, minced	8 oz. dried rigatoni, rotini, or cavatelli pasta
1 fresh rosemary sprig (about 2 inches long)	1 medium tomato, seeded and chopped (1/2 cup)
2 tsp. olive oil	1/3 cup crumbled feta cheese
2 cups chopped fresh tomatoes (about 3 medium tomatoes)	Freshly ground black pepper
1 15-oz. can chickpeas (garbanzo beans), rinsed and drained	
3/4 tsp. salt	

Start to finish: 30 min.

1. For sauce, in a medium saucepan, cook onion, garlic, and rosemary sprig in hot oil about 5 minutes or until tender. Stir in the 2 cups chopped tomatoes, half of the chickpeas, the salt, and black pepper. Bring to boiling; reduce heat. Simmer, uncovered, for 5 minutes. Remove from heat. Remove and discard rosemary.

2. Carefully transfer about half of the tomato mixture to a blender container or food processor bowl. Cover and blend or process until smooth.

Repeat with remaining tomato mixture. Return all to saucepan. Stir in remaining chickpeas. Cook and stir over low heat until sauce is heated through.

3. Meanwhile, cook pasta according to package directions. Drain pasta. To serve, toss cooked pasta with sauce. Top with the seeded, chopped tomato and feta cheese. Sprinkle with freshly ground black pepper.

Makes 3 to 4 servings.
Per serving: 523 cal., 10 g total fat (3 g sat. fat), 12 mg chol., 1,199 mg sodium, 89 g carbo., 10 g fiber, 21 g pro. Dietary exchanges: 1 vegetable, 5½ starch, ½ fat.

Pasta Invierno Salad

*From Taste the Good Life, cookbook of the
Assistance League of Omaha, Nebraska*

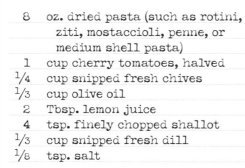

8	oz. dried pasta (such as rotini, ziti, mostaccioli, penne, or medium shell pasta)
1	cup cherry tomatoes, halved
1/4	cup snipped fresh chives
1/3	cup olive oil
2	Tbsp. lemon juice
4	tsp. finely chopped shallot
1/3	cup snipped fresh dill
1/8	tsp. salt

	Dash freshly ground black pepper
4	oz. smoked salmon, flaked, and skin and bones removed
1	small red onion, thinly sliced and separated into rings
1/2	cup dairy sour cream
	Snipped fresh chives and/or fresh dill (optional)

Start to finish: 25 min.

1. Cook pasta according to package directions. Drain pasta. Rinse with cold water; drain again. In a large bowl, combine pasta, cherry tomatoes, and the 1/4 cup chives.

2. For dressing, in a small bowl, stir together oil, lemon juice, shallot, the 1/3 cup dill, salt, and black pepper. Pour the dressing over the pasta mixture. Toss lightly to coat. Spoon pasta into a serving dish. Top with salmon, onion, and sour cream. Sprinkle with additional chives and/or dill, if desired.

Makes 4 servings.
Per serving: 474 cal., 25 g total fat (6 g sat. fat), 17 mg chol., 316 mg sodium, 48 g carbo., 2 g fiber, 14 g pro. Dietary exchanges: 2 vegetable, 2½ starch, ½ very lean meat, 4 fat.

Killer Omelet, p. 142

Straker Carryer, left, of Pittsburgh, submitted his recipe for Killer Omelet to The Heart of Pittsburgh, a cookbook benefiting Sacred Heart Elementary School. Straker's dad taught him how to make omelets.

Herbed Egg and Cheese Casserole, below, is the favorite Christmas Day casserole of Rex Tackett, inset, of San Antonio, Texas.

Herbed Egg and Cheese Casserole, p. 144

Airy Mock Cheese Soufflé has been the most-requested main dish of recipe contributor and community cook Monte Claire Carpenter of Lynnville, Tennessee.

Mock Cheese Soufflé, p. 145

Maple-Bacon Oven Pancake, p. 148

Summer Squash Primavera, p. 162

Proceeds from the sale of I'll Cook When Pigs Fly—
And They Do in Cincinnati! (in which Summer Squash
Primavera, above, appeared) benefit a Cincinnati
program to help kids stay in school. Mary Seay,
right, organizes the Junior League's FLIGHT
Program (Families Learning Is Our Greatest Hope
for the Future).

Pierogi Casserole, p. 163

Broccoli Kugel, p. 166

Broccoli-Cauliflower Tetrazzini, p. 164

Light Vegetable Lasagna, p. 168

Light Vegetable Lasagna, above, is just the sort of thing you'd expect to find in a cookbook published by a gardening club. Betsy Crowley, left, of the Southborough Gardeners of Southborough, Massachusetts, is sharing her passion for pots of dirt and seeds with her daughters.

Pasta with Tomato-Vegetable Sauce and Ricotta

From The Creekside: A Celebration of Cedarburg Cooking,

cookbook of the Junior Women's Club, Cedarburg, Wisconsin

1	Tbsp. olive oil
1	cup chopped onion
1	cup chopped red sweet pepper
1	cup chopped green sweet pepper
1	cup chopped zucchini
1	Tbsp. bottled minced garlic or 6 cloves garlic, minced
1	28-oz. can whole Italian-style (plum) tomatoes, cut up
1/3	cup (half of a 6-oz. can) tomato paste

3/4	tsp. dried oregano, crushed
1/2	tsp. salt
1/2	tsp. dried basil, crushed
12	oz. dried bow-tie pasta
1	cup part-skim ricotta cheese
2	Tbsp. snipped fresh parsley

Prep: 25 min. **Cook:** 20 min.

1. In a large saucepan, heat oil over medium-high heat. Add onion, sweet peppers, zucchini, and garlic. Cook and stir for 4 to 5 minutes or until tender. Stir in undrained tomatoes, tomato paste, oregano, salt, and basil. Bring to boiling; reduce heat. Cover and simmer for 20 minutes.

2. Meanwhile, cook pasta according to package directions. Drain and return to saucepan. Add half of the sauce to the pasta; toss to coat. Divide among six dinner plates. Top with remaining sauce, the ricotta cheese, and parsley.

Makes 6 servings.
Per serving: 354 cal., 7 g total fat (2 g sat. fat), 13 mg chol., 500 mg sodium, 59 g carbo., 5 g fiber, 15 g pro. Dietary exchanges: 5 vegetable, 2 starch, 1 fat.

Around Town
Cedarburg,
Wisconsin (pop.
10,908)
Located 20 miles
north of Milwaukee,
Cedarburg developed
along Cedar Creek.
Limestone from
nearby quarries was
used in mills along
the creek and in other
businesses. Now these
structures house gift
and antiques shops,
bed-and-breakfasts,
and restaurants.
Some eateries offer a
Friday night fish fry,
and one restaurant
serves German
dinners, a reflection of
the German
immigrants who, along
with the Irish, settled
the town.

Summer Squash Primavera

From I'll Cook When Pigs Fly—And They Do in Cincinnati!,
cookbook of the Junior League of Cincinnati, Ohio

12	oz. dried linguine, spiral macaroni, ziti, or penne pasta
5	cloves garlic, minced
2	green onions, sliced
2	Tbsp. olive oil
2	to 3 medium carrots, sliced
1	medium red sweet pepper, sliced
1	medium yellow sweet pepper, sliced
1	small zucchini, chopped

1/4	tsp. salt
1/4	tsp. black pepper
1	cup chicken broth
1	cup snipped fresh basil
1/2	cup finely shredded Parmesan cheese (2 oz.)
2	Tbsp. pine nuts, toasted

Start to finish: 25 min.

**To Market,
To Market**

A kaleidoscope of fresh fruit, vegetables, and flowers beckons patrons to nostalgic Findlay Market in Cincinnati, where a bustling array of loquacious shopkeepers sell their wares, just as their forefathers did, all the way back to 1852. The freshest meat, seafood, poultry, pork, cheese, and bread are available year-round on Wednesdays, Fridays, and Saturdays.

1. Cook pasta according to package directions. Drain; return to saucepan and keep warm.

2. Meanwhile, in a large skillet, cook garlic and green onions in hot oil for 30 seconds. Stir in carrots and sweet peppers. Cook and stir 3 minutes more.

3. Stir in zucchini, salt, and black pepper. Cook and stir for 3 minutes more. Stir in chicken broth. Bring to boiling; reduce heat. Simmer, covered, for 1 minute or until vegetables are just tender.

4. Stir vegetable mixture and basil into pasta and toss. Transfer to serving dish. Sprinkle with Parmesan cheese and pine nuts.

Makes 4 to 6 main-dish servings or 8 to 10 side-dish servings.
Per main-dish serving: 513 cal., 15 g total fat (4 g sat. fat), 13 mg chol., 512 mg sodium, 75 g carbo., 5 g fiber, 20 g pro. Dietary exchanges: 2½ vegetable, 4 starch, ½ high-fat meat, 2 fat.

Pierogi Casserole

From The Heart of Pittsburgh, a cookbook benefiting
Sacred Heart Elementary School, Pittsburgh, Pennsylvania

12	dried lasagna noodles
8	medium potatoes, peeled and cubed (2²/₃ lbs.)
4	to 6 large onions, sliced
²/₃	cup butter
¹/₃	cup milk

1	tsp. salt
¹/₂	tsp. black pepper
1¹/₄	cups shredded cheddar cheese (5 oz.)

Prep: 45 min. **Bake:** 30 min. **Stand:** 15 min.

1. Cook noodles according to package directions. Drain and rinse with cold water. Drain again and set aside.

2. Cook potatoes in boiling water about 20 minutes or until tender. Drain and place in a large mixing bowl.

3. Meanwhile, in a large skillet, cook onions in half of the butter about 10 minutes or until tender. Set aside.

4. Add the remaining butter, the milk, salt, and black pepper to the potatoes. Using electric mixer or potato masher, beat or mash potatoes until smooth. Stir in ¹/₂ cup of the cheese.

5. Lightly grease a 3-quart rectangular baking dish. Stir one-fourth of the mashed potato mixture into the onions; spread in bottom of prepared baking dish. Top with three cooked lasagna noodles. Spread with one-third of the remaining potato mixture; repeat layering of lasagna noodles and potato mixture two more times. Top with remaining lasagna noodles. Cover and bake in a 350°F oven for 30 to 40 minutes or until heated through. Uncover and sprinkle with the remaining ³/₄ cup cheese. Let stand for 15 minutes before serving.

Makes 15 side-dish servings.
Per serving: 267 cal., 12 g total fat (7 g sat. fat), 52 mg chol., 295 mg sodium, 33 g carbo., 2 g fiber, 7 g pro. Dietary exchanges: 2 starch, 2 fat.

Polish Pride Pittsburghers celebrate their city and its ethnic heritages. Many recipes are handed down from generation to generation. This one was inspired by a Polish specialty, a half-moon noodle dumpling called a pierogi that is often filled with cabbage, potatoes, or rice.

Broccoli-Cauliflower Tetrazzini

From Barbara Van Itallie of Poughkeepsie, New York,
competitor in the 1988 Pillsbury Bake-Off

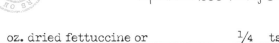

8 oz. dried fettuccine or spaghetti, broken	1/4 tsp. salt
1 16-oz. pkg. loose-pack frozen broccoli, carrots, and cauliflower	1/4 tsp. black pepper
2 Tbsp. margarine or butter	1 4 1/2-oz. jar sliced mushrooms, drained
3 Tbsp. all-purpose flour	2 Tbsp. grated Parmesan cheese
2 1/2 cups reduced-fat milk	
1/2 cup grated Parmesan cheese	

Prep: 35 min. **Bake:** 15 min.

Favorites Forever

Barbara Van Itallie thinks her recipe is as fitting for cooks today as it was when she was a contestant in the Pillsbury Bake-Off in 1988 because it's easy and pleases lots of folks. This recipe—though not a top prizewinner—was voted by home cooks via mail and the Internet as a Pillsbury Bake-Off Hall of Fame favorite.

1. Lightly grease a 3-quart rectangular baking dish; set aside. Cook pasta according to package directions; drain. Cook vegetables according to package directions; drain and set aside.

2. Meanwhile, for cheese sauce, in a saucepan, melt margarine. Stir in flour. Add milk. Cook and stir over medium heat until slightly thickened and bubbly. Cook and stir for 1 minute more. Remove from heat. Stir in the 1/2 cup Parmesan cheese, salt, and black pepper.

3. In a bowl, toss pasta with 1/2 cup of the cheese sauce. Spread pasta evenly in prepared dish. Top with vegetables and mushrooms. Pour remaining cheese sauce over all. Sprinkle with the 2 tablespoons Parmesan cheese. Bake, uncovered, in a 400°F oven about 15 minutes or until heated through.

Make-ahead Tip: Prepare and assemble as above. Chill, covered, in refrigerator for up to 24 hours. To serve, bake, covered, in a 400°F oven for 15 minutes. Uncover and bake for 10 to 15 minutes more.

Makes 8 side-dish or 4 main-dish servings.
Per side-dish serving: 239 cal., 7 g total fat (3 g sat. fat), 12 mg chol., 500 mg sodium, 33 g carbo., 3 g fiber, 11 g pro. Dietary exchanges: 2 vegetable, 1 1/2 starch, 1/2 lean meat, 1 fat.

UFO Phenomenon Macaroni Mousse

From Savoring the Southwest Again, cookbook of the
Roswell Symphony Guild, Roswell, New Mexico

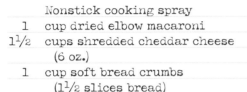

	Nonstick cooking spray
1	cup dried elbow macaroni
1½	cups shredded cheddar cheese (6 oz.)
1	cup soft bread crumbs (1½ slices bread)
¼	cup butter, melted
1	4-oz. jar diced pimiento, drained

1	Tbsp. snipped fresh parsley
1	Tbsp. dried minced onion
½	tsp. salt
1½	cups warm milk
3	beaten eggs
	Paprika

Prep: 20 min. **Bake:** 1 hr.

1. Coat a 1½-quart casserole with nonstick cooking spray; set aside. Cook macaroni according to package directions. Drain. Spoon into the bottom of prepared casserole. In a bowl, combine cheese, bread crumbs, melted butter, pimiento, parsley, onion, and salt. Pour milk over crumb mixture; stir in eggs. Pour egg mixture over macaroni. Sprinkle with paprika. Bake in a 300°F oven about 1 hour or until a knife inserted near the center comes out clean.

Makes 6 to 8 servings.
Per serving: 341 cal., 22 g total fat (13 g sat. fat), 162 mg chol., 551 mg sodium, 21 g carbo., 1 g fiber, 15 g pro. Dietary exchanges: ½ milk, 1 starch, 1 high-fat meat, 2 fat.

Space Food

In 1947 something crashed near Roswell, New Mexico. It could have been a flying saucer. It could have been a weather balloon. Nobody knows for sure. But ever since the "Roswell Incident," the town has been known as the UFO (Unidentified Flying Object) Capital of the World. To acknowledge Roswell's alien connection, the cookbook committee included a UFO (Ungourmet and Unusual Food Offerings) chapter in the book. It includes recipes with titles such as Great Cover-Up BBQ Sauce, Crash Site Chicken Chowder, Flying Saucer Monster Cookies, and Conspiracy Two-Tone Slaw.

Broccoli Kugel

From A Taste of Tradition, cookbook of Temple Emanu-El,
Providence, Rhode Island

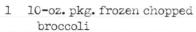

PHOTO APPEARS ON PAGE 158

1	10-oz. pkg. frozen chopped broccoli
1	cup pareve light cream
3	slightly beaten eggs
1/4	cup pareve margarine, melted

1	envelope onion soup mix (half of a 2$\frac{1}{2}$-oz. box)
8	oz. cooked pasta

Prep: 15 min. **Bake:** 35 min.

READ THE LABEL
Foods labeled as "pareve," such as the light cream called for in this recipe, meet the standards of Jewish dietary laws.

1. Cook broccoli according to package directions; drain well. Combine broccoli, cream, eggs, margarine, and soup mix. Stir in pasta. Spoon mixture into a 2-quart square baking dish. Bake in a 350°F oven about 35 minutes or until hot.

Makes 8 main-dish servings.
Per serving: 180 cal., 12 g total fat (4 g sat. fat), 91 mg chol., 507 mg sodium, 14 g carbo., 2 g fiber, 6 g pro. Dietary exchanges: 2 vegetable, $\frac{1}{2}$ starch, 2 fat.

Italian Linguine Bake

From Women Who Can Dish It Out, cookbook of the
Junior League of Springfield, Missouri

	Nonstick cooking spray		2	Tbsp. snipped fresh basil
12	oz. dried linguine		1½	tsp. snipped fresh oregano
1	cup sliced mushrooms		1	26- to 29-oz. jar marinara sauce
1	large onion, quartered and thinly sliced (1 cup)		4	oz. thinly sliced pepperoni
1	medium red or green sweet pepper, sliced into strips		1	cup shredded mozzarella cheese (4 oz.)
5	oz. sliced Canadian-style bacon, cut into thin strips		¼	cup grated Parmesan cheese (1 oz.)
1	Tbsp. bottled minced garlic			
1	Tbsp. olive oil or cooking oil			

Prep: 20 min. **Bake:** 20 min.

1. Lightly coat a 3-quart rectangular baking dish with cooking spray. Cook pasta according to package directions. Meanwhile, in a large skillet, cook mushrooms, onion, sweet pepper, Canadian bacon, and garlic in hot oil for 3 minutes. Add basil and oregano.

2. Drain pasta and return it to saucepan. Add marinara sauce and toss to coat. Spread pasta evenly in prepared baking dish. Top with vegetable mixture. Cover with foil. Bake in a 350°F oven for 15 minutes. Uncover; top with pepperoni and sprinkle with mozzarella cheese and Parmesan cheese. Bake, uncovered, about 5 minutes more or until cheese is melted and pepperoni is hot.

Makes 8 main-dish servings.
Per serving: 402 cal., 16 g total fat (5 g sat. fat), 35 mg chol., 1,167 mg sodium, 48 g carbo., 2 g fiber, 18 g pro. Dietary exchanges: 3 vegetable, 2 starch, 1 lean meat, 2½ fat.

Light Vegetable Lasagna

From *Perennial Palette*, cookbook of the *Southborough Gardeners*, *Southborough, Massachusetts*

PAGE PHOTO APPEARS ON 160

9	dried lasagna noodles
6	cups broccoli florets
1	large red sweet pepper, cut into bite-size strips
1	medium zucchini, sliced
1	medium yellow summer squash, sliced (1¼ cups)
2	beaten eggs
1	16-oz. container low-fat cottage cheese (2 cups)
1	15-oz. container light ricotta cheese (2 cups)
½	cup snipped fresh basil
2	Tbsp. snipped fresh thyme
3	cloves garlic, minced
½	tsp. salt
¼	tsp. black pepper
¼	tsp. bottled hot pepper sauce
3	cups shredded mozzarella cheese (12 oz.)

Prep: 45 min. **Bake:** 45 min. **Stand:** 10 min.

1. Grease a 3-quart rectangular baking dish; set aside. In a large saucepan, cook lasagna noodles in boiling lightly salted water for 10 to 12 minutes or until tender but still firm. Drain noodles; rinse with cold water. Drain well.

2. Meanwhile, place a steamer basket in a Dutch oven. Add water to just below the bottom of the steamer basket. Bring to boiling. Add broccoli, sweet pepper, zucchini, and yellow squash. Reduce heat; cover and steam for 6 to 8 minutes or until vegetables are crisp-tender. Remove from heat.

3. In a medium bowl, combine eggs, cottage cheese, ricotta cheese, basil, thyme, garlic, salt, black pepper, and hot pepper sauce.

4. Layer three of the cooked noodles in prepared dish. Spread with one-third of the ricotta cheese mixture. Top with one-third of the vegetable mixture and 1 cup of the mozzarella cheese. Repeat layers twice more.

5. Bake, covered, in a 375°F oven for 45 to 50 minutes or until heated through. Uncover; let stand for 10 minutes before cutting to serve.

Test Kitchen Tip: Light Vegetable Lasagna is a great make-ahead recipe. After assembling the dish, cover with foil and refrigerate for up to 24 hours. Bake as directed, adding an extra 10 to 15 minutes to the baking time to heat through.

Makes 8 main-dish servings.
Per serving: 388 cal., 15 g total fat (8 g sat. fat), 101 mg chol., 683 mg sodium, 32 g carbo., 4 g fiber, 32 g pro. Dietary exchanges: 2 vegetable, 1½ starch, 3 very lean meat, 2 fat.

Rice Lasagna

From A+ Cooking, Friends and Family Favorites, cookbook of the
North Plains Elementary School, North Plains, Oregon

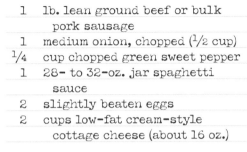

1	lb. lean ground beef or bulk pork sausage		1	8-oz. pkg. shredded mozzarella cheese (2 cups)
1	medium onion, chopped (1/2 cup)		4	cups hot cooked rice
1/4	cup chopped green sweet pepper		1/4	cup grated Parmesan cheese
1	28- to 32-oz. jar spaghetti sauce			
2	slightly beaten eggs			
2	cups low-fat cream-style cottage cheese (about 16 oz.)			

Prep: 30 min. **Bake:** 50 min. **Stand:** 10 min.

1. In a large skillet, cook ground beef, onion, and green pepper until meat is brown. Drain off fat. Stir in spaghetti sauce; heat through.

2. Meanwhile, in a medium bowl, stir together the eggs, cottage cheese, and mozzarella cheese; set aside.

3. In a 3-quart rectangular baking dish, layer half of the meat-sauce mixture, half of the cooked rice, and half of the cottage cheese mixture. Repeat layers. Sprinkle with Parmesan cheese. Bake, uncovered, in a 350°F oven about 50 minutes or until top is golden. Let stand for 10 minutes before serving.

Makes 8 main-dish servings.

Per serving: 427 cal., 16 g total fat (7 g sat. fat), 112 mg chol., 1,109 mg sodium, 37 g carbo., 3 g fiber, 31 g pro. Dietary exchanges: 1½ vegetable, 2 starch, 3 lean meat.

Cuban Black Beans

From De Nuestra Mesa: Our Food, Wine, and Tradition, a cookbook benefiting
New Hope Charities, Palm Beach, Florida

Latin Eats

New Hope Charities provides food and services to some of the poorest families in Palm Beach County. Cookbook volunteers called upon the strength of their community and its Latin roots to create De Nuestra Mesa [From Our Table]: Our Food, Wine, and Tradition. To collect the rich mix of dishes with origins in Spain and the Caribbean, committee members asked acquaintances—both in and out of the United States—to send their best recipes. Along with the recipes came wonderful stories about the origin of the dishes and tales of traditions handed down through the kitchens of the cooks.

1	lb. dry black beans
18	cups water
1	cup finely chopped onion
3/4	cup finely chopped green sweet pepper
4	cloves garlic, minced
1/4	cup olive oil
1 1/2	tsp. salt
1/2	tsp. black pepper
1/4	tsp. dried oregano, crushed

1	bay leaf
2	Tbsp. sugar
2	Tbsp. red wine vinegar
2	Tbsp. dry sherry
2	Tbsp. olive oil

Prep: 25 min. **Stand:** 1 hr. **Cook:** 2 hr.

1. Rinse beans. In a 4- to 4 1/2-quart Dutch oven, combine beans and 10 cups of the water. Bring to boiling; reduce heat. Simmer, uncovered, for 2 minutes. Remove from heat. Cover and let stand for 1 hour. (Or place beans in water in Dutch oven. Cover and let soak in a cool place for 6 to 8 hours or overnight.) Drain and rinse beans.

2. In the same Dutch oven, combine beans and 8 cups of the water. Bring to boiling; reduce heat. Cover and simmer for 1 hour.

3. Meanwhile, in a large saucepan, cook the onion, green pepper, and garlic in the 1/4 cup hot oil for 7 minutes, stirring occasionally.

4. Remove 1 cup of the cooked beans and a little of the liquid from the Dutch oven. Add to vegetable mixture in saucepan; cook about 5 minutes, stirring occasionally. Using a wooden spoon or a potato masher, slightly mash beans. Return bean-and-vegetable mixture to the Dutch oven. Stir in salt, black pepper, oregano, and bay leaf. Bring to boiling; reduce heat. Cover and simmer for 1 hour. Discard bay leaf. Before serving, stir in sugar, vinegar, sherry, and the 2 tablespoons olive oil.

Makes 6 to 8 main-dish servings.
Per serving: 418 cal., 15 g total fat (2 g sat. fat), 0 mg chol., 596 mg sodium, 56 g carbo., 12 g fiber, 17 g pro. Dietary exchanges: 1 vegetable, 2½ starch, 2 fat.

8.

Soups and Stews

Hearty Mushroom and Beef Soup

From The Heart of Pittsburgh, a cookbook benefiting
Sacred Heart Elementary School, Pittsburgh, Pennsylvania

1	Tbsp. cooking oil
1	lb. boneless beef chuck, cut into ½-inch cubes
1	medium onion, chopped (½ cup)
3	cups beef broth
½	of a 28-oz. can (1¾ cups) crushed tomatoes
8	oz. fresh mushrooms, sliced
¾	tsp. dried oregano, crushed
¾	tsp. bottled minced garlic
1	bay leaf

½	cup sliced carrot
2	Tbsp. cold water
4	tsp. cornstarch
1	cup cooked rice
¼	cup dry red wine (optional)
	Fresh rosemary sprigs or snipped parsley (optional)

Prep: 20 min. **Cook:** 1 hr. 10 min.

RICE IS NICE
The cup of cooked rice in this recipe adds a little texture and interest to the soup, but it also has a practical function. The starch in the rice, like the starch in pasta, helps thicken the soup just enough so it has some body.

1. In a large saucepan or Dutch oven, heat oil over medium-high heat; add half of the meat. Cook and stir for 2 to 3 minutes or until brown. Remove with slotted spoon. Repeat with remaining meat and the onion. Return all meat to pan. Stir in beef broth, crushed tomatoes, mushrooms, oregano, garlic, and bay leaf. Bring to boiling; reduce heat. Cover and simmer for 1 hour.

2. Add carrot. Return to boiling; reduce heat. Cover and simmer soup for 7 minutes. Combine cold water and cornstarch; add to pan along with rice. Cook and stir until slightly thickened. Add wine, if desired; heat for 2 minutes more. Discard bay leaf. Garnish with rosemary or parsley, if desired.

Makes 4 servings.
Per serving: 351 cal., 13 g total fat (4 g sat. fat), 82 mg chol., 914 mg sodium, 26 g carbo., 3 g fiber, 32 g pro. Dietary exchanges: 2 vegetable, 1 starch, 3 medium-fat meat.

New Mexico Beef Stew

*From Savoring the Southwest Again, cookbook of the
Roswell Symphony Guild, Roswell, New Mexico*

1/3	cup cornmeal
1	tsp. salt
1/2	tsp. black pepper
1/2	tsp. dried thyme, crushed
1 1/2	lb. boneless beef chuck, cut into 3/4-inch pieces
2	to 3 Tbsp. cooking oil
3	cloves garlic, minced
1 1/2	cups water
2	cups fresh corn kernels
1	28-oz. can tomatoes, cut up

1	15-oz. can chickpeas (garbanzo beans), drained
2	cups chopped, peeled celery root or 1 cup sliced celery
1	cup chopped onion
2	fresh jalapeño peppers, seeded and chopped
1	chipotle pepper in adobo sauce, chopped

Prep: 35 min. **Cook:** 1 1/2 hr.

WHERE THERE'S SMOKE . . .
A chipotle pepper is a dried, smoked jalapeño. Chipotles have a smoky, sweet, almost chocolaty flavor. Chipotles in adobo sauce can be found in some supermarkets and at Mexican grocery stores. Adobo sauce is a dark red sauce made from ground chiles, herbs, and vinegar.

1. In a large plastic bag, combine cornmeal, salt, black pepper, and thyme. Add half of the meat to bag; shake to coat.

2. In a Dutch oven, heat 2 tablespoons of the oil over medium heat; add coated meat cubes and cook until brown on all sides. Remove meat from pan. Repeat with remaining meat and cornmeal mixture, adding remaining oil, if necessary. Return all meat to Dutch oven; add garlic. Cook and stir for 30 seconds. Add water. Bring to boiling; reduce heat. Cover and simmer about 1 hour or until meat is almost tender.

3. Add corn, undrained tomatoes, chickpeas, celery root, onion, jalapeño peppers, and chipotle pepper. Return to boiling; reduce heat. Cover and simmer for 30 minutes more or until meat and vegetables are tender.

Slow-cooker directions: Brown meat as above, adding garlic with second half of meat. In a 3 1/2-, 4-, or 5-quart crockery cooker, place corn, chickpeas, celery root, onion, and jalapeño peppers. Add browned beef. Sprinkle with any leftover cornmeal mixture. Using only 1/4 cup water, combine water with tomatoes and chipotle pepper. Pour over beef. Cover; cook on low-heat setting for 8 to 10 hours. (Or cook on high-heat setting for 4 to 5 hours.) Stir before serving.

Makes 6 servings.
Per serving: 471 cal., 21 g total fat (6 g sat. fat), 73 mg chol., 962 mg sodium, 42 g carbo., 8 g fiber, 30 g pro. Dietary exchanges: 2 vegetable, 2 starch, 3 lean meat, 2 fat.

Beer, Cheese, and Bacon Soup

From *Recipes of Note for Entertaining*, cookbook of the
Rochester Civic Music Guild, Rochester, Minnesota

1/2	cup finely chopped onion
1/2	cup butter or margarine
2/3	cup all-purpose flour
1	tsp. dry mustard
1	tsp. paprika
1/8	tsp. ground red pepper
4	cups milk
1	12-oz. can beer
1	10 1/2-oz. can condensed chicken broth
3	cups shredded sharp cheddar cheese
10	slices bacon, crisp-cooked, drained, and crumbled
	Popcorn (optional)

Start to finish: 15 min.

SLOW AND LOW
The key to a smooth soup with no masses of melted cheese is to add the cheese with the heat on low or turned off. Low-fat cheeses, in particular, require this treatment to melt into the soup.

1. In a large saucepan, cook onion in hot butter until tender. Stir in flour, mustard, paprika, and red pepper. Gradually stir in milk, beer, and broth. Cook, stirring constantly, over medium heat until mixture comes to a boil. Cook and stir for 1 minute more. Reduce heat and stir in cheese until smooth. Stir in bacon. Ladle into bowls; top with popcorn, if desired.

Test Kitchen Tip: For a lighter soup, substitute 2 cups shredded reduced-fat cheddar cheese for the 3 cups sharp cheddar cheese, and 6 slices turkey bacon for the 10 slices bacon. Also use low-fat milk and light beer.

Makes 8 servings.
Per serving: 469 cal., 31 g total fat (14 g sat. fat), 76 mg chol., 1,186 mg sodium, 27 g carbo., 1 g fiber, 16 g pro. Dietary exchanges: 1 milk, 1 starch, 1 high-fat meat, 3 fat.

Potato Soup

*From Beyond Burlap, cookbook of the
Boise Junior League, Boise, Idaho*

195

6	slices bacon, halved crosswise (about 1/4 lb.)
1/2	cup chopped onion
1/2	cup chopped celery
2	large potatoes, peeled and coarsely chopped
1	cup water
1	tsp. mustard seed or Dijon-style mustard

1 1/2	cups light cream or milk
1	10 3/4-oz. can condensed cream of chicken or golden mushroom soup
	Fresh snipped parsley (optional)

Prep: 25 min. **Cook:** 15 min.

1. In a large saucepan, cook bacon over medium heat until crisp. Remove bacon, reserving 1 tablespoon drippings in pan. Drain bacon on paper towels. Crumble bacon and set aside, reserving several pieces for garnish, if desired.

2. Add onion and celery to saucepan. Cook until tender. Stir in the potatoes, water, and mustard. Bring to boiling; reduce heat. Simmer, covered, for 15 minutes or until the potatoes are just tender.

3. Stir in light cream and condensed soup. Heat through; do not boil. Stir in bacon. Garnish with fresh parsley and reserved bacon, if desired.

Makes 6 servings.
Per serving: 317 cal., 22 g total fat (9 g sat. fat), 44 mg chol., 728 mg sodium, 20 g carbo., 2 g fiber, 11 g pro. Dietary exchanges: 1/2 vegetable, 1 1/2 starch, 4 fat.

Around Town
Boise, Idaho (pop. 126,000) You can spot a Gem State license plate by the slogan "Famous Potatoes," which has been on Idaho plates since 1948.

Pink's Fresh Okra Soup

*From 'Pon Top Edisto: Cookin' 'Tweenst the Rivers, cookbook of
Trinity Episcopal Church, Edisto Island, South Carolina*

1	lb. fresh okra, sliced (4 cups), or one 16-oz. pkg. frozen okra
1	medium onion, chopped
1	Tbsp. cooking oil
1	lb. meaty smoked pork hocks
3	medium tomatoes, peeled and chopped (2 cups)
1	8-oz. can tomato sauce
1/2	cup water
1	small green sweet pepper, chopped (1/2 cup)
1/4	tsp. black pepper
	Hot cooked rice (optional)
	Corn bread (optional)

Prep: 45 min. **Cook:** 1 hr.

In the Pink

The pink in the title of this recipe refers to Pink Brown, whose produce stand is the place to shop for fresh vegetables on Edisto Island. She likes to make this soup—the recipe has been handed down for generations in her family—in the late summer and fall, when fresh island-grown okra is available.

1. In a large saucepan, cook okra and onion in hot oil for 5 minutes; remove and set aside. Add pork hocks, tomatoes, tomato sauce, water, and sweet pepper. Bring to boiling; reduce heat. Cover and simmer for 20 minutes. Add okra-onion mixture and black pepper. Return to boiling; reduce heat. Cover and simmer for 1 hour.

2. Remove pork hocks and cool slightly. Cut meat off bones. Coarsely chop meat and return to pan; heat through. Discard bones. Serve soup with rice and corn bread, if desired.

Test Kitchen Tip: If the soup becomes too thick during cooking, stir in a little additional water.

Makes 6 to 8 servings.
Per serving: 125 cal., 4 g total fat (1 g sat. fat), 13 mg chol., 552 mg sodium, 16 g carbo., 3 g fiber, 9 g pro. Dietary exchanges: 3 vegetable, 1/2 medium-fat meat.

Kielbasa Soup

From The Heart of Pittsburgh, a cookbook benefiting
Sacred Heart Elementary School, Pittsburgh, Pennsylvania

6¼	cups reduced-sodium chicken broth
4	cups water
¾	lb. cooked kielbasa or Polish sausage (Polska kielbasa), cut into ¼- to ½-inch-thick slices
1	cup chopped celery

1	cup thinly sliced carrot
2	bay leaves
¼	tsp. black pepper
4	oz. wide noodles (about 2 cups)

Start to finish: 23 min.

SAUSAGE SUB
Kielbasa is a mainstay in Pittsburgh's Polish neighborhoods. Individual butchers have their own special recipes. Typically, this cooked and smoked sausage is made of pork. Polish sausage would make a suitable substitute.

1. In a 4- to 5-quart Dutch oven, combine all ingredients except noodles. Bring to boiling. Add noodles. Return to boiling. Cook for 8 to 10 minutes or until noodles and vegetables are just tender. Discard bay leaves.

Makes 5 servings.
Per serving: 352 cal., 23 g total fat (8 g sat. fat), 77 mg chol., 1,484 mg sodium, 23 g carbo., 2 g fiber, 14 g pro. Dietary exchanges: 1 vegetable, 1 starch, 1 high-fat meat, 2 fat.

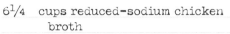

178

Black Bean Soup

From West of the Rockies, cookbook of the
Junior Service League of Grand Junction, Colorado

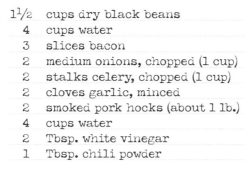

1½	cups dry black beans		¾	tsp. instant beef bouillon
4	cups water			granules
3	slices bacon		½	tsp. black pepper
2	medium onions, chopped (1 cup)		¼	cup dry vermouth or dry sherry
2	stalks celery, chopped (1 cup)			(optional)
2	cloves garlic, minced		1	Tbsp. snipped fresh cilantro
2	smoked pork hocks (about 1 lb.)			Snipped fresh cilantro
4	cups water			(optional)
2	Tbsp. white vinegar			
1	Tbsp. chili powder			

Prep: 25 min. **Cook:** 1½ hr. **Stand:** 1 hr.

1. Rinse beans. In a large saucepan, combine beans and 4 cups water. Bring to boiling; reduce heat. Simmer, uncovered, for 2 minutes. Remove from heat. Cover and let stand for 1 hour. (Or place beans and 4 cups water in large saucepan. Cover and let soak in a cool place for 6 to 8 hours or overnight.) Drain and rinse beans; set aside.

2. In a large saucepan or Dutch oven, cook bacon over medium heat until crisp. Remove bacon; drain on paper towels. Set aside. Cook onions, celery, and garlic in hot drippings about 5 minutes or until tender. Add black beans, pork hocks, 4 cups water, vinegar, chili powder, beef bouillon, and black pepper. Bring to boiling; reduce heat. Cover and simmer about 1½ hours or until beans are tender. Add water during cooking, if necessary. Skim off fat. Remove meat. When cool enough to handle, cut meat off bones; coarsely chop meat. Discard bones.

3. Meanwhile, using a potato masher or fork, lightly mash bean mixture. Return chopped meat to pan. Stir in vermouth, if desired, and the 1 tablespoon cilantro; heat through. To serve, crumble bacon over soup. Top with additional snipped fresh cilantro, if desired.

Makes 6 servings.
Per serving: 187 cal., 5 g total fat (2 g sat. fat), 11 mg chol., 339 mg sodium, 25 g carbo., 3 g fiber, 12 g pro. Dietary exchanges: 1½ starch, 1 medium-fat meat.

Ranch Chicken Chowder

From Savoring the Southwest Again, cookbook of the
Roswell Symphony Guild, Roswell, New Mexico

1	lb. skinless, boneless chicken breast halves, cut into bite-size pieces
2	Tbsp. butter or margarine
1	large sweet potato, peeled and sliced (about 8 oz.)
1	medium onion, chopped ($1/2$ cup)
1	to 2 fresh serrano chile peppers, seeded*
$1/2$	tsp. ground coriander
$1/4$	tsp. ground cumin

3	cups chicken broth
1	$14^1/2$-oz. can hominy, rinsed and drained, or 1 cup frozen whole kernel corn, thawed
	Snipped fresh cilantro (optional)
	Dairy sour cream (optional)

Prep: 15 min. **Cook:** 30 min.

HOT STUFF
For such a small thing (about 1½ inches long), the slightly pointed serrano pepper packs a lot of heat. If you can't find fresh serrano chiles in your supermarket, look for them in Mexican markets.

1. In a large saucepan or Dutch oven, cook chicken, half at a time, in hot butter until no longer pink. Remove chicken with a slotted spoon, reserving drippings in saucepan. Set aside.

2. Add sweet potato, onion, serrano peppers, coriander, and cumin to saucepan; add 1½ cups of the chicken broth. Bring to boiling; reduce heat. Cover and simmer about 20 minutes or until vegetables are very tender. Cool slightly.

3. Add sweet potato mixture to blender container. Cover and blend until smooth. Return to saucepan along with chicken, remaining 1½ cups chicken broth, and hominy. Heat through.

4. Serve in bowls. Garnish with cilantro and sour cream, if desired.

*Test Kitchen Tip: Because chile peppers contain volatile oils that can burn your skin and eyes, avoid direct contact with them as much as possible. When working with chile peppers, wear plastic bags over your hands or wear plastic or rubber gloves. If your bare hands do touch the chile peppers, wash your hands well with soap and warm water.

Makes 5 or 6 servings.
Per serving: 265 cal., 7 g total fat (1 g sat. fat), 53 mg chol., 1,085 mg sodium, 27 g carbo., 4 g fiber, 25 g pro. Dietary exchanges: 1½ starch, 3 very lean meat, ½ fat.

Travel to Seattle and you can sample some of the world's most delicious seafood, stroll through bustling markets, peek into ethnic food stores of almost every kind—and, of course, get a great cup of coffee. The Junior League of Seattle no doubt enjoyed countless cups of coffee as its members compiled *Simply Classic*, a cookbook that celebrates the bounty of the Northwest. This hearty meal-in-a-pot is named after one of Washington's most famous landmarks.

Mount Rainier Chili

From *Simply Classic*, cookbook of the
Junior League of Seattle, Washington

1	lb. dry Great Northern beans
8	cups water
1	Tbsp. cooking oil
2	cups chopped onion
4	cloves garlic, minced
2	4-oz. cans chopped green chiles
2	tsp. ground cumin
1½	tsp. dried oregano, crushed
¼	tsp. ground cloves
¼	tsp. ground red pepper
8	cups chicken broth

2	lb. boneless, skinless chicken breasts or 4 cups coarsely chopped cooked chicken
1	12-oz. can beer
1	cup shredded Monterey Jack cheese or Monterey Jack cheese with jalapeño peppers (4 oz.)

Prep: 30 min. **Stand:** 1 hr. **Cook:** 2 hr.

1. Rinse beans. In a Dutch oven, combine beans and water. Bring to boiling; reduce heat. Simmer, uncovered, for 2 minutes. Remove from heat. Cover and let stand for 1 hour. (Or place beans and water in Dutch oven. Cover and let soak in a cool place overnight.) Drain and rinse beans. Set aside.

2. In the same Dutch oven, heat oil over medium heat; add onion and cook for 5 to 8 minutes or until tender. Stir in garlic, chiles, cumin, oregano, cloves, and ground red pepper. Cook and stir for 2 minutes more. Stir in beans and chicken broth. Bring to boiling; reduce heat. Cover and simmer about 2 hours or until beans are very tender.

3. Meanwhile, if using chicken breasts, place them in a large skillet or saucepan; add enough water to cover. Bring to boiling; reduce heat. Cover and simmer for 15 to 20 minutes or until chicken is tender and no longer pink. Drain; cool slightly. Coarsely chop chicken.

4. Stir chopped chicken, beer, and the 1 cup cheese into bean mixture; cook and stir until cheese is melted. Serve with sour cream, salsa, cilantro, and additional cheese, if desired.

Makes 12 servings.
Per serving: 306 cal., 7 g total fat (3 g sat. fat), 52 mg chol., 834 mg sodium, 29 g carbo., 9 g fiber, 30 g pro. Dietary exchanges: 2 starch, 3 very lean meat, ½ fat.

Caldo Maya (Chicken Tortilla Soup)

From Mesquite Country, cookbook of the
Hidalgo County Historical Museum, Edinburg, Texas

2	to 2½ lb. meaty chicken pieces (breasts, thighs, drumsticks)	¼	to ½ tsp. black pepper
6	cups water	1½	cups chopped carrots (3 medium)
2	cups coarsely chopped onion	1	or 2 poblano chile peppers
2	cups coarsely chopped celery		Sliced avocado (optional)
1	large tomato, coarsely chopped (1 cup)		Chopped fresh cilantro (optional)
½	cup snipped fresh cilantro		Sliced green onions (optional)
1½	tsp. salt		Fried Corn Tortilla Strips (optional)
1	tsp. ground cumin		
¼	to ½ tsp. ground red pepper		

Prep: 20 min. **Cook:** 1 hr.

WARM OR HOT? Choose your level of heat in this traditional Mexican chicken soup by varying the amount of ground red, ground black, and fresh roasted poblano peppers.

1. Skin chicken. In a 4½-quart pot, place chicken, water, half the onion, half the celery, the tomato, cilantro, salt, cumin, red pepper, and black pepper. Bring to a boil; reduce heat. Cover and simmer for 40 to 50 minutes or until chicken is tender. Remove chicken; set aside to cool slightly. Strain broth mixture, reserving broth; discard vegetables. Return broth to pot. Add remaining onion and celery and the carrots. Bring to boiling; reduce heat. Simmer, covered, for 20 minutes or until vegetables are tender.

2. Meanwhile, cut poblano peppers in half lengthwise; remove stems, membranes, and seeds. Place peppers, cut-side down, on a foil-lined baking sheet. Bake in a 425°F oven for 20 to 25 minutes or until skins are dark. Wrap in foil; let stand until cool enough to handle. Pull skin off gently using a paring knife; discard. Chop peppers.

3. Remove chicken from bones; discard bones. Chop chicken. Stir chicken and poblano peppers into broth. Heat through. Ladle into bowls. If desired, garnish with avocado, cilantro, green onions, and tortilla strips.

Fried Corn Tortilla Strips: Cut six 6-inch corn tortillas into thin strips. In a large skillet over medium heat, cook about one-third of the tortilla strips in 3 tablespoons hot cooking oil until crisp, about 2 to 3 minutes, stirring occasionally. Lift strips from skillet with a slotted spoon, reserving oil in skillet. Drain strips on paper towels. Repeat with remaining tortilla strips, one-third at a time, adding a little additional, oil if necessary.

Makes 6 servings.
Per serving: 158 cal., 5 g total fat (1 g sat. fat), 61 mg chol., 638 mg sodium, 7 g carbo., 2 g fiber, 21 g pro.
Dietary exchanges: 2 vegetable, 2½ lean meat.

Hingham Fish Chowder

*From Out of the Ordinary, cookbook of the
Hingham Historical Society, Hingham, Massachusetts*

1	lb. fresh or frozen fish fillets (such as cod, haddock, or orange roughy)
2	medium potatoes, peeled and chopped
1	large onion, chopped (1 cup)
1/4	cup chopped celery
2	Tbsp. butter or margarine, cut up
1	bay leaf
1	tsp. salt

1/4	tsp. black pepper
1/4	tsp. dried dillweed
4	whole cloves (optional)
1	cup water
1/4	cup dry vermouth, dry white wine, or water
1	cup whipping cream or evaporated milk

Prep: 20 min. **Bake:** 1 hr.

Hingham's History

Out of the Ordinary, not surprisingly, is filled with tidbits about the history of Hingham. Here's a sampling:

• In the 19th century, there were so many bucket and pail makers in Hingham, the town was known as "Bucket Town." Hingham buckets often were distinguished by their brass hoops.

• When the industrial boom of the 19th century faded, the shrinking town became a summer resort for Irish, Dutch, and Italian immigrants.

• In the post-World War II suburban explosion, the town's ancient character appeared doomed. Alarmed conservationists mobilized to save a heritage of colonial homes and open green spaces.

1. Thaw fish, if frozen. Cut fish into 2-inch pieces; set aside. In a large bowl, combine fish, potatoes, onion, celery, butter, bay leaf, salt, black pepper, and dillweed. If using whole cloves, place cloves on a double-thick, 3-inch square of 100 percent cotton cheesecloth. Bring corners together and tie with a clean kitchen string. Add bag to fish mixture. Transfer fish mixture to a 2-quart casserole.

2. Stir together the 1 cup water and the vermouth, wine, or water. Pour over fish mixture.

3. Bake, covered, in a 350°F oven about 1 hour or until potatoes are tender, stirring halfway through cooking time. Remove bay leaf and spice bag, if using. Stir in whipping cream.

Makes 4 servings.
Per serving: 417 cal., 29 g total fat (18 g sat. fat), 147 mg chol., 739 mg sodium, 13 g carbo., 1 g fiber, 23 g pro. Dietary exchanges: 1 starch, 3 very lean meat, 5 fat.

More Than Minestrone

From *Simply Classic*, cookbook of the
Junior League of Seattle, Washington

5	slices bacon, cut into bite-size pieces
1	cup chopped onion
1	cup chopped celery
1/3	cup finely chopped carrot
3	cloves garlic, minced
8	cups chicken broth
1	28-oz. can whole Italian-style tomatoes, cut up
1	15$\frac{1}{2}$-oz. can red kidney beans, rinsed and drained

1	15-oz. can white kidney (cannellini) beans, rinsed and drained
1	15-oz. can chickpeas (garbanzo beans), rinsed and drained
1/2	cup snipped fresh parsley
1$\frac{1}{2}$	tsp. dried basil, crushed
1	tsp. dried oregano, crushed
1$\frac{1}{2}$	cups dried tiny shell macaroni
	Grated Parmesan cheese

Start to finish: 55 min.

SODIUM WATCH
To lower the sodium by 222 mg per serving, use reduced-sodium chicken broth instead of regular chicken broth.

1. In a 6-quart Dutch oven, cook bacon over medium heat just until crisp. Add onion and celery. Cook about 5 minutes or until tender. Add carrot and garlic; cook for 2 minutes more. Stir in chicken broth, tomatoes, beans, chickpeas, parsley, basil, and oregano. Bring to boiling; reduce heat. Cover and simmer for 20 minutes, stirring occasionally. Stir in macaroni. Cook, uncovered, for 8 to 10 minutes more or until macaroni is just tender, stirring frequently. Sprinkle Parmesan cheese over top.

Makes 8 to 10 servings.
Per serving: 307 cal., 5 g total fat (1 g sat. fat), 3 mg chol., 1,342 mg sodium, 50 g carbo., 10 g fiber, 19 g pro. Dietary exchanges: 3 bread, 1 vegetable.

"Creamless" Creamy Wild Rice Soup

From Recipes of Note for Entertaining, cookbook of the
Rochester Civic Music Guild, Rochester, Minnesota

½	cup chopped onion
½	cup finely chopped celery
½	cup finely chopped carrots
1	Tbsp. butter
⅔	cup uncooked wild rice, rinsed and drained
4	cups chicken broth
1	tsp. dried rosemary, crushed
½	tsp. dried thyme, crushed
1½	cups fat-free milk

½	cup nonfat dry milk powder
4	tsp. all-purpose flour
1	Tbsp. butter, softened
3	to 4 strips bacon, crisp-cooked, drained, and crumbled
	Black pepper

Prep: 20 min. **Cook:** 45 min.

WILD RICE
What we call wild rice is actually the seed of a marsh grass native to Minnesota. To cook wild rice for use in salads, breads, and other dishes, rinse it to remove tiny particles left after processing. To rinse, place 1 cup rice in a pan of warm water. Stir, then remove any particles that float to the top; drain. Repeat. To cook, bring 2 cups water to boiling in a medium sauce pan. Add ¼ teaspoon salt if desired. Add 1 cup wild rice. Return to boiling. Reduce heat. Simmer, covered, about 40 minutes or until most of the water is absorbed. Drain, if necessary. Makes 2⅔ cups of cooked wild rice.

1. In a large saucepan, cook onion, celery, and carrots in 1 tablespoon hot butter for 3 to 4 minutes or until tender. Stir in wild rice; cook and stir for 1 minute. Add chicken broth, rosemary, and thyme. Bring to boiling; reduce heat. Cover and simmer for 40 minutes or until rice is tender. Stir in milk and milk powder. Combine flour and 1 tablespoon softened butter; whisk into soup. Cook and stir until slightly thickened and bubbly. Cook and stir 1 minute more. Stir in bacon. Season with black pepper to taste.

Makes 6 servings.
Per serving: 208 cal., 7 g total fat (2 g sat. fat), 10 mg chol., 781 mg sodium, 25 g carbo., 1 g fiber, 12 g pro. Dietary exchanges: 1 starch, 1 milk, 1 fat.

9.

Vegetables, Salads, and Sides

Fresh Corn Skillet

From Picnics, Potlucks & Prizewinners:
Celebrating Indiana Hospitality with 4-H Families and Friends

4	fresh ears of corn or one 10-oz. pkg. frozen whole kernel corn, thawed		1	tsp. sugar (optional)
2	Tbsp. olive oil		1	cup fresh pea pods
1½	tsp. instant chicken bouillon granules		1	medium red sweet pepper, cut into thin, bite-size strips
1	tsp. snipped fresh thyme or rosemary		¼	cup sliced green onions Freshly ground black pepper

Prep: 25 min. **Chill:** 1 hr.

1. If using fresh corn, remove husks. Scrub with a stiff brush to remove the silks. Rinse. Use a sharp knife to cut corn from the cob at three-quarters depth of kernels; do not scrape. (You should have about 2 cups corn.) Set aside.

2. In a large skillet, combine oil, bouillon, thyme, and, if desired, sugar. Cook for 30 seconds over medium-high heat. Stir in corn, pea pods, sweet pepper, and green onions. Cook over medium-high heat for 4 minutes or until the vegetables are crisp-tender, stirring occasionally. Transfer to a serving bowl. Chill in refrigerator for at least 1 hour. Sprinkle with black pepper before serving.

Makes 6 servings.
Per serving: 108 cal., 5 g total fat (1 g sat. fat), 0 mg chol., 227 mg sodium, 15 g carbo., 3 g fiber, 3 g pro. Dietary exchanges: 1 starch, ½ fat.

Around the State

Hoosiers are sold on 4-H. About 252,000 youth and 15,000 adult leaders participate in programs in the state's 92 counties. It's estimated that one of every six Indiana residents is a 4-H alumnus. A state resident can even buy a 4-H license plate, which sends a $25 donation to 4-H Foundation programs.

Herbed-Yogurt Baked Tomatoes

From Sharing Our Best, cookbook of the
Junior Women's Club of Clayton, North Carolina

2	large tomatoes
1/2	cup plain fat-free yogurt
2	tsp. all-purpose flour
1/2	tsp. dried marjoram, crushed
1/8	to 1/4 tsp. black pepper

3   Tbsp. grated Romano or
      Parmesan cheese

Prep: 10 min. **Bake:** 20 min.

1. Remove cores from tomatoes; halve tomatoes crosswise. Place tomato halves, cut side up, in an ungreased 2-quart square baking dish.

2. In a small bowl, combine yogurt, flour, marjoram, and black pepper. Spoon about 2 tablespoons of the yogurt mixture onto each tomato half.

Sprinkle Romano cheese over the yogurt mixture.

3. Bake in a 375°F oven for 20 to 25 minutes or until tomatoes are heated through.

Makes 4 servings.

Per serving: 51 cal., 1 g total fat (1 g sat. fat), 4 mg chol., 75 mg sodium, 7 g carbo., 1 g fiber, 4 g pro. Dietary exchanges: 1½ vegetable.

THE BIG CHEESE
Parmesan cheese is a pale yellow, hard cow's-milk cheese that has a sharp, salty taste. It's available in domestic and imported versions in chunked, shredded, and grated forms. The granddaddy of all Parmesans is Parmigiano-Reggiano. It comes only from the Italian provinces of Reggio-Emilia and Parma. It's expensive, but its buttery, nutty flavor is incredible.

Roasted Green Beans in Dill Vinaigrette

From Perennial Palette, cookbook of the Southborough Gardeners,
Southborough, Massachusetts

2	lb. fresh green beans, trimmed		$1/2$	tsp. coarsely ground black pepper
1	Tbsp. olive oil		$1/4$	tsp. salt
$1/2$	tsp. salt		1	Tbsp. olive oil
2	Tbsp. water		2	Tbsp. snipped fresh dill
2	Tbsp. white wine vinegar			
$1\frac{1}{2}$	tsp. Dijon-style mustard			
$1/2$	tsp. sugar			

Prep: 20 min. **Roast:** 20 min.

1. In a large roasting pan, toss together green beans, 1 tablespoon olive oil, and the $1/2$ teaspoon salt. Drizzle water over. Roast, uncovered, in a 450°F oven for 20 to 25 minutes or until the beans are tender, stirring once or twice.

2. Meanwhile, in a small bowl, whisk together the vinegar, mustard, sugar, black pepper, and the $1/4$ teaspoon salt. Whisk in 1 tablespoon olive oil. Stir in dill. Toss cooked beans with vinegar mixture. Serve warm or cooled to room temperature.

Makes 8 to 10 servings.
Per serving: 69 cal., 4 g total fat (0 g sat. fat), 0 mg chol., 248 mg sodium, 8 g carbo., 4 g fiber, 2 g pro. Dietary exchanges: 1½ vegetable, ½ fat.

Summer Vegetable Gratin

From *Perennial Palette*, cookbook of the Southborough Gardeners.
Southborough, Massachusetts

PAGE 197 PHOTO APPEARS ON

Nonstick cooking spray	Salt
2 large leeks, sliced ¼ inch thick (1 cup)*	Black pepper
1 medium zucchini, sliced ¼ inch thick (1¼ cups)	2 Tbsp. fine dry bread crumbs
1 medium yellow summer squash, sliced ¼ inch thick (1¼ cups)	2 Tbsp. finely shredded Parmesan cheese
2 Tbsp. olive oil	2 tsp. snipped fresh thyme
	1 clove garlic, minced

Prep: 15 min. **Bake:** 20 min.

1. Coat a shallow 2-quart baking dish with cooking spray; set aside. Rinse and trim leeks; pat dry with paper towel. In a medium bowl, combine leeks, zucchini, yellow squash, and 1 tablespoon of the oil. Sprinkle with salt and black pepper. Transfer vegetables to prepared dish.

2. In a small bowl, stir together bread crumbs, cheese, thyme, garlic, and the remaining 1 tablespoon oil. Sprinkle crumb mixture evenly over vegetables. Bake in a 425°F oven for 20 to 25 minutes or until vegetables are tender.

*Test Kitchen Tip: Unlike green onions (or scallions), the long green tops of leeks are not tender and not recommended for cooking. To trim a leek, cut off and discard the green tops. Trim off roots from the white stalk. Remove and discard any outer layers of the white stalk that appear tough. Rinse the stalk to remove any dirt or sand. Slice the stalk crosswise; if you notice bits of dirt between the white layers, rinse again.

Makes 4 servings.
Per serving: 117 cal., 8 g total fat (1 g sat. fat), 2 mg chol., 104 mg sodium, 10 g carbo., 3 g fiber, 3 g pro. Dietary exchanges: 2 vegetable, 1½ fat.

Super Cook
Debbie Stutman of Southborough, Massachusetts, lived up to her reputation as a great cook by contributing more recipes to *Perennial Palette* than any other gardening club member. A "gratin" is simply a casserole that's topped with bread crumbs and cheese.

Carrots au Gratin

From the Greenfield Village School Cookbook.
Greenfield, New Hampshire

1	lb. carrots, sliced $1/2$ inch thick (about 3 cups)
$1/4$	cup fine dry bread crumbs
1	Tbsp. butter or margarine, melted
1	$10^{3}/4$-oz. can condensed cream of celery soup or reduced-fat condensed cream of celery soup

1	cup shredded cheddar cheese (4 oz.)
1	Tbsp. snipped fresh parsley
1	to 2 tsp. snipped fresh rosemary

Prep: 15 min. **Bake:** 20 min.

1. Grease a 1-quart casserole; set aside. In a covered medium saucepan, cook carrots in a small amount of boiling water for 10 to 12 minutes or just until tender. Drain well.
2. Meanwhile, in a small bowl, combine bread crumbs and butter; set aside.
3. In a medium bowl, combine carrots, soup, cheddar cheese, parsley, and rosemary. Spoon into prepared casserole. Sprinkle with bread crumb mixture. Bake casserole, uncovered, in a 350°F oven for 20 to 25 minutes or until heated through.

Makes 6 servings.
Per serving: 177 cal., 11 g total fat (6 g sat. fat), 31 mg chol., 598 mg sodium, 14 g carbo., 3 g fiber, 7 g pro. Dietary exchanges: 2 vegetable, $1/2$ starch, 2 fat.

Baked 1015 Onions

From Beneath the Palms, cookbook of the
Junior Service League of Brownsville, Texas

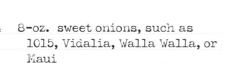

4	8-oz. sweet onions, such as 1015, Vidalia, Walla Walla, or Maui
4	Tbsp. butter
	Bottled hot pepper sauce
	Salt
	Black pepper

Prep: 10 min. **Bake:** 40 min.

1. Peel and trim onions. Score each onion by making deep cuts in a checkerboard pattern at $\frac{1}{2}$-inch intervals across surface of onion. Tear off four 12-inch squares of foil. Place an onion in center of each piece of foil. Press butter into the cuts of each onion. Sprinkle with hot pepper sauce, then with salt and black pepper. Loosely wrap the foil around onions. Bake in a 350°F oven for 40 to 45 minutes or until tender.

Makes 4 servings.

Per serving: 204 cal., 12 g total fat (8 g sat. fat), 33 mg chol., 171 mg sodium, 21 g carbo., 4 g fiber, 3 g pro. Dietary exchanges: 4 vegetable, 2 fat.

Around Town

Brownsville, Texas (pop. 136,000) Brownsville is known to history buffs as the site of two important battles in United States history: the first battle of the Mexican-American War and the last land battle of the Civil War. These days, the city exists in harmony with Mexico. Some Brownsville residents can see Mexico from their windows; others speak proudly of wonderful seafood culled from the gulf waters nearby. Both regional distinctions bear on this gentle town's motto: "On the border by the sea."

Herbed Potatoes

From the Waldorf Ladies Auxiliary Cookbook II. benefiting the
Waldorf Volunteer Fire Department & Rescue Squad. Waldorf. Maryland

Recipes to the
Rescue

Whenever there's a fire in the section of southern Maryland served by the Waldorf Volunteer Fire Department & Rescue Squad. you're likely to find members of the Ladies' Auxiliary there supplying food and beverages for the firefighters. To help fund their work in support of the fire department. the women compiled the Waldorf Ladies Auxiliary Cookbook II. The 200-page volume is filled with more than 600 recipes.

1   lb. baking potatoes (3 medium)
2   Tbsp. butter, melted
1   Tbsp. lemon juice
1   Tbsp. snipped fresh basil or
      fresh thyme
1/4   tsp. black pepper

1/3   cup shredded cheddar cheese or
      2 Tbsp. grated Parmesan
      cheese

Prep: 15 min.   **Bake:** 25 min.

1. Lightly grease a 15×10×1-inch baking pan; set aside.

2. Scrub potatoes with a brush. Pat dry. Cut potatoes crosswise into slices a little more than 1/4 inch thick.

3. In a large bowl, combine melted butter, lemon juice, basil, and black pepper. Add sliced potatoes; toss gently to coat. Place potato slices in a single layer in prepared baking pan.

4. Bake in a 450°F oven for 25 to 30 minutes or until potato slices are tender and bottoms are lightly browned. (For more even browning, turn potato slices over after 15 minutes of baking.) Remove from oven. Sprinkle with cheese. Let stand for 5 minutes. Transfer slices to a double thickness of paper towels to drain. Serve warm.

Makes 4 servings.
Per serving: 176 cal., 9 g total fat (6 g sat. fat), 26 mg chol., 124 mg sodium, 18 g carbo., 2 g fiber, 5 g pro. Dietary exchanges: 1½ starch, 1 fat.

Pam D'Alessandro, left, loves to cook Italian food—as evidenced by the gallons of olive oil and huge tins of tomatoes in her pantry. She shared more than a dozen recipes, including Hearty Mushroom and Beef Soup, below, in The Heart of Pittsburgh cookbook.

Hearty Mushroom and Beef Soup, p. 172

194

New Mexico Beef Stew, p. 173

Serve hearty New Mexico Beef Stew with Cheddar-Corn Rolls (see recipe, page 49). Both recipes are from Savoring the Southwest Again, a cookbook benefiting the Roswell Symphony. Co-chairs Billie Michaud, left, and Patricia Eckert show off the cookbook in front of Pearson Auditorium at the New Mexico Military Institute, where the symphony performs.

Potato Soup, p. 175

Serve Fresh Corn Skillet hot out of the pan as a vegetable side dish or chilled as a vegetable salad. It's terrific either way, say the folks who put together Picnics, Potlucks & Prizewinners: Celebrating Indiana Hospitality with 4-H Families and Friends.

Fresh Corn Skillet, p. 186

Debbie Stutman, inset, of Southborough, Massachusetts, learned how to cook Summer Vegetable Gratin, below, from her grandmother, who had a prolific vegetable garden.

Summer Vegetable Gratin, p. 189

Strawberry Spinach Toss, p. 206

Sweet Potato **Salad, p.** 209

Jackie George, above, of Santiago, Iowa, says she reaches for the Santiago Community Centennial Cookbook at least once a week. She created Sweet Potato Salad, top left, in memory of her grandfather. Sweet potatoes were a popular food at picnics at his home. Cheesy Wild Rice Casserole, bottom left, is so creamy, so good, and so easy! Serve it with ham, beef, or poultry.

Cheesy Wild Rice Casserole, p. 213

Weslaco Grapefruit Salad, p. 211

Clare and Bill Braden, left, owners of a 44-acre citrus orchard outside Harlingen, Texas, claim their favorite ways to enjoy oranges and grapefruit are "with friends or alone. At mealtime or in between." Their Weslaco Grapefruit Salad, above, is named for a Texas town.

Margaret's Company Refrigerator Mashed Potatoes

From the Waldorf Ladies Auxiliary Cookbook II. benefiting the Waldorf Volunteer Fire Department & Rescue Squad. Waldorf. Maryland

5	lb. baking potatoes
1	8-oz. pkg. cream cheese, softened
1	8-oz. carton dairy sour cream
1	tsp. salt
1	tsp. dried parsley
1/2	tsp. garlic powder
1/4	tsp. black pepper

2	Tbsp. butter or margarine, cut up
	Paprika

Prep: 50 min. **Chill:** 6 hr. **Bake:** 1 hr. 20 min.

1. Peel and quarter potatoes. In covered large saucepan, cook potatoes in a moderate amount of boiling water for 20 to 25 minutes or until tender. Drain and mash.

2. Add cream cheese to hot mashed potatoes and stir until combined. Stir in sour cream, salt, parsley, garlic powder, and black pepper. Spread mashed potatoes in a lightly greased 3-quart casserole. Dot with butter; sprinkle with paprika. Cover and chill in refrigerator for at least 6 hours or up to 24 hours.

3. To serve, bake, covered, in a 350°F oven about 1 hour and 20 minutes or until an instant-read thermometer inserted in center registers 165°F.

Makes about 12 servings.
Per serving: 262 cal., 13 g total fat (8 g sat. fat), 35 mg chol., 286 mg sodium, 31 g carbo., 3 g fiber, 7 g pro. Dietary exchanges: 2 starch, 2 fat.

Carrot Potato Boats

From Balancing Acts, cookbook of the
American Gold Gymnastics program, Fargo, North Dakota

3	medium baking potatoes (5½ to 6 oz. each)
1	cup chopped carrots (about 2 medium)
½	of an 8-oz. pkg. fat-free cream cheese, softened

2	Tbsp. thinly sliced green onion
¼	tsp. salt
	Black pepper
1	to 2 tablespoons milk (optional)
	Sliced green onion (optional)

Prep: 30 min. **Bake:** 1 hr. 12 min.

PICK A POTATO
Whether you're in the mood for mashed, baked, boiled, or fried potatoes will determine which potato is the best type to use. High-starch potatoes, such as russets—which have a light, mealy texture—are best for baked potatoes, potato pancakes, French fries, and mashed potatoes. Medium-starch potatoes, such as yellow Finns and Yukon golds, are a good choice for roasting or making into gratins. Low-starch potatoes, often called waxy potatoes, are dense and hold their shape, making them ideal for roasting and potato salads. Most red and round white varieties are low-starch potatoes.

1. Scrub potatoes thoroughly with a brush; pat dry. Prick with a fork. Bake in a 375°F oven for 60 to 70 minutes or until tender. Cool until easy to handle. Halve potatoes lengthwise; scoop out pulp, leaving ¼-inch-thick shells. Meanwhile, cook carrots in a small amount of boiling water about 15 minutes. Drain. Mash carrots and set aside.

2. Mash potato pulp. Combine with cream cheese, the 2 tablespoons green onion, the salt, and black pepper. Stir in mashed carrots. If necessary, add 1 or 2 tablespoons milk to make a fluffy consistency. Spoon into potato shells. Bake in a 375°F oven for 12 to 15 minutes or until heated through. Garnish with additional green onion, if desired.

Makes 6 servings.
Per serving: 108 cal., 0 g total fat (0 g sat. fat), 3 mg chol., 109 mg sodium, 22 g carbo., 1 g fiber, 5 g pro. Dietary exchanges: 1 vegetable, 1 starch.

Potato-Cabbage Casserole

*From Cooking at the Irish Settlement, cookbook of
St. Patrick's Church, Cumming, Iowa*

1	lb. potatoes, sliced
1/3	cup chopped onion
2	Tbsp. butter or margarine
8	cups shredded cabbage
1	10¾-oz. can condensed cream of mushroom soup
¾	cup milk
½	cup shredded cheddar cheese (2 oz.)
½	tsp. black pepper

1/4	tsp. dried rosemary, crushed
1/8	tsp. garlic salt
1	cup soft bread crumbs
2	Tbsp. butter or margarine, melted

Prep: 25 min. **Bake:** 30 min.

1. Place potatoes in a large saucepan; add enough water to cover. Bring to boiling; reduce heat. Cover and simmer about 10 minutes or just until tender. Drain; set aside.

2. Meanwhile, in a large saucepan or Dutch oven, cook onion in 2 tablespoons butter until tender. Add cabbage; cover and cook about 5 minutes or just until cabbage wilts. Stir in condensed soup, milk, cheddar cheese, black pepper, rosemary, and garlic salt. Cook and stir until cheese melts. Carefully stir in potatoes.

3. Lightly grease a 2-quart square baking dish; spoon potato mixture into dish. Combine bread crumbs and 2 tablespoons melted butter; sprinkle over casserole. Bake, uncovered, in a 350°F oven for 30 minutes.

Makes 6 servings.

Per serving: 275 cal., 16 g total fat (5 g sat. fat), 13 mg chol., 594 mg sodium, 27 g carbo., 4 g fiber, 8 g pro. Dietary exchanges: 1 vegetable, 1 starch, 3 fat.

TOMATO TIPS
Before using tomatoes in pasta sauce or salsa, the tomatoes' peels and seeds often need to be removed. Here's an easy way: Make a shallow "X" on the bottom of the tomato, then place the tomato on a slotted spoon. Dip it into a pan of boiling water for 15 seconds; rinse with cold water. After the tomato has cooled slightly, use a paring knife to gently pull on the peel where the scored skin has begun to split. The skin will slip off easily. To remove the seeds, cut the tomato in half crosswise. Holding one half over a bowl, use the tip of a spoon to scoop out the seeds.

Marinated Tomatoes Edisto

From 'Pon Top Edisto: Cookin' 'Tweenst the Rivers, cookbook of Trinity Episcopal Church, Edisto Island, South Carolina

1½	lbs. tomatoes (such as red and/or yellow regular, plum, and/or cherry tomatoes), sliced
⅓	cup olive oil
¼	cup red wine vinegar
½	of a small red onion, cut into thin strips
1	Tbsp. shredded fresh basil or 1 tsp. dried basil, crushed
½	tsp. salt
¼	tsp. black pepper
1	small clove garlic, minced, or ¼ tsp. garlic powder
	Fresh basil leaves (optional)

Prep: 15 min. **Chill:** 4 hr.

1. Arrange tomatoes in a single layer in a large shallow dish. In screw-top jar, combine oil, vinegar, onion, basil, salt, black pepper, and garlic. Cover; shake well. Pour dressing over tomatoes. Cover and refrigerate for at least 4 hours or up to 24 hours. Garnish with fresh basil leaves, if desired.

Makes 4 to 6 servings.

Per serving: 198 cal., 19 g total fat (2 g sat. fat), 0 mg chol., 282 mg sodium, 10 g carbo., 2 g fiber, 2 g pro. Dietary exchanges: 2 vegetable, 3 fat.

Orange Almond Salad

From Cooks Extraordinaires, cookbook of the
Service League of Green Bay, Wisconsin

¼	cup rice vinegar
¼	cup salad oil
3	Tbsp. sugar
½	tsp. salt
½	tsp. black pepper
½	tsp. almond extract
	Butter
¼	cup sugar
¼	cup slivered almonds

6	cups torn mixed greens or fresh spinach
2	11-oz. cans mandarin oranges, chilled and drained
1	cup chopped celery
2	green onions, coarsely chopped

Prep: 20 min. **Chill:** 2 hr.

For the Children
The members of the Service League of Green Bay, Wisconsin, are devoted to helping children. As a fund-raising project, the league put together Cooks Extraordinaires, a 300-plus-page cookbook, first published in celebration of the league's 60th anniversary.

1. For dressing, in a screw-top jar, combine the vinegar, oil, the 3 tablespoons sugar, the salt, black pepper, and almond extract. Cover and shake well. Chill in the refrigerator for at least 2 hours or up to 24 hours.

2. For candied almonds, butter a large piece of foil; set aside. In a small skillet, cook the ¼ cup sugar and slivered almonds over medium-high heat until the sugar begins to melt. Do not stir. Once the sugar begins to melt, reduce heat to low; cook for 3 to 5 minutes more or until all the sugar is melted and golden, stirring occasionally. Pour almond mixture onto buttered foil; cool completely. Break into pieces; set aside.

3. In a large salad bowl, toss together the greens, oranges, celery, green onions, and candied almonds. Drizzle some of the dressing over salad; toss to coat. Pass remaining dressing. Cover and store any leftover dressing in the refrigerator for up to 2 weeks.

Makes 4 servings.
Per serving: 321 cal., 18 g total fat (2 g sat. fat), 0 mg chol., 324 mg sodium, 38 g carbo., 4 g fiber, 4 g pro. Dietary exchanges: 3 vegetable, 1 fruit, ½ starch, 3 fat.

Strawberry Spinach Toss

From Balancing Acts, cookbook of the
American Gold Gymnastics program, Fargo, North Dakota

PHOTO APPEARS ON PAGE 198

5	cups torn spinach	2	Tbsp. lime juice
1	cup sliced strawberries	2	Tbsp. honey
1	cup honeydew melon or cantaloupe balls	1	Tbsp. salad oil
2	oz. Gouda or Edam cheese, cut into thin, bite-size strips	1/2	tsp. fresh ginger or 1/4 tsp. ground ginger
1/3	cup coarsely chopped pecans, toasted		

Start to finish: 25 min.

Around Town

Fargo-Moorhead, North Dakota-Minnesota (pop. 125,000) These sister towns straddle the Red River and sit in the middle of rich, fertile farmland that produces an abundance of potatoes, sugar beets, wheat, corn, and soybeans.

1. In a salad bowl, toss together spinach, strawberries, melon, cheese, and pecans. For dressing, in a screw-top jar, combine remaining ingredients. Cover; shake well. Pour some dressing over spinach mixture. Toss to coat.

Pass remaining dressing.

Makes 6 servings.
Per serving: 145 cal., 9 g total fat (2 g sat. fat), 11 mg chol., 119 mg sodium, 13 g carbo., 2 g fiber, 4 g pro.
Dietary exchanges: 1 vegetable, 1/2 fruit, 2 fat.

Coleslaw Crunch Salad

*From Cooks Extraordinaires, cookbook of the
Service League of Green Bay, Wisconsin*

¾	cup salad oil
⅓	cup sugar
⅓	cup white vinegar
2	2.8-oz. pkgs. beef-flavored ramen noodles
1	16-oz. pkg. shredded cabbage with carrot (coleslaw mix) (about 8 cups)

1	cup slivered almonds, toasted
2	medium carrots, chopped or shredded (1 cup)
½	cup sliced green onions
½	cup shelled sunflower seeds

Start to finish: 20 min.

TOAST 'EM
Toasting nuts, seeds, and coconut enhances their flavor and gives them a mouth-pleasing crunch. Spread the correctly measured amount of nuts, seeds, or coconut in a single layer in a shallow pan. Bake in a 350°F oven for 7 to 10 minutes, stirring once, until golden brown. Watch carefully to prevent burning.

1. For dressing, in a medium bowl, whisk together oil, sugar, vinegar, and the seasoning packets from the ramen noodles. Set aside.

2. In an extra-large bowl, combine the dry ramen noodles, cabbage, almonds, carrots, green onions, and sunflower seeds. Drizzle dressing over the cabbage mixture. Toss to coat.

Makes 8 servings.
Per serving: 486 cal., 38 g total fat (4 g sat. fat), 0 mg chol., 395 mg sodium, 32 g carbo., 5 g fiber, 9 g pro.
Dietary exchanges: 3 vegetable, 1 starch, 6 fat.

Vegetable Salad

From Garden of Eatin'. 50th anniversary cookbook of the
First Evangelical Free Church of Wichita, Kansas

1	15- to 17-oz. can peas, drained
1	14½- to 17-oz. can white or yellow whole kernel corn, drained
1	14½- to 16-oz. can French-cut green beans, drained
1	cup chopped celery (2 stalks)
½	cup chopped green sweet pepper (1 small)
½	cup sliced green onions

1	4-oz. jar diced pimiento, drained
½	cup sugar
¼	cup olive oil
¼	cup vinegar

Prep: 10 min. **Chill:** 6 hr. **Stand:** 15 min.

Anniversary Gift
To commemorate their church's 50th anniversary, the members of the First Evangelical Free Church of Wichita compiled Garden of Eatin'. The book, which the authors say is full of the love of good cooking, features everything from a tongue-in-cheek version of Pastor Tom's Grilled Cheese Sandwich to Baked Chicken Dijon to High Top 10-inch Apple Pie.

1. In a large bowl, combine peas, corn, green beans, celery, sweet pepper, green onions, and pimiento. In a small bowl, combine sugar, oil, and vinegar, stirring until sugar is dissolved. Pour sugar mixture over vegetable mixture, stirring well to combine. Cover and chill in the refrigerator for at least 6 hours or up to 24 hours, stirring occasionally. Let stand for 15 minutes before serving; stir. Serve with a slotted spoon.

Test Kitchen Tip: If you have any of the salad left over, cover and store it in the refrigerator for up to 3 days.

Makes 10 servings.
Per serving: 140 cal., 6 g total fat (1 g sat. fat), 0 mg chol., 350 mg sodium, 20 g carbo., 3 g fiber, 2 g pro. Dietary exchanges: 1 vegetable, 1 fat.

Sweet Potato Salad

*From the Santiago Community Centennial Cookbook, cookbook of
The Friends and Neighbors of Santiago, Iowa*

4	lb. sweet potatoes, peeled and cubed (about 9 cups)
1/4	tsp. salt (optional)
2	cups light mayonnaise dressing or salad dressing
2	Tbsp. finely shredded orange peel
2/3	cup orange juice
2	Tbsp. honey
1/2	tsp. grated fresh ginger or 1/8 tsp. ground ginger
1/4	tsp. ground nutmeg
2	cups sliced celery
1/2	cup snipped dried apricots
1	cup chopped walnuts or pecans
1	8-oz. can pineapple tidbits, drained
	Celery leaves (optional)

Prep: 40 min. **Chill:** 8 hr.

1. Place potatoes in a large pot; add water to cover and, if desired, salt. Bring to boiling; reduce heat. Simmer, covered, for 15 minutes or until potatoes are just tender. Drain well and cool slightly.

2. Meanwhile, for dressing, in a very large mixing bowl, combine mayonnaise, orange peel, orange juice, honey, ginger, and nutmeg. Stir in celery and apricots. Add potatoes. Toss lightly to coat. Cover; chill in the refrigerator for 8 to 24 hours.

3. To serve, stir in nuts and pineapple. Garnish with celery leaves, if desired.

Makes 16 to 20 servings.

Per serving: 274 cal., 15 g total fat (2 g sat. fat), 0 mg chol., 244 mg sodium, 34 g carbo., 4 g fiber, 3 g pro. Dietary exchanges: 1/2 fruit, 2 starch, 2 fat.

From the Heart of Iowa
Published in 1991 to raise money for the 100th birthday celebration of the central Iowa town of Santiago, the Santiago Community Centennial Cookbook is a hefty collection of favorite recipes from local cooks. The Friends and Neighbors of Santiago (FANS) handpicked the heavenly tastes of Iowa to fill the 350-page cookbook.

Fruit and Cream Layered Salad

From *Women Who Can Dish It Out*, cookbook of the
Junior League of Springfield, Missouri

1/2	of an 8-oz. container fat-free or reduced-fat frozen whipped dessert topping, thawed
1	8-oz. carton strawberry low-fat yogurt
1/2	of an 8-oz. pkg. reduced-fat cream cheese, softened
1	Tbsp. sugar
2	tsp. lemon juice
1/4	tsp. almond extract
8	cups bite-size pieces of fresh

and/or canned, drained fruit (such as melon, strawberries, seedless grapes, apples, pears, peeled peaches, apricots, and/or bananas)
Whole strawberries (optional)

2 Tbsp. sliced, toasted almonds

Start to finish: 30 min.

STRAWBERRY SMARTS
The best way to keep fresh strawberries looking and tasting their best is to choose brightly colored, plump berries with the leaves still attached. Wash strawberries only right before you're ready to eat them—and store them in a moistureproof container in the refrigerator for 2 to 3 days.

1. Set aside 2 tablespoons of the whipped dessert topping for garnish. In a medium bowl, gradually stir or whisk yogurt into cream cheese until smooth. Stir in sugar, lemon juice, and almond extract; fold in the remaining whipped dessert topping.

2. In a large (about 2 1/2-quart) clear glass serving bowl, layer half of the fruit. Top with half of the yogurt mixture. Repeat layers, spreading yogurt mixture to edge of bowl. Serve immediately or cover and chill in the refrigerator for up to 1 hour. Before serving, garnish with reserved whipped topping and, if desired, whole strawberries. Sprinkle with almonds.

Makes 12 to 14 servings.
Per serving: 102 cal., 3 g total fat (2 g sat. fat), 8 mg chol., 55 mg sodium, 15 g carbo., 2 g fiber, 3 g pro. Dietary exchanges: 1/2 milk, 1/2 fruit, 1/2 fat.

Weslaco Grapefruit Salad

From Clare and Bill Braden.
Harlingen, Texas

PHOTO APPEARS ON PAGE 200

4	cups grapefruit sections (9 to 10 grapefruit)
1	cup sugar
2	envelopes unflavored gelatin
3/4	cup cold water

1/2	cup chopped pecans
1	or 2 drops red food coloring (optional)
	Whipped cream (optional)
	Grapefruit peel curls (optional)

Prep: 30 min. **Chill:** 6 hr.

1. In a mixing bowl, combine grapefruit sections and 3/4 cup of the sugar. Set aside. In a small mixing bowl, combine gelatin and 1/2 cup of the cold water. Let stand for 5 minutes.

2. Meanwhile, in a medium saucepan, combine the 1/4 cup remaining sugar and remaining 1/4 cup cold water. Heat and stir until sugar dissolves. Add gelatin mixture, grapefruit mixture, pecans, and, if desired, food coloring.

Cook and stir until sugar is completely dissolved. Pour grapefruit mixture into a 2-quart mold or square baking dish. Cover; chill for at least 6 hours. If using mold, unmold salad. Serve with whipped cream, if desired. Garnish with grapefruit peel curls, if desired.

Makes 9 servings.

Per serving: 170 cal., 4 g total fat (0 g sat. fat), 0 mg chol., 3 mg sodium, 33 g carbo., 2 g fiber, 2 g pro. Dietary exchanges: 2 fruit, 1 fat.

At Home in the Grove

Retirees Clare and Bill Braden decided to buy a citrus orchard in 1987, after living aboard an oceangoing sailboat for seven years. They wanted to build a house somewhere warm that would be surrounded by trees. What the couple got—they realized later—was a rundown orchard in sad shape. Then, in 1989, their dream was wiped out in the Christmas freeze. They rebuilt. Two years later, the Bradens had their first crop. Now they send grapefruit all over the country.

Green Rice
From the Damen Kegel-Verein Cookbook,
Austin, Texas

Bowling, Anyone?
The Damen Kegel-Verein (German for Ladies' Bowling Club) Cookbook supports the charitable and social activities of the club. Dating back to 1935, Damen Kegel-Verein is for the wives of the members of Saengerrunde, a singing society for men of German heritage in the Austin, Texas, area.

⅓	cup long grain rice
⅔	cup water
¾	cup chopped green sweet pepper
⅓	cup snipped fresh parsley
¼	cup chopped green onion tops
1	8-oz. pkg. process cheese spread, cubed
1	beaten egg
¼	cup milk

Prep: 25 min. **Bake:** 30 min. **Stand:** 5 min.

1. In a small saucepan, stir together rice and water. Bring to boiling; reduce heat. Cover and simmer about 15 minutes or until rice is tender. In a medium bowl, stir together the cooked rice, sweet pepper, parsley, and green onion tops. Add cheese, egg, and milk. Stir until combined. Turn into a greased 1-quart casserole. Bake, uncovered, in a 350°F oven for 15 minutes; stir. Bake, uncovered, about 15 minutes more or until golden and bubbly around edges. Let stand 5 minutes before serving.

Makes 4 or 5 servings.

Per serving: 258 cal., 14 g total fat (8 g sat. fat), 86 mg chol., 951 mg sodium, 21 g carbo., 1 g fiber, 13 g pro. Dietary exchanges: 1 vegetable, 1 starch, 1 high-fat meat, 1 fat.

Cheesy Wild Rice Casserole

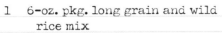

From *Out of the Ordinary*, cookbook of the
Hingham Historical Society, Hingham, Massachusetts

1 6-oz. pkg. long grain and wild
   rice mix
1 4-oz. can sliced mushrooms,
   drained
2½ cups water
1 10-oz. pkg. frozen chopped
   spinach
¾ cup chopped onion

1 Tbsp. butter or margarine
2 tsp. prepared mustard
¼ tsp. ground nutmeg
1 8-oz. pkg. cream cheese, cut
   into cubes

Prep: 20 min. **Bake:** 35 min. **Stand:** 5 min.

Hingham's History
Founded in 1635, the 17th-century Puritan village of Hingham, Massachusetts, grew into an 18th-century town of traders, shipbuilders, and farmers, whose spacious square houses still line the town's streets.

1. In a 2-quart casserole, combine rice mix and seasoning packet with mushrooms. In a medium saucepan, combine water, spinach, onion, butter, mustard, and nutmeg. Bring to boiling; remove from heat. Stir; pour over rice mixture. Stir in cream cheese.

2. Bake, covered, in a 375°F oven for 20 minutes. Stir mixture. Cover; bake 15 to 20 minutes more or until rice is tender. Stir again. Let stand 5 minutes before serving.

Test Kitchen Tip: This rice dish tastes just as creamy when you make it with reduced-fat cream cheese (Neufchâtel). And the casserole can be assembled ahead and refrigerated for up to 2 hours before baking. Add a few extra minutes to the baking time to heat the casserole through.

Makes 6 to 8 servings.
Per serving: 271 cal., 16 g total fat (10 g sat. fat), 47 mg chol., 692 mg sodium, 26 g carbo., 3 g fiber, 7 g pro. Dietary exchanges: 2 vegetable, 1 starch, 3 fat.

Cornbelt Special

From *West of the Rockies*, cookbook of the
Junior Service League of Grand Junction, Colorado

The family dinner hour is as important as ever in Grand Junction, Colorado, thanks to the Junior Service League and its cookbook, West of the Rockies. In 1995, the league created its first-ever cookbook to help fund local charities. The book was an instant hit, but just as successful has been the league's mission to see that Grand Junction's households eat dinner together regularly as families. They call the project the Discover Dinnertime Challenge. The league teamed up with a local grocery store and a TV station to promote the Dinnertime Challenge.

1	$15^1/4$-oz. can cream-style corn
2	beaten eggs
1	8-oz. carton dairy sour cream
$^1/4$	cup butter or margarine, melted
1	$14^3/4$-oz. can whole kernel corn, drained
$1^1/2$	cups shredded cheddar cheese (6 oz.)
1	medium onion, chopped ($^1/2$ cup)
1	$4^1/2$-oz. can chopped green chiles, drained
1	$8^1/2$-oz. pkg. corn muffin mix

Prep: 10 min. **Bake:** $1^1/4$ hr. **Stand:** 5 min.

1. Grease a 2-quart casserole; set aside. In a large bowl, combine cream-style corn, eggs, sour cream, and melted butter. Stir in corn, cheddar cheese, onion, and green chiles. Add corn muffin mix, stirring just until moistened. Turn into prepared 2-quart casserole.

2. Bake in a 350°F oven for $1^1/4$ hours or until knife inserted in center comes out clean and top is golden. Let stand for 5 minutes before serving.

Makes 8 to 10 servings.
Per serving: 407 cal., 24 g total fat (12 g sat. fat), 104 mg chol., 730 mg sodium, 40 g carbo., 1 g fiber, 12 g pro. Dietary exchanges: 2½ starch, 1 medium-fat meat, 3 fat.

10.

Sweets

Fannie's Fudge

From the St. James at Sag Bridge Church Cookbook,
Lemont, Illinois

2	cups sugar
1/2	cup butter
1/2	cup milk
1	cup semisweet chocolate pieces (6 oz.)
1	cup milk chocolate pieces (6 oz.)

12	large marshmallows or 1 1/4 cups tiny marshmallows
1	tsp. vanilla
1/2	cup chopped nuts (optional)

Prep: 20 min. **Chill:** 4 hr.

Visions of Sugarplums

At the St. James at Sag Bridge parish's annual Christmas party, dinner is catered—except for dessert. For this congregation, there are no sweets as delicious as the host of heavenly specialties prepared by the Ladies Guild. St. James has 700 families, and it's blessed with a lot of good cooks. The evidence is in the St. James at Sag Bridge Church Cookbook.

1. Butter a 9×9×2-inch baking pan, or line pan with foil and butter foil. Set aside.

2. In a large saucepan, combine sugar, butter, and milk. Bring mixture to a full rolling boil over medium heat; reduce heat. Boil for 2 minutes. Remove from heat.

3. Stir in chocolate pieces, marshmallows, and vanilla. Continue stirring until smooth. Stir in nuts, if desired. Spread in prepared pan. Chill in the refrigerator about 4 hours or until firm. Cut into 1-inch squares. Store in covered container in refrigerator or freezer.

Makes about 2 pounds (72 pieces).
Per piece: 61 cal., 3 g total fat (2 g sat. fat), 4 mg chol., 17 mg sodium, 9 g carbo., 0 g fiber, 0 g pro. Dietary exchanges: 1/2 other carbo., 1/2 fat.

Caramels

From the St. James at Sag Bridge Church Cookbook.
Lemont, Illinois

	Butter		
½	cup chopped pecans	1	cup light-colored corn syrup
3	Tbsp. butter	½	of a 12-oz. can evaporated milk
1½	cups sugar		(³⁄₄ cup)
1½	cups whipping cream	¼	tsp. salt
		½	tsp. vanilla

Prep: 10 min. **Cook:** 45 min.

1. Line a 9×9×2-inch baking pan with foil, extending foil over edges of pan. Butter foil. Sprinkle pecans onto bottom of pan; set aside. Butter the sides of a large saucepan.

2. In the saucepan, melt the 3 tablespoons butter over low heat. Stir in sugar, whipping cream, corn syrup, evaporated milk, and salt, mixing well. Cook and stir mixture over medium-high heat until boiling.

3. Clip a candy thermometer to side of pan. Reduce heat to medium. (If necessary, reduce heat to medium-low to prevent mixture from boiling over.)

Continue boiling at a moderate, steady rate, stirring frequently, until the thermometer registers 248°F, firm-ball stage (45 to 55 minutes).

4. Remove pan from heat; remove thermometer. Stir in vanilla. Quickly pour mixture into the prepared pan. When mixture is firm, use foil to lift it out of pan. Use a buttered knife to cut into 1-inch squares. Wrap each square in plastic wrap or make decorative wrappers.

Makes 1³⁄₄ pounds (about 64 pieces).
Per piece: 66 cal., 4 g total fat (2 g sat. fat), 11 mg chol., 27 mg sodium, 9 g carbo., 0 g fiber, 0 g pro. Dietary exchanges: ½ other carbo., ½ fat.

Ol' South Pralines

From the Jack Daniel Distillery,
Lynchburg, Tennessee

2	cups sugar	2½	cups pecan halves
1	cup buttermilk or sour milk	2	Tbsp. butter
1	tsp. baking soda	¼	cup whiskey
⅛	tsp. salt	1	tsp. vanilla

Prep: 15 min. **Cook:** 20 min.

IF YOU DON'T HAVE BUTTERMILK
Sour milk can be substituted for buttermilk in most recipes. If you don't happen to have sour milk sitting around, here's a quick and easy way to make it. For each cup of sour milk you need, place 1 tablespoon lemon juice or vinegar in a glass measuring cup; add enough milk to make 1 cup total liquid. Let the mixture stand for 5 minutes before using it in your recipe.

1. Line two large baking sheets with foil; lightly grease foil. Set aside. In a heavy large saucepan, combine sugar, buttermilk, baking soda, and salt. Cook and stir over medium-high heat until mixture boils, stirring constantly. Reduce heat to medium. Clip candy thermometer to side of pan.

2. Stir in pecans and butter; cook and stir until thermometer registers 234°F, about 20 minutes. Watch carefully and reduce heat, if necessary, to prevent mixture from boiling over. Remove from heat. Stir in whiskey and vanilla. Immediately beat the mixture vigorously with a wooden spoon about 7 minutes or until mixture begins to thicken. Quickly drop candy by spoonfuls onto prepared baking sheets.

Makes about 36 pralines.
Per praline: 104 cal., 6 g total fat (1 g sat. fat), 2 mg chol., 57 mg sodium, 12 g carbo., 1 g fiber, 1 g pro.
Dietary exchanges: 1 fat.

English Toffee

*From Around the World, Around Our Town, cookbook of
Friends of the San Pedro Library, San Pedro, California*

2	cups	butter (1 lb.)
2	cups	sugar
1/3	cup	water
2	Tbsp.	light-colored corn syrup

1	cup chopped, toasted almonds
1	7- or 8-oz. bar milk chocolate

Prep: 10 min. **Cook:** 25 min.

1. Line a 9×9×2-inch baking pan with foil, extending foil over edges of pan; set aside.

2. In a large saucepan, melt butter; add sugar, water, and corn syrup. Bring to boiling, stirring to dissolve sugar. Clip candy thermometer to side of pan. Cook over medium heat, stirring frequently, until thermometer registers 290°F, soft-crack stage. (Mixture should boil at a moderate, steady rate over the entire surface.) Reaching 290°F should take 25 to 30 minutes. (Watch carefully after candy mixture reaches 280°F to prevent scorching.) Remove saucepan from heat.

3. Stir in 1/2 cup of the almonds. Pour mixture into prepared pan. Set aside to cool.

4. In a heavy small saucepan, melt chocolate over low heat; spread half of the melted chocolate over toffee. Sprinkle with 1/4 cup of the remaining almonds. Place in the refrigerator for a few minutes to allow chocolate to harden.

5. Turn candy out of pan. Remove foil. Spread second side with the remaining melted chocolate; sprinkle with the remaining 1/4 cup almonds. Chill in refrigerator for a few minutes or until chocolate is set. Break into pieces. Store tightly covered for up to 2 weeks.

Makes about 2½ pounds (60 servings).
Per serving: 115 cal., 9 g total fat (4 g sat. fat), 18 mg chol., 70 mg sodium, 9 g carbo., 0 g fiber, 1 g pro. Dietary exchanges: 1 other carbo., 1 fat.

Port of Flavors
Explore the southern edge of Los Angeles and you'll find a little bit of Norway, or Ireland, or Croatia, or Mexico—depending on whom you ask. What you've discovered is San Pedro, California—an historic port of entry and shipping center that's grown into the busiest harbor in the United States. Today it's home to a lively mix of nationalities—new arrivals and descendants of families from all over the world who have settled here. So when Friends of the San Pedro Library proposed a fund-raising cookbook, an international theme was the obvious choice.

Apple-Cheese Bars

From *Slices & Bites of the Wenatchee Valley,*
cookbook of the Applarians, Wenatchee, Washington

2	cups all-purpose flour		1	cup shredded cheddar cheese (4 oz.)
1	cup butter, softened		3/4	cup granulated sugar
1/2	cup granulated sugar		1/4	cup all-purpose flour
2	egg yolks		1	tsp. ground cinnamon
1	tsp. baking powder		2	egg whites
4	medium cooking apples, such as Golden Delicious, Rome, Granny Smith, Jonathan, or Newtown pippin, peeled and shredded		1 1/2	cups sifted powdered sugar
			1/4	cup cream cheese, softened (about 2 oz.)

Prep: 25 min. **Bake:** 40 min.

Around Town
Wenatchee,
Washington
(pop. 24,000)
From late June to
mid-October, fresh
fruit is harvested in
the Wenatchee Valley.
Cherries begin the
harvest season,
followed by apricots,
peaches, pears, and,
finally, apples.

1. For crust, in a medium bowl, combine the 2 cups flour, butter, the 1/2 cup granulated sugar, the egg yolks, and baking powder; beat with an electric mixer until mixture is crumbly. Press half of the crumb mixture into a 13×9×2-inch baking pan. Bake in a 350°F oven for 10 to 12 minutes or until lightly browned. Set aside.

2. Combine apples, cheddar cheese, the 3/4 cup granulated sugar, the 1/4 cup flour, and the cinnamon. Spread on crust. Sprinkle with the remaining crumb mixture. Set aside.

3. Beat egg whites with electric mixer until soft peaks form. Gradually beat in powdered sugar and cream cheese. Spoon over crumb mixture. Bake for 30 to 35 minutes more. Cool completely.

Makes 36 bars.
Per bar: 147 cal., 7 g total fat (4 g sat. fat), 31 mg chol., 94 mg sodium, 19 g carbo., 0 g fiber, 2 g pro. Dietary exchanges: 1/2 fruit, 1 starch, 1 fat.

Lemon Gooey Bars

From Chautauqua Celebrations, cookbook of the
Chautauqua Arts Festival, Wytheville, Virginia

1   beaten egg
1/3 cup butter, melted
4   tsp. finely shredded lemon peel
3   Tbsp. lemon juice
1   2-layer-size pkg. white cake
    mix
1   cup chopped nuts
1   8-oz. pkg. cream cheese,
    softened

3   cups sifted powdered sugar
2   eggs
    Sifted powdered sugar

Prep: 20 min. **Bake:** 30 min.

1. Grease a 13×9×2-inch baking pan; set aside.

2. For crust, in medium bowl, stir together the 1 egg, the butter, lemon peel, and lemon juice. Stir in dry cake mix and nuts until combined. (Mixture will be thick.) Press evenly into the bottom of prepared pan. Bake in a 350°F oven about 15 minutes or until crust is lightly browned.

3. Meanwhile, for topping, in a large mixing bowl beat cream cheese with an electric mixer until fluffy. Gradually beat in the 3 cups powdered sugar until smooth. Add eggs, one at a time, beating on low speed after each addition just until combined. Pour evenly over the hot crust.

4. Bake for 15 to 20 minutes more or until top is golden and set. Cool in pan on a wire rack. Sprinkle with additional powdered sugar. Cut into bars.

Makes 24 bars.
Per bar: 238 cal., 12 g total fat (5 g sat. fat), 44 mg chol., 213 mg sodium, 31 g carbo., 0 g fiber, 2 g pro. Dietary exchanges: 2 other carbo., 2 fat.

The Arts are Alive
Theodore Roosevelt once said that chautauquas (lectures, concerts, and plays presented in open-air venues) were "the most American thing about America." Back in the late 19th century, touring chautauquas began as places for people to enrich themselves through art, education, and recreation. By the 1920s, about 12,000 chautauquas criss-crossed the country. Wytheville, Virginia, was one stop on the circuit. Like many chautauquas, Wytheville's was discontinued during the Great Depression. In 1985, however, residents there revived the tradition.

Cherry Walnut Bars

From A Christmas Carroll: Have a Dickens of a Time in the Kitchen,
community cookbook of Carroll, Iowa

2 1/4	cups all-purpose flour
1/2	cup granulated sugar
1	cup butter, softened
3	eggs
1 1/2	cups packed brown sugar
3/4	tsp. baking powder
3/4	tsp. salt
3/4	tsp. vanilla

1	6-oz. jar maraschino cherries, drained and chopped (reserving 1/4 cup liquid)
1/2	cup chopped walnuts
2	cups sifted powdered sugar
2	Tbsp. butter or margarine, softened

Prep: 25 min. **Bake:** 45 min.

1. Lightly grease a 13×9×2-inch baking pan; set aside. In a large bowl, combine flour and granulated sugar; cut in the 1 cup butter until crumbly. Press into prepared pan. Bake in a 350°F oven for 20 minutes.

2. Meanwhile, in a medium bowl stir together eggs, brown sugar, baking powder, salt, and vanilla. Add cherries and walnuts. Spoon on top of baked crust. Bake for 25 minutes more. Cool on wire rack.

3. Combine the powdered sugar, the 2 tablespoons butter, and enough of the reserved cherry liquid (3 to 4 tablespoons) to make icing of spreading consistency. Spread or pipe over bars.

Makes 48 bars.

Per bar: 119 cal., 5 g total fat (3 g sat. fat), 25 mg chol., 88 mg sodium, 17 g carbo., 0 g fiber, 1 g pro. Dietary exchanges: 1/2 fruit, 1/2 starch, 1 fat.

Streusel Strawberry Bars

From Robin Deyo,
Barre, Vermont

PAGE PHOTO APPEARS ON 233

1	cup butter, softened
1	cup granulated sugar
1	egg
2	cups all-purpose flour
3/4	cup pecans, coarsely chopped
1	10-oz. jar strawberry or raspberry preserves
	Powdered Sugar Icing or sifted powdered sugar

Prep: 20 min. **Bake:** 45 min.

1. In a medium mixing bowl, beat butter and granulated sugar with an electric mixer on medium speed until combined, scraping sides of bowl occasionally. Beat in egg.

2. Beat in as much flour as you can with the mixer. Stir in any remaining flour. Stir in pecans. Set aside 1 cup of the pecan mixture.

3. Press the remaining pecan mixture into the bottom of an ungreased 9×9×2-inch baking pan. Spread preserves to within 1/2 inch of the edges of the bottom crust. Dot the 1 cup reserved pecan mixture on top of preserves. Bake in a 350°F oven about 45 minutes or until top is golden brown. Cool on a wire rack. Drizzle with Powdered Sugar Icing or sprinkle with powdered sugar. Cut into bars.

Powdered Sugar Icing: In a small mixing bowl, combine 1 cup sifted powdered sugar, 1 tablespoon milk, and 1/4 teaspoon vanilla. Stir in additional milk, 1 teaspoon at a time, until icing is of drizzling consistency.

Makes 24 bars.
Per bar: 209 cal., 11 g total fat (5 g sat. fat), 31 mg chol., 91 mg sodium, 28 g carbo., 1 g fiber, 2 g pro. Dietary exchanges: 1 starch, 1/2 fat.

Grandma's Brownies

From The Pleasant Hill United Methodist Church Women's
Favorite Recipes Cookbook, Topeka, Kansas

2	cups all-purpose flour		1	1-lb. pkg. powdered sugar
2	cups granulated sugar			Dash salt
1	tsp. baking soda		1/2	cup butter
1/2	tsp. salt		1/3	cup buttermilk or sour milk
1	cup water		1/4	cup unsweetened cocoa powder
1/2	cup butter, cut up		1	tsp. vanilla
1/2	cup cooking oil		1/2	cup chopped pecans or walnuts
1/4	cup unsweetened cocoa powder			(optional)
1/2	cup buttermilk or sour milk			
2	eggs			
1	tsp. vanilla			

Prep: 20 min. **Bake:** 25 min.

Love and Brownies

The pages of the Pleasant Hill United Methodist Church Women's Favorite Recipes Cookbook are as full of old-fashioned advice as they are of tempting home-style recipes. A sample: "My mom's the finest cook around, and she told me long ago, 'That bread's no good unless you add some loving to the dough'."

---

1. Grease a 15×10×1-inch baking pan; set aside. In a large bowl, stir together flour, granulated sugar, baking soda, and the 1/2 teaspoon salt; set aside. In a medium saucepan, combine the water, 1/2 cup butter, the oil, and 1/4 cup cocoa powder. Heat just to boiling, stirring to melt butter; add hot liquid to flour mixture. Beat with an electric mixer on low speed just until dry ingredients are moistened. Add the 1/2 cup buttermilk, the eggs, and 1 teaspoon vanilla. Beat on low speed for 1 minute without overbeating. (Batter will be thin.)

2. Pour into the prepared baking pan. Bake in a 350°F oven for 25 to 30 minutes or until a toothpick inserted in center comes out clean. Place pan on a wire rack.

3. For frosting, in a large bowl, combine powdered sugar and salt; set aside. In a medium saucepan, combine 1/2 cup butter, the 1/3 cup buttermilk, and 1/4 cup cocoa powder; beat and stir over medium heat until butter is melted. Pour hot buttermilk mixture over powdered sugar mixture. Add 1 teaspoon vanilla. Beat with an electric mixer on low speed just until combined; beat on medium speed until smooth. By hand, stir in nuts, if desired. Carefully pour the warm frosting over the warm brownies; spread evenly. Cool completely. Cut into bars.

Makes 48 brownies.

Per brownie: 150 cal., 7 g total fat (3 g sat. fat), 20 mg chol., 102 mg sodium, 22 g carbo., 0 g fiber, 1 g pro. Dietary exchanges: 1½ other carbo., ½ fat.

Chocolate Goody Bars

From Lynn Lhotka, winner of the Betty Crocker
50th Anniversary of Cake-Mix Bake Sales Competition

1	19.8-oz. pkg. fudge brownie mix
1/2	cup cooking oil
2	eggs
1/4	cup water
1	16-oz. can vanilla frosting
3/4	cup chopped peanuts
3	cups crisp rice cereal

1	cup creamy peanut butter
1	12-oz. pkg. semisweet chocolate pieces

Prep: 20 min. **Bake:** 28 min.

1. Grease a 13×9×2-inch baking pan; set aside.

2. In a large bowl, stir together brownie mix, oil, eggs, and water until well mixed. Spread mixture into prepared pan.

3. Bake in a 350°F oven for 28 to 30 minutes or until toothpick inserted 2 inches from side of pan comes out clean. Cool completely on wire rack.

4. Frost with frosting. Sprinkle with peanuts. Cover; chill in the refrigerator.

5. Meanwhile, place rice cereal in a medium bowl. In a small saucepan, combine peanut butter and chocolate pieces. Heat and stir over low heat until chocolate is melted. Pour over cereal. Stir to coat evenly. Spread over frosting. Cover; chill in the refrigerator until chocolate layer is set. Refrigerate leftover bars, covered.

Makes 36 bars.
Per bar: 261 cal., 14 g total fat (2 g sat. fat), 12 mg chol., 150 mg sodium, 33 g carbo., 1 g fiber, 4 g pro. Dietary exchanges: 2 starch, 2 fat.

Bake Sale Success

The women of Trinity Lutheran Church in Birchwood, Wisconsin, offer these prizewinning tips on making your next bake sale a smashing success:

• Pick the best place in town to hold your sale, and be consistent with the location and date.

• Let people know how the bake sale proceeds will be used.

• Seek matching funds. The church women got additional money from Lutheran insurance and fraternal organizations.

• Make items look special. For their autumn sale, the church women decorate the price tags with raffia ribbon and colorful leaves that buyers can use to create fall arrangements at home.

Peanut Butter Cup Bars

From Balancing Acts, cookbook of the
American Gold Gymnastics program, Fargo, North Dakota

3/4	cup butter or margarine
1	cup creamy peanut butter
2	cups graham cracker crumbs
2	cups sifted powdered sugar
1	cup milk chocolate pieces

Prep: 10 min. **Chill:** 5 min.

1. Line a 13×9×2-inch baking pan with foil. In a large saucepan, melt butter over low heat. Add peanut butter; stir until smooth. Remove from heat. Stir in graham cracker crumbs and sugar until combined. Press mixture firmly and evenly in bottom of prepared pan.

2. In a small saucepan, melt chocolate pieces over very low heat, stirring until smooth. Spread over crumb layer. Place in refrigerator for 5 minutes or until chocolate is firm. Lift foil from pan; cut into bars.

Makes 48 bars.
Per bar: 106 cal., 7 g total fat (2 g sat. fat), 8 mg chol., 77 mg sodium, 10 g carbo., 0 g fiber, 2 g pro. Dietary exchanges: 1 starch, ½ fat.

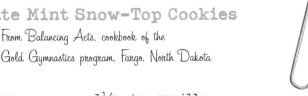

Chocolate Mint Snow-Top Cookies

From Balancing Acts, cookbook of the
American Gold Gymnastics program, Fargo, North Dakota

1¹/₃	cups all-purpose flour
1¹/₂	tsp. baking powder
¹/₄	tsp. salt
1¹/₂	cups semisweet chocolate pieces
6	Tbsp. butter, softened
1	cup granulated sugar
2	eggs

1¹/₂	tsp. vanilla
¹/₄	tsp. mint flavoring
	Powdered sugar

Prep: 15 min. **Chill:** 30 min.
Bake: 10 min. per batch

1. Combine flour, baking powder, and salt; set aside.

2. In a small saucepan, heat 1 cup of the chocolate pieces over low heat until melted, stirring constantly.

3. In a large bowl, beat butter with electric mixer on medium speed for 30 seconds. Beat in granulated sugar until fluffy. Beat in melted chocolate, eggs, vanilla, and mint flavoring.

4. Gradually beat in the flour mixture and remaining ¹/₂ cup chocolate pieces.

Wrap dough in plastic wrap. Freeze for 30 minutes or until firm enough to shape into balls. Shape dough into 1-inch balls; roll in powdered sugar. Place about 2 inches apart on ungreased cookie sheet. Bake in a 350°F oven for 10 to 12 minutes or until tops are crackled. Cool for 2 minutes. Transfer to wire rack; cool.

Makes 42 cookies.
Per cookie: 83 cal., 4 g total fat (1 g sat. fat), 15 mg chol., 46 mg sodium, 3 g carbo., 0 g fiber, 1 g pro. Dietary exchanges: 1 starch.

HOMETOWN Tip

A CHOCOLATE GUIDE
Here are the main types of chocolate you'll see on the supermarket shelf:

•**Unsweetened chocolate** is the basic type of chocolate from which all others are made. Sometimes called baking or butter chocolate, unsweetened chocolate is pure chocolate with no sugar or flavoring added.

•**Semisweet chocolate** is pure chocolate with cocoa butter and sugar added to it.

•**Sweet baking chocolate** is similar to semisweet but has a higher sugar content.

•**Milk chocolate** is made of pure chocolate, extra cocoa butter, sugar, and milk solids.

Waffle Cookies

From the 125th Anniversary Cookbook of
Zion Lutheran Church, Hampton, Nebraska

2	oz. unsweetened chocolate, cut up		2	Tbsp. light-colored corn syrup
1/3	cup butter or margarine		1	Tbsp. cooking oil
3/4	cup sugar		1/2	cup chopped pecans
2	beaten eggs			
1	tsp. vanilla			
1	cup all-purpose flour			
1	cup semisweet chocolate pieces (6 oz.)			

Start to finish: 50 min.

Pride Guides Them

Hampton, Nebraska, is a quiet little town, surrounded by cornfields on the Great Plains. It's a place where you'd expect a tidy church that beckons townsfolk with its tall white steeple. It's also a place where you'd expect to find some great home cooking. The steeple belongs to Zion Lutheran Church. The great cooking is found in the church's 125th Anniversary Cookbook. It's full of recipes that members have served at socials and on their own family tables through the years.

1. Preheat waffle iron. In a medium saucepan, melt unsweetened chocolate and butter over low heat. Cool slightly. Stir in sugar, eggs, and vanilla. Add flour; stir just until combined.

2. Drop rounded teaspoonfuls of batter into center of each waffle grid. Bake on medium heat about 75 seconds. Using a fork, transfer cookies to rack; cool. Repeat with remaining batter.

3. In a small saucepan, combine semisweet chocolate pieces, corn syrup, and oil. Cook and stir over low heat just until smooth. Cool before using. Spread over cookies; sprinkle with pecans.

Makes 24 cookies.
Per cookie: 140 cal., 8 g total fat (2 g sat. fat), 25 mg chol., 33 mg sodium, 17 g carbo., 0 g fiber, 2 g pro. Dietary exchanges: 1½ starch, 1½ fat.

Pecan Shortbread Raspberry Cookies

From Peggy Russell of Ojai, California, winner of the Land O'Lakes Best Cookie Contest at the Los Angeles County Fair

1	cup butter
2/3	cup granulated sugar
1	tsp. vanilla
1/2	tsp. almond extract
2	cups all-purpose flour
1	cup ground pecans

	Powdered sugar
1/3	cup seedless raspberry preserves

Prep: 40 min.   **Chill:** 1 hr.   **Bake:** 7 min.

1. In a large bowl, beat butter with electric mixer on medium to high speed for 30 seconds. Add granulated sugar, vanilla, and almond extract; beat until fluffy, scraping bowl often. Beat in flour and pecans until combined. Wrap dough in plastic wrap; chill for 1 to 2 hours or until dough is easy to handle.

2. On a slightly floured surface, roll dough, half at a time, to 1/8-inch thickness. Using a 2-inch round scalloped cookie cutter, cut rounds from dough. Place 1 inch apart on ungreased cookie sheets. Using a 1-inch round cutter, cut centers from half of the unbaked cookies. Remove centers; reroll dough to make more cookies. Bake in a 350°F oven for 7 to 9 minutes or until edges are firm and bottoms are lightly browned. Cool on racks.

3. To assemble, sift powdered sugar over tops of cookies with holes; set aside. Spread about 1/2 teaspoon of the preserves onto top of each cookie without a hole. Top with a cookie with a hole, sugar side up.

Makes about 40 cookies.
Per cookie: 100 cal., 6 g total fat (3 g sat. fat), 12 mg chol., 47 mg sodium, 10 g carbo., 0 g fiber, 1 g pro. Dietary exchanges: 1 starch, ½ fat.

Queen of Cookies
Peggy Russell loves to bake cookies. From Thanksgiving to Christmas, she produces more than 2,000! She also loves to show off her talents at the Los Angeles County Fair. In a Land O'Lakes-sponsored contest, her cookie version of an Austrian torte won first place and was named national state fair winner in 1999. Peggy's prizes from Land O'Lakes included $500 and a year's supply of butter, sour cream, and cheese. She baked every day and took the treats to the office.

The Ultimate Ginger Cookies

From Heritage Recipes, cookbook of the
Oregon Genealogical Society, Eugene, Oregon

3/4	cup butter, softened
1	cup packed brown sugar
1/4	cup mild-flavored molasses
1	egg
2 1/4	cups all-purpose flour
2	tsp. baking soda
2	tsp. ground ginger
1/2	tsp. salt

1	2.7-oz. jar crystallized ginger, finely chopped (1/2 cup)
4	tsp. grated fresh ginger

Prep: 20 min. **Chill:** 2 hr.
Bake: 10 min. per batch

CANDIED GINGER
Crystallized ginger (also called candied ginger) is fresh ginger that's been boiled in a sugar syrup, then dipped in sugar and dried. It imparts a fiery sweetness to foods. For a sweet-hot treat, it can be dipped in melted bittersweet chocolate, allowed to dry, and served as part of a dessert tray. Look for crystallized ginger in the baking aisle or near the herbs and spices in your local supermarket. Don't buy pieces that are hard, stuck together, or missing their sugar coating; these signs indicate the ginger is old or of poor quality.

1. In a large bowl, beat butter with an electric mixer on medium to high speed for 30 seconds. Beat in brown sugar until fluffy. Beat in molasses and egg.

2. In a medium bowl, stir together flour, baking soda, ground ginger, and salt. Beat as much of the flour mixture into the butter mixture as you can with the mixer; stir in any remaining flour mixture. Stir in crystallized ginger and fresh ginger. Wrap dough in plastic wrap and chill in the refrigerator for 2 hours or until easy to handle. (Or chill for up to 24 hours. If dough becomes too stiff, let stand at room temperature for 20 to 30 minutes before using.)

3. Shape dough into 1-inch balls. Place balls, 2 inches apart, on ungreased cookie sheets. Bake in a 350°F oven for 10 minutes or until browned and set. Cool on wire racks. Store in airtight container for up to 3 days or freeze for up to 1 month.

Makes 60 cookies.
Per cookie: 60 cal., 3 g total fat (2 g sat. fat), 10 mg chol., 89 mg sodium, 9 g carbo., 0 g fiber, 1 g pro. Dietary exchanges: 1/2 other carbo.

Coconut Dreams

From the Barnebirkie Cookie Book.
Hayward. Wisconsin

½	cup butter, softened
½	cup sugar
¼	tsp. baking soda
1	egg yolk
1	cup all-purpose flour
1	cup flaked coconut

Prep: 20 min. **Chill:** 8 hr.
Bake: 8 min. per batch

1. In a large bowl, beat butter with an electric mixer on medium to high speed for 30 seconds. Add sugar and baking soda. Beat until combined, scraping sides of bowl occasionally. Beat in egg yolk. Beat in as much of the flour as you can with the mixer; stir in any remaining flour and coconut. Shape into a 10-inch-long log. Wrap in plastic wrap or waxed paper. Chill in refrigerator for 8 hours or overnight.

2. Using a sharp knife, cut log into ¼ inch-thick slices. Place 1 inch apart on ungreased cookie sheets. Bake in a 350°F oven for 8 to 9 minutes or until edges are firm. Cool on cookie sheet for 1 minute; transfer to wire racks; cool.

Makes 36 cookies.
Per cookie: 57 cal., 4 g total fat (2 g sat. fat), 13 mg chol., 37 mg sodium, 6 g carbo., 0 g fiber, 1 g pro. Dietary exchanges: ½ other carbo., ½ fat.

Ready. Set. Ski! Each February. the Barnebirkie (BAR-nah-byeer-kee). a children's cross-country ski race. is held in Hayward. Wisconsin. It's followed by the American Birkebeiner (BYEER-kah-biner) for adults. The American Birkebeiner is the largest cross-country ski marathon in North America. The 43-kilometer course attracts men and women from around the world. Competitors ski from Telemark Lodge in Cable. Wisconsin. to Main Street in Hayward.

Honey-Roasted Chocolate Chippers

From I'll Cook When Pigs Fly—And They Do in Cincinnati!,
cookbook of the Junior League of Cincinnati, Ohio

3/4	cup butter-flavored shortening		1	cup semisweet chocolate pieces (6 oz.)
1	cup packed brown sugar		1/2	cup honey-roasted peanuts
1 1/2	tsp. ground cinnamon		3	1.6- to 2-oz. chocolate-coated
1	tsp. baking powder			caramel candy bars or
1/2	tsp. baking soda			chocolate-coated caramel-
1	tsp. salt			topped nougat bars with
1	egg			peanuts, chopped
1	tsp. milk			
1	tsp. vanilla			
1 3/4	cups all-purpose flour			**Prep:** 25 min. **Bake:** 10 min. per batch
1/2	cup rolled oats			

1. In a large bowl, beat shortening with an electric mixer on medium to high speed for 30 seconds. Add brown sugar, cinnamon, baking powder, baking soda, and salt. Beat until combined, scraping side of bowl occasionally. Beat in egg, milk, and vanilla; beat in as much flour as you can with the mixer. Stir in remaining flour and oats. Stir in chocolate pieces, peanuts, and chopped candy bars.

2. Grease cookie sheets; set aside. Roll dough into balls about 2 inches in diameter. Place 1 inch apart on prepared cookie sheets. Bake in a 350°F oven about 10 minutes or until golden brown. Cool on cookie sheets for 2 minutes. Transfer to wire rack; cool.

Makes 36 cookies.
Per cookie: 144 cal., 8 g total fat (2 g sat. fat), 7 mg chol., 118 mg sodium, 16 g carbo., 1 g fiber, 2 g pro. Dietary exchanges: 1 1/2 other carbo.

Streusel Strawberry Bars, p. 223

For a town festival one summer, the women of Trinity Lutheran Church in Birchwood, Wisconsin, announced they were serving two of their prizewinners from the Betty Crocker 50th Anniversary of Cake-Mix Bake Sales Competition at an ice cream social. Chocolate Goody Bars, right, was one of them. Twice as many people as they expected came to enjoy the goodies.

Chocolate Goody Bars, p. 225

Peanut Butter Cup Bars, p. 226

Chocolate Mint Snow-Top Cookies, p. 227

A sweet or two is a well-earned reward for the girls of the American Gold Gymnastics program of Fargo, North Dakota. Recipes for Peanut Butter Cup Bars and Chocolate Mint Snow-Top Cookies, left, come from Balancing Acts, a cookbook benefiting the AGG program.

Pecan Shortbread Raspberry Cookies, p. 229

Peggy Russell, top, of Ojai, California, loves to bake cookies. Pecan Shortbread Raspberry Cookies won her first place at the Land O'Lakes-sponsored contest at the Los Angeles County Fair. If you don't want to fuss with a filled cookie, just make cutouts of the dough. These cookies can stand on their own without the jam.

Angel Food Cake with Lemon Cream and Berries, p. 248

Committee members (from left) Kim Erdel, Darlene McCrachen, and Martha Gaska helped update Ozark cooking in Women Who Can Dish It Out, the cookbook of the Junior League of Springfield, Missouri. Angel Food Cake with Lemon Cream and Berries, above, is one of the book's desserts.

Chocolate Caramel Cheesecake, p. 250

Heavenly Raspberry Pie, right, brings out the best flavor of raspberries because it's a divine combination of cooked and fresh berries. Strawberries with Cannoli Cream, below right, has the flavor of the famous Italian pastry and the freshness of lush strawberries. It's a quick, elegant dessert for company that goes together in less than 10 minutes.

Heavenly Raspberry Pie, p. 253

Strawberries with Cannoli Cream, p. 257

Honey-Cardamom Crunch, p. 265

Rebecca Vancuren, above, of Edwards, Colorado, created colorful, sweet-and-tart Honey-Cardamom Crunch, above left, for the Chex Recipe Contest. Her creation won her $5,000. Vary the flavor of dreamy Chocolate and Sherry Cream Bars, below left, by choosing a different liqueur each time you make them.

Chocolate and Sherry Cream Bars, p. 274

Christmas Pound Cake, p. 278

Fuss Cookies

From *Linen Napkins to Paper Plates*, cookbook of the
Junior Auxiliary of Clarksville, Tennessee

1	cup butter, softened
1/3	cup granulated sugar
1	tsp. vanilla
1/4	tsp. salt
2 1/2	cups all-purpose flour
	Apple jelly (about 1/4 cup)

Pecan halves (about 48)
Powdered sugar (optional)

Prep: 25 min. **Bake:** 8 min. per batch

1. In a large mixing bowl, beat butter with an electric mixer on medium to high speed for 30 seconds. Add granulated sugar, vanilla, and salt. Beat until well combined. Beat in as much of the flour as you can. With a wooden spoon, stir in the remaining flour.

2. Shape dough into 1-inch balls. Place 1 inch apart on an ungreased cookie sheet. Flatten balls slightly with the palm of your hand. Press your thumb into the center of each ball. (Edges will have cracks.) Place about 1/4 teaspoon of the apple jelly in center of each ball. Top with a pecan half.

3. Bake in a 400°F oven for 8 to 10 minutes or until edges are lightly browned. Transfer cookies to a wire rack and let cool. Just before serving, sprinkle cookies with powdered sugar, if desired.

Makes 48 cookies.
Per cookie: 76 cal., 5 g total fat (3 g sat. fat), 11 mg chol., 54 mg sodium, 7 g carbo., 0 g fiber, 1 g pro. Dietary exchanges: 1/2 starch, 1 fat.

Colorful History
In their book *Linen Napkins to Paper Plates*, the members of the Junior Auxiliary of Clarksville, Tennessee, combine Southern-style cooking with a helping of local reminiscences and recipe history. An example is the story of Fuss Cookies. In the 1920s, two women quarreled at a club luncheon about the recipe, causing quite a "fuss" around Clarksville. From then on, the cookies had a new name.

Eleven-Cup Cookies

From Biggest Hits, cookbook of the
Elk Grove Renegades softball team, Elk Grove, California

1 cup butter, softened	1 cup raisins
1 cup peanut butter	1 cup semisweet chocolate pieces (8 oz.)
1 cup granulated sugar	
1 cup packed light brown sugar	1 cup cereal (such as crisp rice cereal, corn flakes, bran cereal flakes, or wheat cereal flakes)
1 tsp. baking soda	
1 tsp. baking powder	
2 eggs	
1 cup all-purpose flour	1 cup chopped walnuts
1 cup quick-cooking rolled oats	
1 cup coconut	**Prep:** 30 min. **Bake:** 9 min. per pan

1. In a very large bowl, beat butter and peanut butter with an electric mixer on medium to high speed for 30 seconds. Add granulated sugar, brown sugar, baking soda, and baking powder. Beat until combined, scraping side of bowl occasionally. Beat in eggs. Beat in as much of the flour as you can with the mixer. Stir in remaining flour, the rolled oats, coconut, raisins, chocolate pieces, cereal, and walnuts.

2. Drop dough by rounded teaspoons 2 inches apart on an ungreased cookie sheet. Bake in a 350°F oven for 9 to 11 minutes or until edges are golden. Cool on cookie sheet for 1 minute. Transfer to a wire rack; cool.

Makes about 60 cookies.
Per cookie: 137 cal., 8 g total fat (3 g sat. fat), 16 mg chol., 90 mg sodium, 14 g carbo., 1 g fiber, 2 g pro. Dietary exchanges: 1 other carbo., 1 fat.

Chocolate Cake with Peanut Butter Frosting

*From Downhome Desserts from the Heart of Iowa, a cookbook benefiting
Exceptional Concepts, Burt, Iowa*

2	cups all-purpose flour
2	cups granulated sugar
2/3	cup unsweetened cocoa powder
1	tsp. baking soda
1/2	tsp. baking powder
1/2	tsp. salt
2	eggs
3/4	cup milk
2/3	cup cooking oil
1	tsp. vanilla
2	tsp. instant coffee crystals

1	cup cold water
1	3-oz. pkg. cream cheese, softened
1/4	cup creamy peanut butter
2	Tbsp. milk
1/2	tsp. vanilla
2 1/4	to 2 1/2 cups sifted powdered sugar

Prep: 10 min. **Bake:** 35 min. **Cool:** 1 hr.

1. For cake, grease a 13×9×2-inch baking pan; set aside. In a large bowl, stir together flour, granulated sugar, cocoa powder, baking soda, baking powder, and salt. Add eggs, the 3/4 cup milk, the oil, and the 1 teaspoon vanilla. Beat with an electric mixer on low speed until combined, then on medium speed for 2 minutes.

2. Dissolve coffee crystals in the cold water; add to flour mixture. Beat on low speed until smooth. (Batter will be thin.) Pour into prepared pan. Bake in a 350°F oven for 35 to 40 minutes or until toothpick inserted in center comes out clean. Cool cake for 1 hour in pan on wire rack.

3. For frosting, in a medium bowl, beat together cream cheese and peanut butter. (Mixture will become thick.) Gradually beat in the 2 tablespoons milk and the 1/2 teaspoon vanilla. Beat in enough of the powdered sugar to make frosting of spreading consistency. Spread on cake. Sprinkle with 3 tablespoons semisweet chocolate pieces, if desired.

Makes 15 servings.
Per serving: 380 cal., 15 g total fat (4 g sat. fat), 36 mg chol., 228 mg sodium, 56 g carbo., 1 g fiber, 5 g pro. Dietary exchanges: 4 other carbo., 3 fat.

Helping Hands
Deep in Iowa farm country, you'll find Burt, a community that bills itself as "the little town with the big heart and helping hand." Living up to that claim are the volunteers of Exceptional Concepts, who for more than 30 years have been assisting local area residents with disabilities. To support its work, the organization put together two cookbooks of favorite recipes from cooks who live in north-central Iowa. In the 230-page Downhome Desserts from the Heart of Iowa, are cookies, pies, cakes, and hundreds of other desserts to tempt even those who claim not to crave sweets.

Mississippi Mud Cake

From *Worth Savoring*, cookbook of the
Union County Historical Society, New Albany, Mississippi

2 cups granulated sugar	1 7-oz. jar marshmallow ice-cream topping
1 cup butter, melted	1/2 cup butter, melted
1/2 cup unsweetened cocoa powder	1/3 cup unsweetened cocoa powder
4 eggs	1/4 cup evaporated milk
1 tsp. vanilla	2 tsp. vanilla
1 1/4 cups all-purpose flour	4 cups sifted powdered sugar
1 cup chopped nuts (such as pecans or walnuts)	
1 cup flaked coconut	

Prep: 20 min. **Bake:** 30 min. **Chill:** Up to 24 hr.

Eat These Words

The folks of New Albany, Mississippi, are proud of their literary heritage, including writer William Faulkner, and their culinary treasures. In fact, they have been gathering recipes for their town cookbooks for at least **65 years.** Their cookbook, *Worth Savoring*, created by the Union County Historical Society, features reflections from native New Albany writers and many old-time family recipes such as *Mississippi Mud Cake*, whose layers of chocolate cake, marshmallow, and cocoa frosting give the gooey cake its name.

1. Grease and lightly flour a 13×9×2-inch baking pan; set aside. In a large bowl, beat together the granulated sugar, the 1 cup butter, and the 1/2 cup cocoa powder with an electric mixer on medium speed until smooth. Add the eggs, one at a time, beating well after each addition. Add the 1 teaspoon vanilla. Beat in the flour until just combined. With a wooden spoon, stir in the nuts and coconut. Spread mixture into the prepared baking pan.

2. Bake in a 350°F oven for 30 minutes or until a toothpick inserted near the center comes out clean. Remove from oven and place on a wire rack. Carefully spread the marshmallow ice cream topping on top. Cool completely.

3. In a large mixing bowl, beat the 1/2 cup melted butter, the 1/3 cup cocoa powder, the evaporated milk, and the 2 teaspoons vanilla with an electric mixer on medium speed until smooth. Slowly beat in powdered sugar. Spread over cake. Cover and chill in the refrigerator for up to 24 hours. Cut just before serving.

Makes 15 servings.
Per serving: 360 cal., 18 g total fat (9 g sat. fat), 69 mg chol., 142 mg sodium, 48 g carbo., 1 g fiber, 4 g pro.
Dietary exchanges: 3 other carbo., 3 fat.

Jam Cake

From Linen Napkins to Paper Plates, cookbook of the
Junior Auxiliary of Clarksville, Tennessee

2 cups self-rising flour*	1/2 cup buttermilk
1 tsp. ground cinnamon	1 cup raisins
1/2 tsp. ground allspice	1 cup pitted, chopped dates
1/2 tsp. ground nutmeg	1 cup chopped nuts
1/4 tsp. ground cloves	1/2 cup butter
1/2 cup butter, softened	1 cup packed brown sugar
1 cup granulated sugar	1/4 cup milk
2 eggs	2 1/2 cups sifted powdered sugar
1 cup seedless blackberry jam	
1 cup unsweetened applesauce	**Prep:** 25 min. **Bake:** 40 min.

1. Grease a 13×9×2-inch baking pan; set aside. Stir together flour, cinnamon, allspice, nutmeg, and cloves; set aside.

2. In a large mixing bowl, beat the softened butter with an electric mixer on medium to high speed for 30 seconds. Add granulated sugar and beat until well combined. Add eggs one at a time, beating well after each. Beat in jam and applesauce until combined. Add the flour mixture and buttermilk alternately to beaten mixture, beating on low speed until combined. Stir in raisins, dates, and nuts. Pour batter into prepared pan.

3. Bake in a 350°F oven for 40 to 45 minutes or until a wooden toothpick inserted in center comes out clean. Place cake in pan on a wire rack and cool completely.

4. In a medium skillet, melt the 1/2 cup butter over medium heat. Stir in brown sugar. Bring boiling; reduce heat. Simmer, uncovered, for 2 minutes, stirring often. Carefully add milk. Cook and stir for 1 minute more. Remove from heat; cool for 5 minutes. In a large bowl, combine powdered sugar and the slightly cooled brown sugar mixture; beat with an electric mixer on low speed until smooth. Frost cooled cake immediately.

*Note: If desired, for the self-rising flour, substitute 2 cups all-purpose flour, 2 teaspoons baking powder, 1 teaspoon salt, and 1/2 teaspoon baking soda.

Makes 12 servings.
Per serving: 676 cal., 24 g total fat (11 g sat. fat), 80 mg chol., 472 mg sodium, 114 g carbo., 4 g fiber, 6 g pro. Dietary exchanges: 1 1/2 fruit, 6 other carbo., 5 fat.

Orange Snacking Cake

From Flavors of Washington County, a cookbook benefiting the
Washington County Historical Society, Washington County, Wisconsin

Town by Town
When members of the Washington County (Wisconsin) Historical Society compiled a cookbook to raise funds for the Old Courthouse Renovation Project, they diligently gathered recipes from the county's 13 towns. It became a labor of love and a way of preserving the life, times, and recipes of the past for generations to come.

1	cup sugar
1/2	cup shortening
2	eggs
2	cups all-purpose flour
1	tsp. baking soda
1/4	tsp. salt
1	cup buttermilk or sour milk*
1	Tbsp. finely shredded orange peel

1	cup raisins
1	cup chopped walnuts or pecans
1/3	cup sugar
1/3	cup orange juice

Prep: 20 min. **Bake:** 30 min. **Cool:** 30 min.

1. Grease a 13×9×2-inch baking pan; set aside.

2. In a large bowl, beat the 1 cup sugar and the shortening with an electric mixer on medium to high speed until well mixed. Add eggs, one at a time, beating well after each. Stir together flour, baking soda, and salt. Add flour mixture and buttermilk alternately to egg mixture, beating on low speed after each addition just until combined. By hand, stir in orange peel; fold in raisins and nuts. Spread batter in prepared pan.

3. Bake in a 350°F oven about 30 minutes or until a toothpick inserted in center comes out clean. Stir together the 1/3 cup sugar and the orange juice; gradually pour over baked cake. Cool in pan on wire rack for 30 minutes. Serve warm, or cool completely on wire rack.

*Note: To make 1 cup sour milk, place 1 tablespoon lemon juice or vinegar in a glass measuring cup. Add enough milk to make 1 cup total liquid; stir. Let the mixture stand in for 5 minutes before using.

Makes 15 servings.
Per serving: 283 cal., 13 g total fat (3 g sat. fat), 29 mg chol., 150 mg sodium, 39 g carbo., 1 g fiber, 5 g pro. Dietary exchanges: 2½ other carbo., 2 fat.

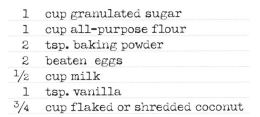

One-Minute Cake Tried and True

From *Downhome Desserts from the Heart of Iowa,* a cookbook benefiting
Exceptional Concepts, Burt, Iowa

1	cup granulated sugar		1/2	cup packed brown sugar
1	cup all-purpose flour		1/2	cup chopped walnuts or pecans
2	tsp. baking powder		1/3	cup butter or margarine
2	beaten eggs		3	Tbsp. milk
1/2	cup milk		1/4	tsp. salt
1	tsp. vanilla			
3/4	cup flaked or shredded coconut			

Prep: 10 min. **Bake:** 30 min.

1. For cake, grease an 8×8×2-inch baking pan; set aside. In a large bowl, combine granulated sugar, flour, and baking powder. In a small bowl, combine eggs, the 1/2 cup milk, and the vanilla. Add all at once to flour mixture; mix well. Turn into prepared pan. Bake in a 375°F oven about 20 minutes or until a toothpick inserted near center comes out clean.

2. Meanwhile, for topping, in a medium saucepan, combine coconut, brown sugar, nuts, butter, the 3 tablespoons milk, and the salt. Cook and stir until butter is melted and brown sugar is dissolved. Spoon over hot cake. Increase oven temperature to 400°F. Bake about 10 minutes more or until topping is golden. Cool in pan on wire rack. Serve warm or at room temperature.

Makes 9 servings.
Per serving: 339 cal., 15 g total fat (7 g sat. fat), 68 mg chol., 255 mg sodium, 48 g carbo., 1 g fiber, 5 g pro. Dietary exchanges: 3 other carbo., 2 fat.

Angel Food Cake with Lemon Cream and Berries

From Women Who Can Dish It Out, cookbook of the
Junior League of Springfield, Missouri

1	16-oz. pkg. angel food cake mix		Strawberries, raspberries, and/or blueberries
2	8-oz. cartons lemon fat-free yogurt		
1	4-serving-size pkg. instant vanilla pudding mix		**Prep:** 15 min. **Bake:** Per package directions
1	8-oz. container frozen light whipped dessert topping, thawed		

PERFECT ANGEL FOOD CAKE
Whether they're made from scratch or from a mix, angel food cakes need to be cooled upside down to set their structures. Most 10-inch tube pans are outfitted with feet so the pan will sit level on the countertop as the cake cools upside down. If your tube pan doesn't have feet, you can turn it upside down and slip the open center of the pan over the neck of a narrow glass bottle.

1. Prepare and bake cake mix in a 10-inch tube pan or a 13×9×2-inch baking pan; bake according to package directions or until golden brown and top appears dry. Cool cake completely according to package directions. (If using the 13×9×2-inch pan, turn cake in pan upside down, resting corners of pan on four cans of equal height; cool completely.)

2. For lemon cream, in a medium bowl, stir together yogurt and one-fourth of the pudding mix until smooth. Gradually add remaining pudding mix to yogurt, stirring until smooth after each addition. Fold in whipped topping. Serve lemon cream and berries over cake.

Test Kitchen Tip: Any leftover lemon cream can be stored in the refrigerator for up to 4 days.

Makes 16 servings.
Per serving: 163 cal., 2 g total fat (2 g sat. fat), 1 mg chol., 325 mg sodium, 33 g carbo., 0 g fiber, 3 g pro. Dietary exchanges: 1 fruit, 1 starch, ½ fat.

Luscious Orange Sponge Cake

From Beneath the Palms, cookbook of the
Junior Service League of Brownsville, Texas

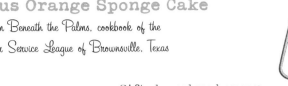

1 cup all-purpose flour	Sifted powdered sugar
1 tsp. baking powder	Orange Whipped Cream
1/4 tsp. salt	3 Tbsp. orange liqueur
3 eggs	
3/4 cup granulated sugar	**Prep:** 45 min. **Bake:** 15 min. **Chill:** 4 hr.
1/3 cup orange juice	
1/2 tsp. orange extract	

1. Grease and flour a 15×10×1-inch baking pan; set aside. Stir together flour, baking powder, and salt.

2. In a large bowl, beat eggs with electric mixer on high speed 4 minutes or until thick. Beat in granulated sugar on medium speed for 5 minutes or until fluffy. Add juice and extract; beat on low speed until combined. Add flour mixture; beat on low speed until combined. Pour batter into pan.

3. Bake in a 375°F oven for 15 minutes or until cake springs back when lightly touched. Loosen edges of cake from pan; turn cake out onto a towel sprinkled with powdered sugar. Transfer towel and cake to wire rack; cool. Prepare Orange Whipped Cream.

4. Cut cake crosswise into three 10×5-inch rectangles. Brush top of each rectangle with liqueur. Place one rectangle on platter. Top with 1 cup Orange Whipped Cream. Add another rectangle; top with 1 cup cream. Add last layer. Frost with remaining cream. Cover; chill for 4 to 24 hours.

Orange Whipped Cream: In a medium saucepan, combine 1 cup sugar, 1/3 cup flour, and dash salt. In a bowl, stir together 3 egg yolks, 1/2 cup orange juice, and 1 tablespoon lemon juice. Whisk yolk mixture into sugar mixture. Cook and stir over medium heat until thickened. Reduce heat; cook and stir 1 minute more. Remove from heat. Stir in 1/4 teaspoon grated orange peel. Set pan in ice water; cool, stirring occasionally. In chilled bowl, beat 1 1/2 cups whipping cream with electric mixer on medium speed until soft peaks form. Fold in egg mixture.

Makes 12 servings.
Per serving: 315 cal., 14 g total fat (8 g sat. fat), 147 mg chol., 124 mg sodium, 42 g carbo., 0 g fiber, 4 g pro. Dietary exchanges: 3 other carbo., 3 fat.

Down in the Valley: The cookbook committee that put together Beneath the Palms started with regional recipes that call on the fruits and vegetables of the Rio Grande Valley. The Valley, as locals call it, is a rich agricultural region where vegetables and fruits flourish year-round, including citrus fruits, mangoes, papayas, tomatillos, and Texas' famous 1015 Super Sweet Onions. With so many local fresh ingredients to cook with, committee members tested close to 2,000 recipes before settling on 250 of them. Every recipe in the book was tested at least three times.

Chocolate Caramel Cheesecake

*From the 125th Anniversary Cookbook of
Zion Lutheran Church, Hampton, Nebraska*

PAGE 237 PHOTO APPEARS ON

2	cups crushed vanilla wafers (about 50 wafers)	1/2	cup sugar
6	Tbsp. butter, melted	1	tsp. vanilla
1	14-oz. pkg. vanilla caramels (about 48 caramels)	2	eggs
1	5-oz. can evaporated milk	1/2	cup semisweet chocolate pieces, melted and slightly cooled
1	cup chopped pecans, toasted		
2	8-oz. pkg. cream cheese, softened		

Prep: 35 min. **Bake:** 40 min. **Chill:** 4 hr.
Stand: 20 min.

Around Town

Hampton, Nebraska (pop. 420) This rural community just off Interstate 80 is in the heart of corn—and Cornhusker—country. Locals head to York, Aurora, or Bradshaw for movies and dining. On football weekends, they keep their eye on the University of Nebraska football team 65 miles down the road in Lincoln.

1. For crust, combine crushed vanilla wafers and melted butter. Press mixture onto the bottom and about 2 inches up the sides of a 9-inch springform pan. Bake in a 350°F oven for 10 minutes. Cool and set aside.

2. In medium saucepan, combine caramels and evaporated milk. Cook and stir over low heat, stirring frequently, until smooth. Pour over prepared crust. Sprinkle with pecans. Chill in refrigerator while preparing filling.

3. For filling, in a medium bowl, beat cream cheese, sugar, and vanilla with an electric mixer on medium speed until combined. Add eggs, beating on low speed just until combined (do not overbeat); stir in melted chocolate. Pour over caramel-nut layer in pan.

4. Bake in a 350°F oven about 40 minutes or until center appears nearly set when shaken. Cool cheesecake in pan on a wire rack for 15 minutes. Loosen from side of springform pan; cool on wire rack. Cover and chill in refrigerator for at least 4 hours.

5. Let cheesecake stand at room temperature for 20 minutes before serving. Garnish each serving with whipped cream, chopped pecans, melted chocolate and/or chocolate curls, and caramel topping, if desired.

Makes 12 servings.
Per serving: 548 cal., 35 g total fat (15 g sat. fat), 106 mg chol., 322 mg sodium, 55 g carbo., 1 g fiber, 8 g pro. Dietary exchanges: 2 starch, 1 other carbo., 6 fat.

Fresh Ginger Cheesecake

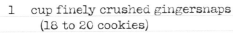

From Food to Light Up Your Life, cookbook of the volunteers of the
Hospice of Morongo Basin, California

1	cup finely crushed gingersnaps (18 to 20 cookies)
2	Tbsp. sugar
1/4	cup butter, melted
3	8-oz. packages cream cheese, softened
1 1/2	cups sugar
2	tsp. grated fresh ginger

1	tsp. lemon juice
1	tsp. vanilla
1/8	tsp. salt
4	eggs
1/2	cup whipping cream

Prep: 30 min. **Bake:** 45 min. **Cool:** 45 min.
Chill: 4 hr.

1. Stir together crushed gingersnaps and the 2 tablespoons sugar; stir in melted butter. Press onto bottom of an 8- or 9-inch springform pan. Bake in a 350°F oven for 10 minutes. Cool in pan on wire rack.

2. For filling, in a large bowl, beat cream cheese with electric mixer on low to medium speed until smooth. Gradually beat in the 1 1/2 cups sugar until smooth and fluffy. Beat in ginger, lemon juice, vanilla, and salt. Add eggs all at once; beat on low speed just until combined. (Do not overbeat.) Stir in whipping cream. Pour into crust-lined pan. Place on a shallow baking pan.

3. Bake in the 350°F oven about 45 minutes for the 9-inch pan or about 55 minutes for the 8-inch pan or until center is just set. Cool in pan on wire rack for 15 minutes. Loosen crust from side of pan; cool for 30 minutes more. Remove side of pan; cool cheesecake completely. (Top of cheesecake may crack during cooling.) Cover; chill in refrigerator for 4 to 24 hours.

Makes 12 servings.
Per serving: 439 cal., 30 g total fat (18 g sat. fat), 158 mg chol., 327 mg sodium, 36 g carbo., 0 g fiber, 7 g pro. Dietary exchanges: 2½ other carbo., 5 fat.

Compassion and Cookery

Although dedicated to giving emotional support and other care to their clients, the volunteers of the Hospice of Morongo Basin in California are also keenly interested in cooking. To take advantage of their volunteers' culinary skills, the hospice decided to put together Food to Light Up Your Life as a fund-raising project. As the call for help went out, all sorts of recipes came in—often with interesting names, such as Methuselah's Cocktail, Lithuanian Luau, and Cathedral Windows. The cheesecakes are eye-catching too. With this recipe, there's no need to go to a fancy bakery for an extra-special dessert.

Prizewinning Rhubarb-Apple Pie

From Belinda Myers of Dallastown, Pennsylvania.
Best of Show winner at the 1999 Lancaster County Rhubarb Festival

4	cups sliced fresh rhubarb		1	Tbsp. butter or margarine
1	cup peeled and chopped apple			Pastry for Double-Crust Pie
1²⁄₃	cups sugar			
¹⁄₃	cup all-purpose flour			
	Dash ground cinnamon			

Prep: 30 min. **Bake:** 50 min.

1. In a large saucepan, combine rhubarb, apple, sugar, flour, and cinnamon. Cook and stir over medium heat until mixture just begins to thicken. Remove from heat. Stir in butter or margarine. Cool.

2. Meanwhile, prepare pastry. On a lightly floured surface, roll out half of the pastry to a 12-inch circle and line a 9-inch pie plate with pastry. Transfer filling to pie plate. Trim pastry even with edge. Roll out remaining pastry to a 12-inch circle. Cut into 1¹⁄₂-inch-wide strips. Weave strips over filling for lattice crust. Press ends of strips into crust rim. Fold bottom pastry over strips; seal and crimp edge. Cover pie edge with foil. Bake in a 400°F oven for 25 minutes. Remove foil. Bake for 25 minutes more. Cool.

Pastry for Double-Crust Pie: Stir together 2 cups all-purpose flour and 1 teaspoon salt. Using a pastry blender, cut in ²⁄₃ cup butter-flavored shortening until pieces are pea-size. Sprinkle 1 tablespoon ice water over part of the mixture; gently toss with a fork. Push moistened dough to side of bowl. Repeat moistening dough, using 1 tablespoon ice water at a time (for a total of 6 to 7 tablespoons). Form dough into two balls.

Makes 8 servings.
Per serving: 482 cal., 21 g total fat (6 g sat. fat), 4 mg chol., 310 mg sodium, 71 g carbo., 2 g fiber, 4 g pro. Dietary exchanges: 2¹⁄₂ fruit, 2 starch, 4 fat.

Heavenly Raspberry Pie

From Perennial Palette, cookbook of the Southborough Gardeners, Southborough, Massachusetts

1	recipe Baked Pastry Shell	3	Tbsp. cornstarch
5	cups fresh or frozen raspberries	3/4	cup whipping cream
3/4	cup sugar	2	Tbsp. sugar
1/2	cup cold water		
3	Tbsp. lemon juice		

Prep: 40 min. **Chill:** 2 hr.

1. Prepare Baked Pastry Shell as directed; set aside.

2. In a medium saucepan, stir together 2 cups of the raspberries, the 3/4 cup sugar, the cold water, lemon juice, and cornstarch. Cook and stir over medium heat until thickened and bubbly; cook and stir for 2 minutes more. Remove from heat. Cool slightly. Cover and refrigerate until thoroughly chilled.

3. Carefully fold 2 cups of the remaining raspberries into the chilled mixture. Spoon into pastry shell. Cover; chill for at least 2 hours or until firm.

4. To serve, in a chilled medium bowl, combine whipping cream and the 2 tablespoons sugar; beat with chilled beaters of an electric mixer on medium speed until soft peaks form. Serve pie with whipped cream and the remaining 1 cup raspberries.

Baked Pastry Shell: Stir together 1 1/4 cups all-purpose flour and 1/4 teaspoon salt. Cut in 1/3 cup shortening. Moisten dough with 4 to 5 tablespoons cold water total, adding 1 tablespoon at a time and tossing with a fork. On a lightly floured surface, roll dough into a 12-inch circle. Ease pastry into a 9-inch pie plate. Trim pastry to 1/2 inch beyond edge of pie plate. Fold under extra pastry. Crimp edge. Prick bottom and side of pastry. Line pastry with a double thickness of foil. Bake in a 450°F oven for 8 minutes. Remove foil. Bake for 5 to 6 minutes more or until golden brown. Cool on wire rack.

Makes 8 servings.
Per serving: 350 cal., 17 g total fat (7 g sat. fat), 31 mg chol., 77 mg sodium, 47 g carbo., 6 g fiber, 3 g pro. Dietary exchanges: 3 other carbo., 2 fat.

Bake Me a Pie as Fast as You Can When recipe contributor Sandy Neff was growing up, she and her mother baked together every Saturday. Her father and three brothers would eat everything they made. One of their favorites was Heavenly Raspberry Pie. It's no wonder!

Sweet Potato Pie

From Blessings, cookbook of First Presbyterian Church, Pine Bluff, Arkansas

2 medium sweet potatoes (about 1 lb.), peeled and cubed	1/4 tsp. ground nutmeg
1 1/4 cups all-purpose flour	Dash salt
1/4 tsp. salt	3 slightly beaten eggs
1/3 cup shortening	1 12-oz. can evaporated milk
4 to 5 Tbsp. cold water	Whipped cream (optional)
1/4 cup butter or margarine	Ground nutmeg (optional)
3/4 to 1 cup packed brown sugar	
1 1/2 tsp. ground cinnamon	

Prep: 35 min. **Bake:** 50 min. **Cool:** 1 hr.

SWEET POTATO BASICS
To microcook sweet potatoes, place 1 pound peeled, cubed sweet potatoes in a casserole with 1/2 cup water. Microwave, covered, on 100 percent power (high) for 10 to 13 minutes. Cool, then mash, using an electric mixer or potato masher.
• 1 medium sweet potato weighs about 7 1/2 ounces.
• 1 medium sweet potato = 1 1/4 cups shredded.
• 1 medium sweet potato = 2/3 cup mashed.
• 1 large sweet potato weighs about 9 ounces.
• One 17-ounce can sweet potatoes = about 2 cups drained and mashed.

1. In a large covered saucepan, cook sweet potatoes in boiling water about 15 minutes or until tender.
2. Meanwhile, in a medium mixing bowl, combine flour and the 1/4 teaspoon salt. Using a pastry blender, cut in shortening until pieces are pea-size. Sprinkle cold water, 1 tablespoon at a time, over part of mixture. Gently toss with a fork just until all dough is moistened. Form dough into a ball.
3. On a lightly floured surface, roll dough from center to edge into a 12-inch circle. Transfer pastry to a 10-inch deep-dish pie plate. Trim pastry to 1/2 inch beyond edge of plate. Fold under extra pastry; crimp edge as desired. Line unpricked pastry shell with a double thickness of foil. Bake in a 450°F oven for 8 minutes. Remove foil; bake for 4 to 5 minutes more or until set and dry. Set aside. Reduce oven temperature to 400°F.
4. Drain potatoes. In a large bowl combine potatoes and butter. Beat with electric mixer until smooth. Add brown sugar, cinnamon, nutmeg, and the dash salt. Beat until combined. Add eggs. Beat on low speed just until combined. Gradually stir in evaporated milk.
5. Pour filling into prepared pastry shell. Cover edge of pie with foil. Bake in 400°F oven for 10 minutes. Reduce heat to 350°F and bake for 40 to 50 minutes more or until knife inserted in center comes out clean. Cool on wire rack for 1 hour. Serve warm. (Or cover and refrigerate after 2 hours.) If desired, serve with whipped cream sprinkled with ground nutmeg.

Makes 8 servings.
Per serving: 386 cal., 20 g total fat (8 g sat. fat), 108 mg chol., 220 mg sodium, 45 g carbo., 2 g fiber, 8 g pro. Dietary exchanges: 3 starch, 3 fat.

Southern Chocolate-Pecan Pie

From Deep in the Heart, cookbook of the
Dallas Junior Forum, Dallas, Texas

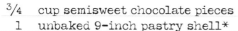

3/4	cup semisweet chocolate pieces
1	unbaked 9-inch pastry shell*
3	slightly beaten eggs
2/3	cup sugar
1/2	cup light-colored corn syrup
1/2	cup dark-flavored corn syrup

1/3	cup butter, melted
	Dash salt
1	cup pecan halves

Prep: 15 min. **Bake:** 45 min.

1. Sprinkle chocolate pieces evenly over bottom of unbaked pastry shell; set aside. For filling, in a medium bowl, combine eggs, sugar, corn syrups, butter, and salt. Stir well. Stir in pecans. Carefully pour the filling over chocolate pieces in pastry shell.

2. To prevent overbrowning, cover edge of pie with foil. Bake in a 350°F oven for 25 minutes. Remove foil. Bake 20 to 25 minutes more or until a knife inserted near the center comes out clean. Cool completely on a wire rack. Refrigerate within 2 hours. Cover pie for longer storage in the refrigerator.

*Test Kitchen Tip: For the 9-inch pastry shell, prepare your favorite single-crust pastry, use 1 unbaked refrigerated piecrust (half of a 15-ounce package), or use one 9-inch frozen deep-dish pastry shell. (If you use a frozen pastry shell, a deep-dish one is essential to hold all of the filling.)

Makes 8 servings.
Per serving: 587 cal., 33 g total fat (11 g sat. fat), 101 mg chol., 239 mg sodium, 68 g carbo., 4 g fiber, 6 g pro. Dietary exchanges: 4½ other carbo., 5 fat.

Meetin' and Eatin'
In the foreword to their cookbook, the members of the Dallas Junior Forum wrote, "In between service and fund-raising, we have many a meeting /and we always provide some really good eating./We've decided to share favorite recipes with you/to help with some of the entertaining you do."

Apple Dumplings

From *Slices & Bites of the Wenatchee Valley*,
cookbook of the Applarians, Wenatchee, Washington

2 cups sugar	¼ cup sugar
2 cups water	½ tsp. ground cinnamon
¼ cup margarine or butter	3 cups shredded, peeled cooking
¼ tsp. ground cinnamon	apples (3 to 4 medium), such as
¼ tsp. ground nutmeg	Golden Delicious, Rome,
2 cups all-purpose flour	Granny Smith, Jonathan, or
2 tsp. baking powder	Newtown pippin
½ tsp. salt	
¾ cup shortening	**Prep:** 30 min. **Bake:** 50 min.
⅔ cup milk	

1. For sauce, in a large saucepan, combine the 2 cups sugar, the water, margarine, the ¼ tsp. cinnamon, and the nutmeg. Bring to boiling and boil for 5 minutes; set aside (you should have about 2 cups sauce).

2. For dough, in a large mixing bowl, combine flour, baking powder, and salt. Using a pastry blender, cut in shortening until pieces are pea-size. Make well in center. Add milk all at once. Stir just until moistened. Knead dough on a lightly floured surface 10 to 12 strokes or until nearly smooth. Roll out to 12×10-inch rectangle.

3. For filling, combine the ¼ cup sugar and the ½ teaspoon cinnamon; set aside. Spread apples evenly over dough. Sprinkle with sugar mixture. Roll dough into spiral, starting from a long side. Pinch seam to seal. Cut into twelve 1-inch-thick pieces. Place in 13×9×2-inch baking pan. Pour sauce over dumplings. Bake in a 350°F oven about 50 minutes or until golden.

Makes 12 servings.
Per serving: 382 cal., 17 g total fat (4 g sat. fat), 1 mg chol., 217 mg sodium, 56 g carbo., 1 g fiber, 3 g pro. Dietary exchanges: 1½ fruit, 2 starch, 3 fat.

Strawberries with Cannoli Cream

From Jean Roczniak
Rochester, Minnesota

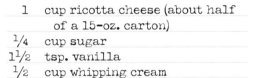

1	cup ricotta cheese (about half of a 15-oz. carton)	1/3	cup miniature semisweet chocolate pieces	
1/4	cup sugar	6	cups fresh strawberries, halved	
1 1/2	tsp. vanilla			
1/2	cup whipping cream			

Start to finish: 10 min.

STRAWBERRIES NEED TLC
Strawberries are a fragile fruit, so handle them carefully. When you bring them in from the you-pick-'em patch, your garden, or the grocery store, place them in the refrigerator in a single layer, loosely covered with paper towels. Strawberries are best eaten within a day or two. Wash or hull fresh berries only when you're ready to eat or cook them. To remove the hulls, use a strawberry huller or a small sharp knife.

1. For cannoli cream, in a medium bowl, stir together ricotta, sugar, and vanilla. In a small chilled bowl, beat whipping cream with an electric mixer on medium speed until soft peaks form. (Do not overbeat.) By hand, gently stir whipped cream and about half of the chocolate pieces into ricotta mixture. (If desired, mixture may be made up to 2 days ahead. Refrigerate, covered.)

2. To serve, divide strawberries among 8 dessert dishes. Spoon cannoli cream over berries. Sprinkle with remaining chocolate pieces.

Makes 8 servings.
Per serving: 198 cal., 12 g total fat (7 g sat. fat), 36 mg chol., 36 mg sodium, 20 g carbo., 3 g fiber, 5 g pro. Dietary exchanges: 1 1/2 fruit, 2 fat.

Pumpkin Pie Squares

From the 125th Anniversary Cookbook of
Zion Lutheran Church, Hampton, Nebraska

1¼ cups all-purpose flour	¾ cup granulated sugar
½ cup quick-cooking rolled oats	1 tsp. ground cinnamon
¾ cup packed brown sugar	½ tsp. ground ginger
½ cup butter or margarine	¼ tsp. ground cloves
1 15-oz. can pumpkin	½ tsp. salt
1 12-oz. can (1½ cups) evaporated milk	2 Tbsp. butter
3 slightly beaten eggs	½ cup chopped pecans
	Whipped dessert topping (optional)

Prep: 20 min. **Bake:** 1 hr. **Chill:** 4 hr.

GREAT PUMPKIN
Canned pumpkin is convenient, but you can make your own pumpkin puree. Cut a medium (about 6 pounds) pie pumpkin into 5-inch-square pieces. Remove the seeds and fibrous strings. Arrange pieces in a single layer, skin side up, in a large shallow baking pan. Cover with foil. Bake in a 375°F oven for 1 to 1½ hours or until tender. Scoop the pulp from the rind. Working with part of the pulp at a time, place pulp in a food processor or blender container. Cover and blend or process until smooth. Place pumpkin in a cheesecloth-lined strainer and press out any liquid. Makes about 2 cups puree.

1. For crust, in a medium bowl, combine 1 cup of the flour, the oats, and ½ cup of the brown sugar. Cut in the ½ cup butter until mixture resembles coarse crumbs. Press into bottom of an ungreased 13×9×2-inch baking pan. Bake in a 350°F oven for 20 minutes. Meanwhile, for filling, in a large bowl, combine pumpkin, evaporated milk, eggs, granulated sugar, cinnamon, ginger, cloves, and salt. Pour filling into crust. Bake for 25 minutes more.

2. Meanwhile, for streusel topping, in small bowl, combine the remaining ¼ cup flour and remaining ¼ cup brown sugar. Cut in the 2 tablespoons butter until mixture resembles coarse crumbs; stir in pecans. Sprinkle over filling. Bake for 15 minutes more or until filling is set. Cool on rack for 1 hour; chill for at least 4 hours. Cut into squares. Top with whipped topping, if desired.

Makes 24 squares.
Per square: 172 cal., 8 g total fat (2 g sat. fat), 37 mg chol., 115 mg sodium, 22 g carbo., 1 g fiber, 3 g pro. Dietary exchanges: 1½ starch, 1 fat.

Rhubarb Crunch

From Cookbook Twenty-Five Years, cookbook of
Women of the Farm Bureau, Madison County, Illinois

1	cup all-purpose flour
1	cup quick-cooking oats
1	cup packed brown sugar
1	tsp. ground cinnamon
1/2	cup butter
4	cups diced rhubarb
1	cup granulated sugar
2	Tbsp. cornstarch

1	cup water
1	tsp. vanilla
	Few drops red food coloring (optional)
	Vanilla ice cream or whipped cream (optional)

Prep: 15 min. **Bake:** 1 hr. **Cool:** 30 min.

For the Farm
Sales of Cookbook Twenty-Five Years by the Women of the Madison County, Illinois, Farm Bureau help support collegiate scholarships for Farm Bureau members or their dependents who plan to major in agriculture.

1. In a large bowl, stir together flour, oats, brown sugar, and cinnamon. Using a pastry blender or two knives, cut in butter until mixture resembles fine crumbs. Press half of the mixture into bottom of a 9×9×2-inch baking pan. Sprinkle rhubarb evenly over crust; set aside.

2. In a small saucepan, stir together granulated sugar and cornstarch; add the water. Cook and stir until mixture is thickened and bubbly. Stir in vanilla and, if desired, red food coloring. Pour evenly over rhubarb. Sprinkle with the remaining crumb mixture. Bake, uncovered, in a 350°F oven for 1 hour or until topping is browned and filling is bubbly. Cool for about 30 minutes. Serve warm with ice cream or whipped cream, if desired.

Makes 9 servings.

Per serving: 379 cal., 12 g total fat (7 g sat. fat), 29 mg chol., 124 mg sodium, 67 g carbo., 3 g fiber, 4 g pro. Dietary exchanges: 2 fruit, 2½ starch, 1½ fat.

Blueberry Crisp

*From Treasured Recipes of the Shipwreck Coast, cookbook of the
Great Lakes Shipwreck Historical Society, Whitefish Point, Michigan*

3	cups fresh blueberries
2	Tbsp. lemon juice
2/3	cup packed brown sugar
1/2	cup all-purpose flour
1/2	cup quick-cooking rolled oats
3/4	tsp. ground cinnamon

1/8	tsp. salt
1/3	cup cold butter
	Half-and-half or light cream (optional)

Prep: 20 min. **Bake:** 25 min.

Superior's Most Famous Shipwreck

On November 10, 1975, the "Edmund Fitzgerald," a ship loaded with iron ore, mysteriously sank 17 miles northwest of Whitefish Point after losing radar contact in a horrific storm. The entire crew of 29 was lost. Twenty years later, divers replaced the bell of the ship with a replica that included the names of the crewmen. The original bell is on display in the Shipwreck Museum at Whitefish Point.

1. Place blueberries in a 2-quart square baking dish. Sprinkle with lemon juice.

2. Combine brown sugar, flour, oats, cinnamon, and salt. Using a pastry blender, cut in butter until mixture resembles coarse crumbs. Sprinkle oat mixture evenly over blueberries.

3. Bake in a 375°F oven for 25 minutes or until topping is golden brown and blueberries are tender. Serve warm with half-and-half, if desired.

Makes 4 to 6 servings.
Per serving: 427 cal., 16 g total fat (10 g sat. fat), 41 mg chol., 243 mg sodium, 70 g carbo., 4 g fiber, 4 g pro.
Dietary exchanges: 3 fruit, 1 starch, 3 fat.

Mayo Shortcake

From Kissimmee Valley Vittles, cookbook of the
Osceola County Historical Society, Osceola County, Florida

2 cups self-rising flour*	Whipped cream or whipped
2 Tbsp. granulated sugar	dessert topping
1 cup milk	Sifted powdered sugar
1 tsp. vanilla	(optional)
1/3 cup mayonnaise	
Sweetened fresh fruit	**Prep:** 10 min. **Bake:** 20 min.

1. Grease an 8×1½-inch round baking pan; set aside. In a medium bowl, stir together flour and granulated sugar. Make a well in the center. Add milk, vanilla, and mayonnaise. Stir just until combined. (Batter will be stiff.) Spread mixture evenly into prepared baking pan. Bake in a 400°F oven for 20 to 25 minutes or until a toothpick inserted near the center comes out clean. Remove from pan; cool slightly. If desired, using a long serrated knife, split shortcake in half horizontally. Serve warm. Top with your favorite sweetened fresh fruit and whipped cream. If desired, sprinkle with sifted powdered sugar.

*Test Kitchen Tip: If you can't find self-rising flour at your supermarket, substitute 2 cups all-purpose flour mixed with 2 teaspoons baking powder, 1 teaspoon salt, and ½ teaspoon baking soda.

Makes 8 servings.
Per shortcake: 204 cal., 8 g total fat (1 g sat. fat), 8 mg chol., 464 mg sodium, 28 g carbo., 1 g fiber, 4 g pro. Dietary exchanges: 1 starch, 3 other carbo., 1 fat.

Bread-and-Butter Custard

From Sterling Service, cookbook of the
Dothan Service League, Dothan, Alabama

Around Dothan,
Alabama, folks
treasure the past.
And to pay tribute to
the rich heritage of
the area, the Dothan
Service League has
published Sterling
Service. The 254-
page cookbook
commemorate
50 years of service
by the league, and
showcases more than
350 recipes of
local cooks. To add to
the cookbook's charm,
photographs of pieces
of heirloom silver are
sprinkled throughout
the pages, some
accompanied by a
brief history of
the pattern.

2	cups whipping cream	4	1/2-inch-thick slices French bread
2	cups milk	1	Tbsp. butter
3	thin strips orange peel (each about 3×1/2 inches)		Powdered sugar
3	eggs		Ground nutmeg
6	egg yolks		
1/2	cup granulated sugar		
1/4	cup orange liqueur		

Prep: 25 min. **Bake:** 30 min. **Cool:** 30 min.

1. Lightly grease a 2-quart square baking dish; set aside.

2. In a heavy large saucepan, combine whipping cream, milk, and orange peel. Heat, stirring frequently, until mixture is steaming. Discard peel.

3. Meanwhile, in a large bowl, beat together eggs and egg yolks. Stir in granulated sugar and orange liqueur. Stir whipping cream mixture into egg mixture. Pour into prepared baking dish. Spread one side of each bread slice with butter. Arrange bread, buttered side up, atop egg mixture in dish, pressing lightly to absorb some of the liquid.

4. Bake in a 325°F oven for 30 to 35 minutes or until puffed and a knife inserted in custard (not in bread) comes out clean. Cool on wire rack about 30 minutes. Sprinkle with powdered sugar and nutmeg. Serve warm.

Makes 6 servings.

Per serving: 555 cal., 41 g total fat (23 g sat. fat), 440 mg chol., 202 mg sodium, 32 g carbo., 0 g fiber, 11 g pro. Dietary exchanges: 2 other carbo., 6 fat.

11.

Holiday Best

Colonial Wassail Bowl

From Out of the Ordinary, cookbook of the
Hingham Historical Society, Hingham, Massachusetts

1	750-ml bottle dry red wine (such as Burgundy)		6	inches stick cinnamon
2	cups cranberry juice		1/4	cup brandy (optional)
1	cup sugar			Lemon slices (optional)
1/2	cup water			
1/4	cup lemon juice			

Prep: 5 min. **Cook:** 10 min.

1. In a large saucepan, combine red wine, cranberry juice, sugar, water, lemon juice, and stick cinnamon. Heat just until bubbly around edges; reduce heat. Simmer, uncovered, for 10 minutes. Remove stick cinnamon with a slotted spoon. Stir in brandy, if desired.

Carefully pour punch into a heatproof punch bowl; garnish with lemon slices, if desired. Ladle into heatproof cups.

Makes twelve to fourteen 4-ounce servings.

Per serving: 132 cal., 0 g total fat (0 g sat. fat), 0 mg chol., 4 mg sodium, 24 g carbo., 0 g fiber, 0 g pro. Dietary exchanges: 1 other carbo.

Honey-Cardamom Crunch

From Rebecca Vancuren of Edwards, Colorado,
winner of the Chex Recipe Contest

1/3 cup packed brown sugar	2 cups tiny pretzel twists
1/4 cup butter	1 cup unblanched whole almonds
1/4 cup honey	1 cup coconut
1/2 to 1 tsp. ground cardamom or 1/4 tsp. allspice	1 cup dried cranberries or snipped dried pineapple
6 cups bite-size rice-square cereal	

Prep: 15 min. **Bake:** 40 min.

1. In a small saucepan, heat and stir brown sugar, butter, honey, and cardamom until butter melts. In a large roasting pan, combine rice-square cereal, pretzels, almonds, and coconut. Drizzle butter mixture over cereal mixture; toss to coat.

2. Bake in a 300°F oven for 40 minutes; stir every 10 minutes. Stir in cranberries. Spread mix on foil; cool. Store in an airtight container.

Makes 13 cups.
Per 1/2-cup serving: 124 cal., 5 g total fat (2 g sat. fat), 5 mg chol., 105 mg sodium, 18 g carbo., 1 g fiber, 2 g pro. Dietary exchanges: 1 starch, 1 fat.

Cardamom Memories

When Rebecca Vancuren was 14 years old, she tasted cardamom in a sweet roll while on vacation in Wisconsin. She never forgot the flavor of that roll, and since then she has looked for ways to include cardamom in her cooking. For the Chex Recipe Contest, she stirred together a buttery syrup lightly spiced with cardamom to coat Chex cereal and dried cranberries. She tried out the recipe on family and friends. They loved it! The Chex judges loved it too.

Grandma's Holiday Punch
From The Purple Pantry Cook Book, cookbook of the
University of Northern Iowa Alumni Association, Cedar Falls, Iowa

1   12-oz. can frozen lemonade
    concentrate
1   10-oz. pkg. frozen strawberries
    in syrup
1   8-oz. can crushed pineapple,
    undrained

3   1-liter bottles ginger ale,
    chilled
1   cup rum or vodka (optional)
    Ice ring (optional)

Start to finish: 10 min.

ADD PUNCH TO YOUR PUNCH
Dress up your holiday punch with a pretty ice ring. Fill a shallow tube mold halfway with water; freeze until firm. Top the ice layer with fruit such as whole strawberries or slices of kiwi, lemons, or limes. Add more water and freeze. Unmold the ring by dipping the bottom of the mold in a sink filled with warm water for 30 seconds or so.

1. In a blender container, combine lemonade concentrate, strawberries with their syrup, and undrained pineapple. Cover and blend until smooth. (May be made ahead and chilled for up to 24 hours, if desired.)

2. To serve, pour strawberry mixture into a large punch bowl. Slowly pour ginger ale down side of bowl. Stir in rum or vodka, if desired. Add ice ring, if desired.

Makes thirty 4-ounce servings.
Per serving: 68 cal., 0 g total fat (0 g sat. fat), 0 mg chol., 8 mg sodium, 17 g carbo., 0 g fiber, 0 g pro. Dietary exchanges: 1 fruit.

Eggnog Bread

From the St. James at Sag Bridge Church cookbook.
Lemont, Illinois

2	cups all-purpose flour		1	cup dairy or canned eggnog
1	cup sugar		1/2	cup butter, melted and cooled slightly
2	tsp. baking powder		1	tsp. vanilla
1/4	tsp. salt		1/2	tsp. rum flavoring
1/8	tsp. ground nutmeg			
1	beaten egg			

Prep: 15 min. **Bake:** 45 min. **Cool:** 10 min.

1. Grease the bottom and 1/2 inch up the sides of a 9×5×3-inch loaf pan; set aside.

2. In a large bowl, stir together flour, sugar, baking powder, salt, and nutmeg. Make a well in the center; set bowl aside.

3. In a medium bowl, combine egg, eggnog, butter, vanilla, and rum flavoring. Add egg mixture all at once to the flour mixture. Stir just until moistened. Batter should be slightly lumpy.

4. Spoon batter into prepared pan. Bake in a 350°F oven for 45 to 50 minutes or until a toothpick inserted near the center comes out clean. Cool in pan on wire rack for 10 minutes. Remove from pan. Cool completely on wire rack. Wrap bread and store overnight before slicing.

Makes 1 loaf (16 slices).

Per slice: 179 cal., 8 g total fat (4 g sat. fat), 30 mg chol., 163 mg sodium, 25 g carbo., 0 g fiber, 2 g pro. Dietary exchanges: 1½ starch, 1 fat.

Cranberry Muffins

From Gracious Goodness Christmas in Charleston, a cookbook benefiting
Bishop England High School, Charleston, South Carolina

1 cup fresh cranberries	1/2 tsp. salt
2 Tbsp. sugar	1 beaten egg
2 cups all-purpose flour	3/4 cup milk
1/4 to 1/2 cup sugar	1/4 cup butter, melted
4 tsp. baking powder	
1 tsp. finely shredded orange peel	

Prep: 15 min. **Bake:** 15 min.

Around Town

Charleston,
South Carolina
(pop. 100,122)
At Christmastime,
festivals throughout the
city feature favorite
low-country dishes,
including plenty of
shrimp, crab, okra,
rice, and grits.
Eggnog specialties,
inspired by plantation
cooks, are the libation
of choice.

1. Grease twelve 2$\frac{1}{2}$-inch muffin cups or line with paper bake cups. In a medium bowl, toss cranberries with the 2 tablespoons sugar. Set aside.

2. In a large bowl, combine flour, the $\frac{1}{4}$ to $\frac{1}{2}$ cup sugar, the baking powder, orange peel, and salt. Stir well. Combine egg, milk, and butter. Make a well in center of flour mixture; add egg mixture and cranberries. Stir just until moistened. Spoon into prepared muffin cups.

3. Bake in a 400°F oven about 15 minutes or until golden. (Or spoon into six 3$\frac{1}{4}$-inch jumbo muffin cups and bake in a 350°F oven for 25 minutes or until golden.) Serve warm.

Makes 12 regular size muffins.
Per muffin: 147 cal., 5 g total fat (3 g sat. fat), 29 mg chol., 262 mg sodium, 23 g carbo., 1 g fiber, 3 g pro. Dietary exchanges: 1/2 fruit, 1 starch, 1 fat.

Chutney-Glazed Ham

From Taste of the Territory, cookbook of the
Service League of Bartlesville, Oklahoma

1	8-lb. cooked ham (shank portion)	1	Tbsp. Dijon-style mustard
	Whole cloves	1	clove garlic, minced
1/2	cup packed brown sugar	1	tsp. rice vinegar
1/4	cup chutney	1/8	tsp. bottled hot pepper sauce
1/4	cup plum jam		

Prep: 20 min. **Bake:** 3 hr. **Stand:** 15 min.

SCORING A HAM
Scoring a ham in a traditional diamond pattern and studding the crosspoints with cloves accomplishes three things. It decorates the ham, tenderizes it, and infuses it with spicy clove flavor and aroma as the ham bakes.

1. Score ham by making shallow diagonal cuts in a diamond pattern. Stud with cloves. Place on a rack in a shallow roasting pan. Insert a meat thermometer in meat, making sure it does not touch bone. Bake in a 325°F oven about 2½ hours or until thermometer registers 125°F.

2. For glaze, in a medium saucepan, combine brown sugar, chutney, plum jam, mustard, garlic, rice vinegar, and hot pepper sauce. Cook and stir over medium heat until mixture is bubbly.

3. Brush ham with some of the glaze. Bake about 30 minutes more or until thermometer registers 135°F. Remove from oven. Cover with foil; let stand for 15 minutes before carving. (The meat's temperature will rise 5°F during standing.) Reheat the remaining glaze, if necessary. Pass with ham.

Makes 20 servings.
Per serving: 207 cal., 6 g total fat (2 g sat. fat), 60 mg chol., 1,455 mg sodium, 9 g carbo., 0 g fiber, 27 g pro. Dietary exchanges: 4 lean meat.

Christmas Raspberry Salad

From the St. James at Sag Bridge Church cookbook,
Lemont, Illinois

1	6-oz. pkg. raspberry-flavored gelatin
2	cups boiling water
1	16-oz. jar applesauce
1	10-oz. pkg. frozen red raspberries in syrup, thawed

1/2	cup tiny marshmallows
1	to 2 Tbsp. milk
1/4	cup dairy sour cream

Prep: 20 min. **Stand:** 40 min. **Chill:** 3 hr.

STAR LIGHT, STAR BRIGHT
This beautiful red molded salad looks lovely in a star shape, but you can also make it into squares and "frost" it with a thick layer of the marshmallow mixture used for the drizzle.

1. Dissolve gelatin in boiling water. Let stand about 30 minutes to cool. Stir in applesauce and raspberries with their syrup. Pour into a 5- to 6-cup mold. Cover and chill in the refrigerator for 2 to 3 hours or until firm. Remove from mold.

2. For drizzle, in a small saucepan, combine marshmallows and milk. Cook and stir over low heat until marshmallows are melted. Remove from heat; let stand about 10 minutes. Stir in the sour cream.

3. Place mixture in a clear plastic bag. Snip off a corner of the bag and drizzle the mixture over the salad. Chill in the refrigerator about 1 hour or until firm. Garnish salad with the drizzle up to 4 hours before serving.

Makes 8 servings.
Per serving: 274 cal., 5 g total fat (3 g sat. fat), 11 mg chol., 84 mg sodium, 56 g carbo., 2 g fiber, 3 g pro. Dietary exchanges: 1½ fruit, 2 other carbo., 1 fat.

Sweet Potato Casserole

From the Vardaman Sweet Potato Recipe Collection,
Vardaman, Mississippi

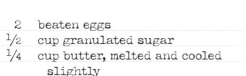

2	beaten eggs	1/2	cup packed brown sugar
1/2	cup granulated sugar	1/4	cup all-purpose flour
1/4	cup butter, melted and cooled slightly	2	Tbsp. cold butter
1	tsp. vanilla	1/2	cup chopped pecans
4	cups mashed, cooked sweet potatoes (about 3 lb.)		
1/2	cup raisins		

Prep: 20 min. **Bake:** 20 min.

1. In a large bowl, stir together eggs, granulated sugar, butter, and vanilla. Stir in sweet potatoes and raisins. Spread the mixture evenly in an ungreased 2-quart square baking dish.
2. For topping, in small bowl, combine brown sugar and flour. Cut in butter until mixture resembles coarse crumbs. Stir in pecans. Sprinkle over sweet potato mixture. Bake in a 350°F oven for 20 minutes or until heated through.

Makes 8 servings.
Per serving: 458 cal., 16 g total fat (7 g sat. fat), 78 mg chol., 137 mg sodium, 77 g carbo., 4 g fiber, 6 g pro. Dietary exchanges: 5 starch, 1½ fat.

Sweet Potatoes for the Sweet
When cooks in Vardaman, Mississippi, get ready to prepare their special sweet potato recipes for the holidays, they reach for the Vardaman Sweet Potato Recipe Collection. It's filled with delicious dishes from their "families." Related or not, everybody in this rural community seems like family. And most of them grow sweet potatoes.

Pistachio Chip Cookies

From Gracious Goodness Christmas, a cookbook benefiting
Bishop England High School, Charleston, South Carolina

½	cup butter
1	4-serving size pkg. instant pistachio pudding mix
1	egg
1	cup all-purpose flour
½	tsp. baking soda
	Several drops green food coloring (optional)

1	cup miniature semisweet chocolate pieces
15	green or red candied cherries

Prep: 15 min. **Bake:** 12 min. per batch

Christmas in Charleston

This Christmas story starts in the 1980s when moms of students at Bishop England High School in Charleston, South Carolina, started delivering hot and cold dishes to the faculty at lunchtime. Before too long, it seemed everyone wanted the recipes for the noontime meals. Volunteers gathered the recipes, plus other family favorites, to sell as a school fund-raiser. The hard work of many culminated in the release of Gracious Goodness Charleston. That was in 1991, and it was only the beginning. A few years later, dedicated volunteers pitched in for Gracious Goodness Christmas—a holiday recipe collection featuring treasured Southern goodies.

1. Lightly grease baking sheets; set aside. In a medium bowl, beat butter and pudding mix with electric mixer on medium to high speed for 30 seconds. Beat in egg. Beat in flour and soda. Stir in food coloring, if desired. Stir in chocolate pieces. Drop by rounded teaspoonfuls 2 inches apart on prepared baking sheets. Press half of a cherry into center of each cookie. Bake in a 350°F oven about 12 minutes or until bottoms are lightly browned. Cool on wire rack.

Makes about 30 cookies.
Per cookie: 87 cal., 5 g total fat (2 g sat. fat), 15 mg chol., 101 mg sodium, 11 g carbo., 0 g fiber, 1 g pro. Dietary exchanges: ½ starch, 1 fat.

Frosted Ginger Stars

From the Barnebirkie Cookie Book,
Hayward, Wisconsin

1	cup butter, softened
1½	cups granulated sugar
2	tsp. baking soda
2	tsp. ground ginger
½	tsp. salt
¼	tsp. ground cloves
1	cup molasses
½	cup cold, strong coffee
1	egg
5½	cups all-purpose flour
2	egg whites

1½	cups granulated sugar
18	large marshmallows, cut up
½	cup water
½	tsp. white vinegar
2	cups sifted powdered sugar

Prep: 1 hr. **Chill:** 8 hr. **Bake:** 8 min. per batch

1. In a large bowl, beat butter with an electric mixer on medium to high speed for 30 seconds. Add 1½ cups granulated sugar, the baking soda, ginger, salt, and cloves. Beat until combined, scraping sides of bowl occasionally. Beat in molasses, coffee, and egg. Beat in as much of the flour as you can with the mixer. Stir in any remaining flour. Divide dough in half. Cover and chill in the refrigerator for 8 hours or overnight.

2. On a lightly floured surface, roll dough, half at a time, to ¼-inch thickness. Using a 2½-inch star or other cutters, cut into desired shapes. Place 1 inch apart on ungreased cookie sheets. Bake in a 350°F oven about 8 minutes or until edges are lightly browned. Cool on cookie sheets for 1 minute. Transfer to wire racks; cool completely.

3. For frosting, let egg whites stand at room temperature for 30 minutes. Meanwhile, in the top of a double boiler, combine 1½ cups granulated sugar, marshmallows, water, and vinegar. Place over boiling water (upper pan should not touch water). Cook, stirring constantly, until marshmallows melt. In a medium bowl, beat egg whites with an electric mixer on high speed until stiff peaks form (tips stand straight). Beat egg whites into marshmallow mixture in double boiler. Cook, beating constantly, for 5 minutes. Remove from heat; add powdered sugar. Beat until smooth. Quickly frost cooled cookies. Let cookies stand until frosting hardens.

Makes about 72 cookies.
Per cookie: 117 cal., 3 g total fat (2 g sat. fat), 10 mg chol., 85 mg sodium, 22 g carbo., 0 g fiber, 1 g pro. Dietary exchanges: 1½ other carbo.

The Great Cookie Race Every entrant is a winner in the Barnebirkie, a children's cross-country ski race held annually in Hayward, Wisconsin. After swooshing across the finish line, the more than 1,000 kids, ages 3 to 16, who finish the 1- to 5-kilometer course are treated to hot cocoa and a smorgasbord of 17,000 cookies baked by the Sons of Norway from Wisconsin, Michigan, Illinois, and Indiana.

Chocolate and Sherry Cream Bars

From A Christmas Carroll: Have a Dickens of a Time in the Kitchen,
community cookbook of Carroll, Iowa

PHOTO APPEARS ON PAGE **240**

1	cup butter or margarine		1/4	cup sherry, orange liqueur, kirsch, clear crème de cacao, or other clear liqueur
4	oz. unsweetened chocolate			
4	slightly beaten eggs		1	cup chopped walnuts
2	cups granulated sugar		1/2	cup semisweet chocolate pieces
1	tsp. vanilla		2	Tbsp. butter
1	cup all-purpose flour		4	tsp. sherry, other desired clear liqueur, or water
4	cups sifted powdered sugar			
1/2	cup butter, softened			
1/2	cup half-and-half or light cream			

Prep: 25 min. **Chill:** 1¾ hr. **Bake:** 25 min.

A Christmas Carroll

Carroll, Iowa, may be a long way from the 19th-century London of Dickens' "A Christmas Carol." Still, it's a place where people go to have a "Dickens of a time" during the Christmas season. That's when this county seat hosts holiday tours for visitors. Festivities have included an Olde English Feast, a local production of A Christmas Carol, and a tour of an inn where President Kennedy once slept.

1. Grease a 15×10×1-inch baking pan; set aside. For crust, in a large saucepan, melt the 1 cup butter and unsweetened chocolate over low heat. Remove from heat. Stir in eggs, granulated sugar, and vanilla. Using a wooden spoon, beat lightly just until combined. Stir in flour. Spread in prepared pan. Bake in 350°F oven for 25 minutes. Cool. (Crust will be moist.)

2. For filling, in a large bowl, combine powdered sugar and the 1/2 cup butter. Beat with an electric mixer on low speed until combined. Gradually add half-and-half and the 1/4 cup sherry; beat well. Stir in walnuts. Spread over crust; chill until firm.

3. For topping, in a small saucepan, melt semisweet chocolate pieces and the 2 tablespoons butter over low heat; remove from heat. Stir in the 4 teaspoons sherry until smooth. Drizzle over chilled filling. Chill slightly (until set but not firm). With knife, score top to outline bars; chill until firm. Cut into bars to serve. Store leftovers in the refrigerator.

Makes 60 bars.
Per bar: 139 cal., 8 g total fat (4 g sat. fat), 28 mg chol., 55 mg sodium, 17 g carbo., 0 g fiber, 1 g pro. Dietary exchanges: 1 starch, 1½ fat.

Fresh Cranberry-Apple Pie

From A Christmas Carroll: Have a Dickens of a Time in the Kitchen, community cookbook of Carroll, Iowa

1	cup sugar		2	Tbsp. butter or margarine
3	Tbsp. cornstarch		1	recipe Pastry for Double-Crust Pie
1/4	tsp. salt			
1/4	cup light corn syrup		4	to 5 cups sliced apples
2	Tbsp. water			Milk (optional)
1 1/2	cups fresh cranberries			Coarse sugar (optional)
1 1/2	tsp. grated orange peel			

Prep: 1 hr. **Bake:** 40 min.

1. In a large saucepan, combine sugar, cornstarch, and salt; stir in corn syrup and water. Cook and stir until mixture thickens slightly and boils. Add cranberries; cook for 3 to 5 minutes more or until skins break. Stir in orange peel and butter. Cool.

2. Line a 9-inch pie plate with half of the pastry. Stir apples into cranberry mixture; spoon into pastry-lined pie plate. Trim pastry to edge of pie plate. Place remaining pastry on filling; trim edge 1/2 inch beyond edge of pie plate. Turn top crust under bottom crust; flute edge. Cut vents for steam. Roll out trimmings and cut into leaf shapes. Place on top of pie. Brush with milk and sprinkle with coarse sugar, if desired. To prevent overbrowning, cover edge of pie with foil. Place a baking sheet under pie to catch drips.

3. Bake in a 425°F oven 20 minutes. Remove foil; bake 20 minutes more or until top is golden. Cool completely.

Pastry for Double-Crust Pie: In a large bowl, stir together 2 cups all-purpose flour and 1/2 teaspoon salt. Using a pastry blender, cut in 2/3 cup shortening until pieces are pea-size. Sprinkle 1 tablespoon cold water over part of mixture; gently toss with a fork. Push moistened dough to side of bowl. Repeat, using 1 tablespoon cold water at a time (6 or 7 tablespoons total), until all dough is moistened. Divide in half. Form each half into a ball. On a lightly floured surface, slightly flatten one ball of dough. Roll from center to edge into a 12-inch circle. Continue recipe as instructed.

Makes 8 servings.
Per serving: 462 cal., 20 g total fat (6 g sat. fat), 8 mg chol., 238 mg sodium, 68 g carbo., 3 g fiber, 3 g pro. Dietary exchanges: 3 fruit, 1 starch, 4 fat.

Around Town
Carroll, Iowa (pop. 10,331) Specialty shops, many featuring country handicrafts, draw rural and city folks for holiday shopping. The best part of shopping here? You won't have to wait in long lines to make a purchase!

Christmas Rice Pudding

From Beatrice Ojakangas,
Duluth, Minnesota

1½	cups water		2/3	cup sugar
½	tsp. salt		1	Tbsp. butter, melted
¾	cup short or medium grain rice		½	tsp. ground cardamom
2	beaten eggs			Raspberry Sauce (see recipe, below)
2	cups half-and-half, or light cream			
1½	cups milk			

Prep: 30 min. **Bake:** 1¼ hr.

Cooking with Beatrice

Beatrice Ojakangas grew up on a farm in northern Minnesota. She taught herself to bake fancy breads so she could win a 5-day trip to the state fair. She also won two national 4-H bread-baking championships. Of Finnish descent, she grew up appreciating heritage breads such as Finnish rye and cardamom bread. While living and traveling in Europe after she married, she began a self-study of Scandinavian cooking—from Iceland to Norway. She's now a food writer and cookbook author.

1. In a medium saucepan, bring water, salt, and rice to boiling; reduce heat. Cover and simmer for 12 to 15 minutes or until rice has absorbed the water. (Rice will still be slightly crunchy.)

2. Butter a 2-quart casserole. Stir together the eggs, half-and-half, milk, sugar, melted butter, cardamom, and cooked rice. Spoon into the prepared casserole.

3. Set the casserole in a large baking pan. Pour boiling water in the larger pan so water reaches about halfway up the side of the casserole dish.

4. Bake, uncovered, in a 325°F oven for 1 hour. Stir mixture. Bake 15 minutes more. Remove casserole from pan of water. Stir mixture once more. (Pudding should have a creamy texture.) Set aside to cool slightly.

5. Serve the rice pudding warm with warm Raspberry Sauce poured over each serving.

Raspberry Sauce: In a medium saucepan, combine 2 tablespoons cornstarch and 2 tablespoons sugar. Stir in 1½ cups cranberry-raspberry juice and 1 teaspoon lemon juice. Cook and stir over medium heat until sauce is thickened and bubbly. Cook and stir 2 minutes more. Remove from heat. Cover surface with plastic wrap; cool slightly without stirring.

Makes 8 to 10 servings.
Per serving: 437 cal., 26 g total fat (16 g sat. fat), 143 mg chol., 230 mg sodium, 47 g carbo., 1 g fiber, 6 g pro. Dietary exchanges: 1 fruit, 2 starch, 4 fat.

Pumpkin Gingerbread

From Recipes and Memories: A Taste of Yesterday for Today,
cookbook of the Romeo Monday Club, Romeo, Michigan

2¼ cups all-purpose flour	1½ tsp. ground ginger
½ cup sugar	1 tsp. baking soda
⅔ cup butter	½ tsp. ground cinnamon
¾ cup chopped pecans	½ tsp. ground cloves
¾ cup buttermilk	¼ tsp. salt
½ cup molasses	1 recipe Caramel Sauce (optional)
½ cup canned pumpkin	Vanilla ice cream (optional)
1 egg	Chopped pecans (optional)

Prep: 35 min. **Bake:** 50 min. **Cool:** 30 min.

1. In a large bowl, combine flour and sugar. Cut in butter until mixture resembles coarse crumbs. Stir in pecans. Press 1¼ cups of the crumb mixture into bottom of an ungreased 2-quart square baking dish. To the remaining crumb mixture, add buttermilk, molasses, pumpkin, egg, ginger, baking soda, cinnamon, cloves, and salt; mix well. Pour over crumb mixture in baking dish. Bake in a 350°F oven about 50 minutes or until center tests done. Cool for 30 minutes. Serve warm with Caramel Sauce, if desired. Top with ice cream and pecans, if desired.

Caramel Sauce: In a medium saucepan, melt ½ cup butter; stir in 1¼ cups packed brown sugar and 2 tablespoons light corn syrup. Cook and stir until boiling. Stir in ½ cup whipping cream; return to boiling. Serve warm.

Makes 9 servings.
Per serving: 394 cal., 21 g total fat (9 g sat. fat), 61 mg chol., 370 mg sodium, 49 g carbo., 2 g fiber, 5 g pro. Dietary exchanges: 1 fruit, 2 starch, 4 fat.

Long Live the Ladies Club
While the beautiful old homes in Romeo, Michigan, are visual reminders of the town's heritage, the Romeo Monday Club is a living link with the town's past. While many such ladies' clubs have gone the way of white gloves and fancy hats, the Romeo Monday Club still thrives. To celebrate their 100th anniversary as a federated women's club and to raise money for the town's library, members compiled Recipes and Memories: A Taste of Yesterday for Today.

Christmas Pound Cake

From Gracious Goodness Christmas in Charleston, a cookbook benefiting Bishop England High School, Charleston, South Carolina

3 cups granulated sugar	1 tsp. orange extract
1 cup butter, softened	1 tsp. vanilla
6 eggs	3/4 tsp. rum flavoring
3 cups all-purpose flour	Powdered sugar
1/2 tsp. baking soda	Raspberry Sauce (optional)
Dash salt	
1 8-oz. carton dairy sour cream	
1/2 cup apricot brandy or apricot nectar	

Prep: 25 min. **Bake:** 1¼ hr. **Cool:** 15 min.

Queen of Cakes
Recipe contributor Dorothy Aikens makes more than 20 Christmas Pound Cakes every year. Apricot brandy—just a half cup or so—makes the cake moist and tasty. Need an endorsement? Just ask Dorothy's friends.

1. Grease and flour a 10-inch fluted tube pan; set aside. In large bowl, beat granulated sugar and butter with electric mixer on medium to high speed until well mixed. Add eggs, one at a time, beating well after each addition. Stir together flour, baking soda, and salt. Combine sour cream, brandy, orange extract, vanilla, and rum flavoring. Add flour and sour cream mixtures alternately to butter mixture, beating on low speed after each addition just until combined. Turn into prepared pan.

2. Bake in a 325°F oven about 1¼ hours or until toothpick inserted in center of cake comes out clean. Cool in pan on wire rack for 15 minutes. Loosen sides. Remove from pan. Turn right side up on rack; cool completely. To serve, sprinkle with powdered sugar; pass Raspberry Sauce, if desired.

Raspberry Sauce: Thaw 3 cups frozen raspberries. Puree raspberries in blender, then sieve. Discard seeds. In a saucepan, combine 1/3 cup sugar and 1 teaspoon cornstarch. Add raspberries. Cook and stir until thickened and bubbly. Cool. Makes 1 cup.

Makes 16 servings.
Per serving: 403 cal., 16 g total fat (10 g sat. fat), 117 mg chol., 196 mg sodium, 55 g carbo., 1 g fiber, 5 g pro. Dietary exchanges: 3½ starch, 3 fat.

Index

TIPS

Want more recipes?

Many of the community cookbooks featured in Hometown Favorites are available for purchase. Before you send a check or money order and a note requesting to buy one of the books listed below, it's a good idea to contact the organization first—by phone or mail—to be sure the book you want is still in print. More cookbook ordering information is available on the Hometown Cooking Web site at www.hometowncook.com

The 125th Anniversary Cookbook (Hampton, Nebraska): Send $16.95, plus $4.05 for postage and handling, to: Zion Lutheran Church, 125th Anniversary Committee, Dept. HC, 2306 E. 16th Road, Hampton, NE 68843. Make checks payable to Zion Lutheran Church.

A+ Cooking, Friends and Family Favorites (North Plains, Oregon): Send $6.50 plus $2.50 shipping and handling for each book to: Cookbook Sales—PTO, P.O. Box 664, North Plains, OR 97133-0664.

Angel Food (Brigham City, Utah): Send $10.00 plus $3.50 shipping and handling for each book to: Angel Food, 226 S. 400 West, Brigham City, Utah 84302. (Make check payable to: St. Michael's Episcopal Church.)

Around the World, Around Our Town (San Pedro, California): The library's 434-page cookbook costs $25 plus $4 shipping and handling. Send your request to: Friends of the San Pedro Library, Attention D. Lisica, Dept. HC, 931 S. Gaffey Street, San Pedro, CA 90731.

Atlanta Cooknotes (Atlanta, Georgia): Send $19.95 plus $2.50 shipping and handling (Georgia residents add 6% sales tax) to: The Junior League of Atlanta, Inc.-Cookbooks, 3154 Northside Parkway, NW, Atlanta, GA 30327.

Balancing Acts (Fargo, North Dakota): Send $15 plus $4 for postage to Balancing Acts, American Gold Gymnastics, Box HC, 2001 17th Ave. South, Fargo, ND 58103. Or call 701/280-0400.

The Barnebirkie Cookie Book (Hayward, Wisconsin): Send a check or money order for $8 plus $2 shipping. Make check or money order payable to Birkebeiner 5-611. Mail to Edith Mahnke, 3112 City Heights Road, Ashland, WI 54806.

Beneath the Palms (Brownsville, Texas): Send $18.95 plus $2.00 postage and handling for each book (Texas residents also add $1.56 sales tax) to: Beneath the Palms, Brownsville Junior Service League, Inc., Dept. HC, P.O. Box 3151, Brownsville, TX 78523-3151.

Beyond Burlap (Boise, Idaho): To order the cookbook, contact the Junior League of Boise, Attn: Beyond Burlap, Dept. HC, 5266 Franklin Rd., Boise, ID 83705. Phone: 888/340-5754 or 208/342-8851. Fax: 208/342-4901. Cost is $19.95, plus $3.00 shipping and handling.

Black Tie & Boots Optional (Colleyville, Texas): Send $19.95 plus $3.50 shipping and handling (Texas residents add $1.55 for the 7.75% sales tax) to: Colleyville Women's Club, P.O. Box 181, Colleyville, TX 76034.

Blessings (Pine Bluff, Arkansas): Write First Presbyterian Church, 717 West 32nd, Dept. HC, Pine Bluff, AR 71603. Phone: 870/534-7831; fax: 870/534-7834. Cost is $16.95 plus $3.05 shipping and handling.

Bully's Best Bites (Starkville, Mississippi): Send $18.95 plus $3.00 postage and handling (MS residents add $1.33 sales tax) to: Bully's Best Bites, P.O. Box 941, Starkville, MS 39760. (Make checks payable to Bully's Best Bites.)

Celebrate San Antonio (San Antonio, Texas): Send $19.95, plus $3.50 shipping and handling, to: Celebrate San Antonio, P.O. Box 791186, San Antonio, TX 78279-1186.

Chautauqua Celebrations (Wytheville, Virginia): For each book, send $21.95 plus $4.00 shipping and handling (Virginia residents also add 4.5 percent sales tax) to: Wythe Arts Council, Ltd., P.O. Box 911, Dept. HC, Wytheville, VA 24382. Make checks payable to Wythe Arts Council, Ltd.

A Christmas Carroll: Have a Dickens of a Time in the Kitchen (Carroll, Iowa): Send $12.00, plus $5.00 for postage and handling, to: Carroll Chamber of Commerce, P.O. Box 307, Dept. HC, 223 West 5th Street, Carroll, IA 51401. Make checks payable to: Carroll Chamber of Commerce.

Cooking at the Irish Settlement (Cumming, Iowa): Send $10 plus $2 shipping and handling for each book to: St. Patrick's Cookbook, P.O. Box 1, Cumming, Iowa 50061. (Make check payable to: St. Patrick's Altar and Rosary Society.)

The Creekside: A Celebration of Cedarburg Cooking (Cedarburg, Wisconsin): Send a check or money order ($15 plus $3 for shipping and handling) to Cedarburg Junior Women's Club, P.O. Box 205, Dept. HC, Cedarburg, WI 53012.

The Damen Kegel-Verein Cookbook (Austin, Texas): Send $10.00 plus $3.50 postage and handling to: Damen Kegel-Verein, Saengerrunde, 1607 San Jacinto Blvd., Austin, TX 78701. (Make check payable to Damen Kegel-Verein.)

Deep in the Heart (Richardson, Texas): Send $18.95 plus $3.50 shipping and handling for each book to: Dallas Junior Forum, Inc., 800 E. Campbell, Suite 199; Richardson, Texas 75081. (Make check payable to: Deep in the Heart.)

Delicious Developments (Rochester, New York): Send $19.95 plus $3.00 postage and handling (NY residents add sales tax) to: Friends of Strong Memorial Hospital, 601 Elmwood Avenue, Box 660, Rochester, New York 14642.

De Nuestra Mesa: Our Foods, Wines, and Tradition (Palm Beach County, Florida): Send a check or money order to: De Nuestra Mesa, Dept. HC, 626 N. Dixie Highway, West Palm Beach, FL 33401. The cost is $19.95 plus $3.50 postage and handling for each book. Checks should be made out to New Hope Charities, Inc.

Downhome Desserts from the Heart of Iowa (Burt, Iowa): Send $10.95 plus $4.95 shipping and handling for each book to Exceptional Concepts, P.O. Box 99, Burt, IA 50522. (Make checks payable to Exceptional Concepts.)

The Edible Palette (Suffolk, Virginia): Send $8.00 plus $2.50 postage and handling (Virginia residents add $0.36 sales tax) to: Suffolk Art League, P.O. Box 1086, Suffolk, Virginia 23439. (Make checks payable to Suffolk Art League.)

Favorite Recipes of Sokol Greater Cleveland (Cleveland, Ohio): Send $8 plus $2 shipping and handling for each book to: Sokol Greater Cleveland, Bohemian National Hall, 4939 Broadway Avenue, Cleveland, Ohio 44127. (Make check payable to Sokol Greater Cleveland.)

Flavors of Washington County (Washington County, Wisconsin): Send $12.50 plus $2.50 shipping and handling for each book to: Washington County Historical Society, Re: Cookbook Order, 340 S. 5th Avenue, West Bend, Wisconsin 53095.

Food to Light Up Your Life (Joshua Tree, California): Send $7.00 plus $1.75 postage and handling to: Hospice of Morongo Basin, 61675 29 Palms Highway, Joshua Tree, CA 92252.

Gracious Goodness Christmas in Charleston (Charleston, South Carolina): To order a copy of either Gracious Goodness Christmas in Charleston or the earlier cookbook, Gracious Goodness Charleston, send $16.95, plus $4.00 postage and handling for each book to: Bishop England Endowment Fund, Dept. HC, 363 Seven Farms Drive, Charleston, SC 29492-7534. Phone: 843/849-9599, ext. 21.

Greenfield Village School Cookbook (Greenfield, New Hampshire): Send $16 plus $4 for postage to: GPTO, P.O. Box 48, Dept. HC, Greenfield, NH 03047-0048.

The Heart of Pittsburgh (Pittsburgh, Pennsylvania): Send $17.95 per book (plus $2.50 shipping and handling for the first book; $0.50 for each additional book) to Sacred Heart Elementary School PTG, 325 Emerson Street, Dept. HC, Pittsburgh, PA 15206. Pennsylvania residents add $1.26 state sales tax.

I'll Cook When Pigs Fly— And They Do in Cincinnati! (Cincinnati, Ohio): Send a check for $19.95, plus $5.20 for sales tax, shipping, and handling for each book to:

Junior League of Cincinnati, Dept. HC, Columbia Center, 3500 Columbia Pkwy., Cincinnati, OH 45226.

Immanuel Lutheran Church Cookbook (Story City, Iowa): Send $10 plus $2 postage and handling to: Immanuel ILCW, Immanuel Lutheran Church, 604 Lafayette Avenue, Story City, IA 50248.

Just Peachey: Cooking Up a Cure (Warsaw, Indiana): Send $15.00 plus $4.50 postage and handling to: *Just Peachey*, P.O. Box 1823, Warsaw, IN 46581-1823. For credit card orders, call 219/268-9015. (Make checks payable to: Just Peachey.)

The Kansas City Barbeque Society Cookbook (Kansas City, Missouri): Send $19.95 plus $4.00 shipping and handling for the hardcover book or $14.95 plus $4.00 shipping for the softcover book to: Kansas City Barbeque Society, Dept. HC, 11514 Hickman Mills Drive, Kansas City, MO 64134. Or call 816/765-5891.

Kissimmee Valley Vittles (Osceola County, Florida): Send $5 plus $2 shipping and handling for each book to: Osceola County Historical Society, 750 N. Bass Road, Kissimmee, Florida 34746. (Make check payable to: Osceola County Historical Society.)

Linen Napkins to Paper Plates (Clarksville, Tennessee): Send $19.95 plus $3.50 shipping and handling (Tennessee residents add sales tax of $1.70) to: Junior Auxiliary of Clarksville, TN, Inc., P.O. Box 30, Clarksville, TN 37041-0030.

Mesquite Country (Edinburg, Texas): Send $19.95 plus $3.50 shipping and handling (Texas residents add $1.64 sales tax) to: Hidalgo County Historical Museum, 121 East McIntyre, Edinburg, TX 78539.

Our Family Favorites (Spring Valley, Wisconsin): Send $5.00 plus $3.50 shipping and handling for each book to: Spring Lake Sunday School, N7845 170th, Spring Valley, WI 54767. (Make check payable to: Spring Lake Sunday School.)

Out of the Ordinary (Hingham, Massachusetts): Send $16.95 plus $3.20 for postage (Massachusetts residents add $0.85 sales tax) to: Out of the Ordinary, c/o Hingham Historical Society, P.O. Box 434, Dept. HC, Hingham, MA 02043.

Perennial Palette (Southborough, Massachusetts): Send $17.00, plus $3.00 for postage (Massachusetts residents add $0.85 sales tax) to: Perennial Palette, c/o Southborough Gardeners, P.O. Box 184, Dept HC, Southborough, MA 01722.

Picnics, Potlucks & Prizewinners (Indiana): The 208-page hardcover book costs $18.95 plus $3.00 for shipping and handling. Send a check, money order, or Visa or MasterCard information to: Indiana 4-H Foundation, Dept. HC, 225 East Street, Suite 760, Indianapolis, IN 46202. Or, call 317/692-7044.

Pleasant Hill United Methodist Women's Favorite Recipes Cookbook (Topeka, Kansas): Send $5 plus $3 postage and handling to Pleasant Hill United Methodist Church, 5919 N. W. Glenwood Drive, Topeka, Kansas 66617. (Make checks payable to Pleasant Hill UMW.)

'Pon Top Edisto: Cookin' 'Tweenst the Rivers (Edisto Island, South Carolina): Send $19.95, plus $5.00 shipping and handling to: 'Pon Top Edisto, c/o Trinity Episcopal Church, P.O. Box 425, Dept. HC, Edisto Island, SC 29438. Make checks payable to 'Pon Top Edisto.

The Purple Pantry Cook Book (Cedar Falls, Iowa): Send $15.00 plus $3.50 postage and handling (Iowa residents add 5% sales tax; Black Hawk County residents add 6% sales tax) to: The UNI Alumni Association, Attn: Cookbook Offer, 204 Commons, Cedar Falls, IA 50614-0284. Or for credit card orders, call 319/773-ALUM or 888/UNI-ALUM.

Puttin' on the Peachtree (DeKalb County, Georgia): Send $16.95 plus $3.00 shipping and handling for each book to: Junior League of DeKalb Publications, P.O. Box 183, Decatur, Georgia 30031-0183. (Make check payable to: JLD Publications.)

Rave Reviews (Ogunquit, Maine): Send $18.95 plus $4.00 shipping and handling (Maine residents also add 95 cents sales tax per book) to Ogunquit Playhouse Foundation, P.O. 1439, Dept. HC, Ogunquit, ME 03907. Make checks payable to the Ogunquit Playhouse Foundation.

Recipes and Memories (Romeo, Michigan): Write the Romeo Monday Club, Dept. HC, P.O. Box 32, Romeo, MI 48065. Enclose a check for $12 plus $2 shipping and handling.

Recipes of Note for Entertaining (Rochester, Minnesota): Send $18 plus $3 shipping and handling (Minnesota residents add 6½% sales tax and Rochester residents add 7% sales tax) to: Rochester Civic Music Guild, P.O. Box 5802, Rochester, MN 55903.

Recipes of Yesterday & Today (Agency, Iowa): Send $12.50 for each book to: Agency United Methodist Church, 119 North College, Agency, Iowa 52530. (Make check payable to: Agency United Methodist Church Cookbook.)

Savoring Cape Cod (South Wellfleet, Massachusetts): Send $14.95 plus $2.50 shipping and handling for each book to: Massachusetts Audubon Society, P.O. Box 236, South Wellfleet, Massachusetts 02663. (Massachusetts residents add $0.75 sales tax for each book.)

Savoring the Southwest Again (Roswell, New Mexico): The cost is $22.50 plus $3.50 for shipping and handling. Make checks payable to Roswell Symphony Guild; send to: Savoring the Southwest Again, Dept. HC, P.O. Box 3078, Roswell, NM 88202. Or call 505/623-7477 or 800/457-0302.

Simply Classic (Seattle, Washington): Send $24.95 for each book to Junior League of Seattle, 4119 E. Madison Street, Seattle, Washington 98112. (Washington residents add $1.62 sales tax for each book; Seattle residents add $2.15 sales tax per book.)

Slices & Bites of the Wenatchee Valley (Wenatchee, Washington): To order *Slices & Bites . . .*, contact the Wenatchee Applarians, Dept. HC, P.O. Box 1625, Wenatchee, WA 98807-1625. Phone: 509-665-0560; fax: 509/665-0347. Cost is $11.85 plus $3.00 shipping and handling.

Southern Settings (Decatur, Alabama): Send $24.95 plus $3.50 for postage and handling or a MasterCard or Visa number (Alabama residents add 8% sales tax) to: Decatur General Foundation Cookbook, Dept. HC, P.O. Box 1461, Decatur, AL 35602-1461. The book also may be ordered via the hospital's Web site: www.decatur-general.org.

Sterling Service (Dothan, Alabama): Send $19.95 plus $3.50 shipping and handling for each book to Dothan Service League, P.O. Box 223, Dothan, Alabama 36302. (Alabama residents add $1.60 sales tax for each book.)

The St. James at Sag Bridge Church cookbook (Lemont, Illinios): Send $25 to St. James at Sag Bridge, 10060 S. Archer Ave., Dept. HC, Lemont, IL 60439.

Taste of History (Hot Springs, South Dakota): Send $12 plus $5 postage and handling for each book to Friends of the Hot Springs Public Library, Dept. HC, 1543 Baltimore Ave., Hot Springs, SD 57747. Phone: 605/745-3151.

A Taste of Oregon (Eugene, Oregon): Send $19.95 plus $6.00 shipping and handling for each book to: Junior League of Eugene, Inc., 2839 Willamette Street, Eugene, Oregon 97405. (Make check payable to: A Taste of Oregon.) For phone orders, call 800/364-4031 between 8:00 a.m. and 12:30 p.m. Pacific time.

Taste of the Territory (Bartlesville, Oklahoma): Send $18.95 plus $5.00 shipping and handling to Service League of Bartlesville, 822 S. Johnstone Street, Bartlesville, OK 74003. (Oklahoma residents add $1.52 sales tax per book.) For phone orders using Visa or MasterCard, call 918/336-4346.

A Taste of Tradition (Providence, Rhode Island): Send a check for $20, plus $3 shipping and handling, to: Temple Emanu-El, 99 Taft Ave., Dept HC, Providence, RI 02906. Rhode Island residents add 7 percent sales tax.

Treasured Recipes of the Shipwreck Coast (Whitefish Point, Michigan): This 143-page book costs $14.95 plus $4.95 for shipping and handling. To order, call 906/635-1742, or write to Shipwreck Museum, 111 Ashmun Street, Dept. HC, Sault St. Marie, MI 49783. Visit the museum's Web site at www.shipwreckmuseum.com.

West of the Rockies (Grand Junction, Colorado): Write Junior Service League, Dept. HC, P.O. Box 3221, Grand Junction, CO 81502. Or use the Web site: www.westoftherockies.org. Enclose a check for $17.95 plus $3.00 shipping and handling.

What Can I Bring? (Northern Virginia): Send $19.95 plus $4.00 shipping and handling (Virginia residents add $0.90 sales tax) to: JNLV, 7921 Jones Branch Drive, Suite 320, McLean, VA 22102.

Women Who Can Dish It Out (Springfield, Missouri): Send $19.95 plus $3.95 postage and handling for each book to: Junior League of Springfield, Dept. HC, 2574 East Bennett, Springfield, MO 65804; phone orders, 417/887-9422; fax orders, 417/887-7705. Make check payable to: JLS Cookbooks.

Worth Savoring (New Albany, Mississippi): Send $19.95 plus $3.00 shipping and handling (Mississippi residents add 7% sales tax) to: Worth Savoring, Union County Historical Society, P.O. Box 657, New Albany, Mississippi 38652.

Metric Cooking Hints

By making a few conversions, cooks in Australia, Canada, and the United Kingdom can use the recipes in this book with confidence. The charts on this page provide a guide for converting measurements from the U.S. customary system, which is used throughout this book, to the imperial and metric systems. There also is a conversion table for oven temperatures to accommodate the differences in oven calibrations.

Product Differences: Most of the ingredients called for in the recipes in this book are available in English-speaking countries. However, some are known by different names. Here are some common U.S. American ingredients and their possible counterparts:
• Sugar is granulated or castor sugar.
• Powdered sugar is icing sugar.
• All-purpose flour is plain household flour or white flour. When self-rising flour is used in place of all-purpose flour in a recipe that calls for leavening, omit the leavening agent (baking soda or baking powder) and salt.
• Light-colored corn syrup is golden syrup.
• Cornstarch is cornflour.
• Baking soda is bicarbonate of soda.
• Vanilla is vanilla essence.
• Green, red, or yellow sweet peppers are capsicums.
• Golden raisins are sultanas.

Volume and Weight: U.S. Americans traditionally use cup measures for liquid and solid ingredients. The chart, above right, shows the approximate imperial and metric equivalents. If you are accustomed to weighing solid ingredients, the following approximate equivalents will help.
• 1 cup butter, castor sugar, or rice = 8 ounces = about 230 grams
• 1 cup flour = 4 ounces = about 115 grams
• 1 cup icing sugar = 5 ounces = about 140 grams

Spoon measures are used for smaller amounts of ingredients. Although the size of the tablespoon varies slightly in different countries, for practical purposes and for recipes in this book, a straight substitution is all that's necessary.
Measurements made using cups or spoons always should be level unless stated otherwise.

Equivalents: U.S. = Australia/U.K.
⅛ teaspoon = 1 ml
¼ teaspoon = 1.25 ml
½ teaspoon = 2.5 ml
1 teaspoon = 5 ml
1 tablespoon = 15 ml
1 fluid ounce = 30 ml
¼ cup = 60 ml
⅓ cup = 80 ml
½ cup = 120 ml
⅔ cup = 160 ml
¾ cup = 180 ml
1 cup = 240 ml
2 cups = 475 ml
1 quart = 1 liter
½ inch = 1.25 cm
1 inch = 2.5 cm

Baking Pan Sizes

U.S.	Metric
8×1½-inch round baking pan	20×4-cm cake tin
9×1½-inch round baking pan	23×4-cm cake tin
11×7×1½-inch baking pan	28×18×4-cm baking tin
13×9×2-inch baking pan	32×23×5-cm baking tin
2-quart rectangular baking dish	28×18×4-cm baking tin
15×10×1-inch baking pan	38×25.5×2.5-cm baking tin (Swiss roll tin)
9-inch pie plate	22×4- or 23×4-cm pie plate
7- or 8-inch springform pan	18- or 20-cm springform or loose-bottom cake tin
9×5×3-inch loaf pan	23×13×8-cm or 2-pound narrow loaf tin or pâté tin
1½-quart casserole	1.5-litre casserole
2-quart casserole	2-litre casserole

OVEN TEMPERATURE EQUIVALENTS

Fahrenheit Setting	Celsius Setting*	Gas Setting
300°F	150°C	Gas mark 2 (very low)
325°F	170°C	Gas mark 3 (low)
350°F	180°C	Gas mark 4 (moderate)
375°F	190°C	Gas mark 5 (moderately hot)
400°F	200°C	Gas mark 6 (hot)
425°F	220°C	Gas mark 7 (hot)
450°F	230°C	Gas mark 8 (very hot)
475°F	240°C	Gas mark 9 (very hot)
Broil		Grill

*Electric and gas ovens may be calibrated using Celsius. However, for an electric oven, increase the Celsius setting 10 to 20 degrees when cooking above 160°C. For convection or forced-air ovens (gas or electric), lower the temperature setting 10°C when cooking at all heat levels.

rush!
free-year request

BUSINESS REPLY MAIL
FIRST-CLASS MAIL PERMIT NO. 120 BOONE, IA

POSTAGE WILL BE PAID BY ADDRESSEE

Better Homes and Gardens®
H◯metown Cooking®

MAGAZINE
PO BOX 37456
BOONE IA 50037-2456

---

rush!
free-year request

BUSINESS REPLY MAIL
FIRST-CLASS MAIL PERMIT NO. 120 BOONE, IA

POSTAGE WILL BE PAID BY ADDRESSEE

Better Homes and Gardens®

MAGAZINE
PO BOX 37428
BOONE IA 50037-2428